'Rosie Boy[...]nd one of
them was[...] ED[...][...]rigorous,
and riveting mem[...] book written
with the kind of honesty and the kind of openness that make
you realise what good writing is all about. The book is a classic
of the examined life. Boycott's search is not only for sobriety, but
for h[...] better self, and she takes the reader every step of the way
in [...]ry human, very powerful confrontation with imper-
fecuo.. A Nice Girl Like Me is the world's best antidote to the
emp[...] narcissism of the celebrity memoir. The book will mean a
gre[...] deal to anyone who ever wished they could start again –
wh[...] means everyone' Andrew O'Hagan

'Yo[...] ame it and she's done it . . . she actually manages to turn
squ[...] r and despair into wry comedy and it's good stuff, proving
one [...] her old doctor's dictums . . . "If you want to know about
alcc[...]lism ask an alcoholic." The humour keeps bubbling to the
surl[...] e in spite of the horror and anguish' Jeffrey Bernard, *Spectator*

'It's [...]t meant to be a moral tale, not an Awful Warning. It's
wha[...] happened to her. And because she writes very well, it
read[...] ike the exciting and hair-raising story it is' Maeve Binchy

'Bra[...], honest and full of all kinds of lessons' Susan Hill, *Good
Hou[...] keeping*

'Thi[...] s a beautiful and brutally honest book. A young woman's
battl[...] with alcohol addiction and struggle for meaning, it's as
brav[...] and fresh as when it was first written. That perpetual,
perp[...] xing question echoes across the decades. What does it
me[...] o be a woman? And how, exactly, do we go about being
[...] ally Brampton

'[...] ce Girl Like Me is the most unflinching personal account of
a[...] tion that I have read. First published in 1984 it remains
a[...] ss, without an ounce of self-pity about it. It serves as both
a[...] iography and documentary history of the women's liber-
a[...] movement in the 1970s. Rosie Boycott is generous, brave,
and hugely compelling' Sophie Dahl

'This extraordinary book remains as fresh and important today as on the day it was written . . . [It is] all the more astonishing as it is written not by a loser seeking to blame the world for her woes, but by someone who has shaped the thinking of a generation while searching restlessly for something just out of reach. The dark melancholy of filling the empty void is something familiar to many, the bravery required to confront the demons and come out the other side still ahead of the game is a testament to a great writer whose honesty is an inspiration. *A Nice Girl Like Me* is about real life being messy, it is also about taking responsibility and has an heroic quality of a punch drunk prizefighter returning from hell to take the title. Optimism runs through it like Brighton through rock. How appropriate that it should be reprinted as Obama becomes President' Tim Smit, Chief Executive (and co-founder) of the Eden Project

'Written with the pacy swing of intelligent literate journalism. The emotions are powerful enough, the characters clearly sketched and the action fast and bizarre enough for topselling fiction, but there's the voyeur addition of knowing it's true and even, for London trendhounds, the recognition factor, as old acquaintances stick their oar in . . . The book has various interests: the underground press, the later seedy stages of the hippy movement, the rise of feminism and its inner conflicts, the pressures peculiar to modern, clever women, the complex hold of addiction, the tyranny of sex as a social counter, tangled family emotions – plus the suspense of a good "plot" and a highly charged heroine' Alex Hamilton, *Guardian*

'The book tells of a bright, tough, ambitious girl, one of the many but perhaps more reckless and driven than most, who flipped out of her straight, middle-class background and Cheltenham Ladies College education through a looking glass into what she and others who followed or watched, hoped might be a brave new liberated world. It is the story of growing up the hard way in an easy age, with a round-the-world ticket in one hand, a glass in the other, and fear and loathing down below' Suzanne Lowry, *Sunday Times*

A NICE GIRL LIKE ME

A BATTLE WITH ADDICTION IN
A DECADE OF DECADENCE

ROSIE BOYCOTT

WITHDRAWN

POCKET
BOOKS

LONDON • SYDNEY • NEW YORK • TORONTO

A NOTE ON THE AUTHOR

In 1972 Rosie Boycott co-founded both *Spare Rib* and Virago Press before becoming the first woman to edit *Esquire Magazine* followed by two broadsheets and a national daily newspaper. For two years she presented *A Good Read* on Radio Four and was a co-host of *Start the Week* in the 1990s. She is a frequent contributor to the *Late Review* and has regularly appeared on *Question Time*, *Any Questions*, *Woman's Hour* and other television and radio programmes.

Rosie is also the author of *Batty, Bloomers and Boycott, All For Love* and *Spotted Pigs and Green Tomatoes* – a year in the life of a Somerset smallholding which she started with her husband, Charles Howard, in 2003. She is the travel editor of *The Oldie Magazine* and a regular contributor to a wide range of newspapers and magazines.

A trustee of the Hay-on-Wye Literary Festival, Rosie has chaired both the Orange and the Samuel Johnson literary prizes, is an ambassador for the Alzheimer's Society and a trustee of the homeless charity Streetsmart.

Currently Chairman of the London Food Board and Food Advisor to the Mayor of London, she has one daughter, Daisy, from her first marriage to the journalist and war-reporter David Leitch, as well as four step-children, and lives in London and Somerset.

First published in Great Britain by Chatto & Windus, 1984
This edition published by Pocket Books, 2009
An imprint of Simon & Schuster UK Ltd
A CBS COMPANY

1 3 5 7 9 10 8 6 4 2

Simon & Schuster UK Ltd
1st Floor
222 Gray's Inn Road
London
WC1X 8HB

www.simonandschuster.co.uk

Simon & Schuster Australia
Sydney

A CIP catalogue record for this book is available
from the British Library

ISBN: 978-1-84739-470-5

Typeset in Palatino by M Rules
Printed by CPI Cox & Wyman, Reading, Berkshire RG1 8EX

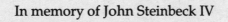

In memory of John Steinbeck IV

FOREWORD

Nice girls, according to the books, don't end up, aged thirty, in bins for alcoholics. Nice girls, as in 'What's a nice girl like you doing in a place like this . . .?' always leave themselves a margin.

I always thought I was good at leaving myself safety margins too – until I suddenly realised they'd all somehow evaporated, like guests at a disastrous party. I began this book when I had little left to lose – by the time it was finished there was a great deal. It is not intended as a manual on how to save your own life – although if anyone reads it this way, that is their prerogative.

The book is also in part memorial. Since I left the Charter Clinic two and a half years ago, three of my fellow patients who appear in the following pages, and another who doesn't, have all died. It was only a return visit to the Charter with my baby daughter which made me realise that statistically I was lucky to be alive.

Eighteen months after I left the Charter, in June 1983, they modified their programme extensively. Nowadays no patients are given drugs after withdrawal, and far stronger links with AA and support groups are encouraged. Bill Morgan, the Programme Director, calls the recovery rate 'phenomenal'.

The book would never have been finished without help.

At the clinic, Dr Max Glatt, Cathy Westward and Bill Morgan all earned my gratitude for their time and, above all, acceptance.

My old school friend 'Snoopy', otherwise Jill Murison, is largely responsible for nudging me towards the painful recollections of Cheltenham.

Jerome Burne, David Jenkins, Andrew Fisher and Lucretia Stewart, Julia and Rachel Shaw, Dave Howsen, Rufus Harris helped enormously with the chapters about the underground press.

Jonathon Green was invaluable, not only with recollections but with generous lending from his copious reference library. Sue Allen and Marsha Rowe gave hours of their time to reconstructing the days of *Spare Rib*, as did my publisher, Carmen Callil. John Steinbeck IV provided the action for large sections – to him, many thanks. And to Chogyam Trungpa Rinpoche, thank you also. Alina Enisteanu checked the chapter on Kuwait, correcting the Arabic spelling and sharpening my facts in crucial areas. Where it was impossible to remember a real name, I have substituted another, and also where I felt that this might save embarrassment.

I was lucky from the outset to have the help and encouragement of my agent, Deborah Rogers, and my publisher, Carmen Callil. Without either of them, I very much doubt that this book would have progressed beyond the scattered notes which I took in the clinic. I am grateful also to my editor, Mike Petty.

Beryl Drinkwater laboriously typed the manuscript, aided by Sue Allen and Ruth Evans.

My father provided a refuge in his home where I first started the book, as well as answering endless questions about my early childhood. For that and for much else, thank you.

A Nice Girl Like Me, ultimately, is not just about surviving, it's about thriving. For that, and for his invaluable advice and encouragement, I am in debt to my husband, David Leitch.

RMB

January 1984

ONE

On Wednesday 19 August 1981, I walked into my doctor's surgery, finally ready to admit defeat.

I had been drunk for the better part of the last eight days, a bender of such enormous proportions that even I, with my alcoholic cunning, could no longer avoid the consequences. The comforting screen that huge excesses throw up between the drunk and reality had failed me.

As I entered his surgery, shaky and desperate, I was even glad that my doctor imposed a no-smoking rule. My hands were shaking so much that lighting a cigarette would have been out of the question.

I negotiated my way to a chair, my legs like jelly, my mouth full of the bitter taste of stale vodka and my brain like steel wool. For the moment, at least, I knew I was beaten; there was no option but to go into a home. At least it would keep the world, in particular my father and my boyfriend, quiet for a while. But really give in? Accept the doctor's inevitable verdict that I could never drink again? Even though I felt like hell, I was still rebellious enough to think I could somehow go on.

The thought of a home terrified me. I had visions of padded cells and straitjackets, of huge quantities of tranquillisers, of being in the company of real lunatics. But then my behaviour had been crazed enough to be called insane.

The doctor looked at me across his mahogany desk. He reached for the telephone and after making a number of calls announced that I was booked into a suitable institution. I could be admitted that afternoon.

I got up to leave, stepping gingerly across the polished floor. Outside the bright sun hurt my eyes. The light bounced off the fashionable terraces of Eaton Square and I regretted shedding my dark glasses in one of those Cyprus bars.

It was eleven-thirty a.m. I wondered whether to go to the nearest off-licence for some vodka but decided against it. I couldn't face the hassle of dealing with the shop assistant. I wasn't even sure if I had enough money for both the taxi home and the booze. The effort to check was beyond me.

'I've been booked into a clinic. I'm going in this afternoon,' I said to William, my boyfriend, when I arrived home.

We had been living together for three years. My drinking habits were starting to affect him too. He had had to cover up for me and turn down invitations, with fragile excuses, when I was too drunk to go. The fear that he would return home and find me pissed had been constantly with him. He had to live with the fact that I appeared to prefer the bottle to him.

His face registered sadness and relief. He said, 'I have to go out, just for a couple of hours, but I'll be back to drive you there. I've locked up all the booze, so don't bother looking for any.'

The door closed behind him and I immediately checked to see if his parting words were true. They were. I began to regret that I had not made a detour on the way home. Now, if I wanted a drink, I would have to manage the two hundred yards to the off-licence. Today it seemed like miles.

As usual, I headed for the bathroom to see if there were any soothing or numbing medicines. My eyes were red from weeping and lack of sleep; sore from too many nights when I had not bothered to clean off the mascara.

I found a full bottle of the codeine-based cold remedy called Night Nurse, lurking amidst half-empty bottles of shampoo and bubble baths. My spirits rose a fraction. Here was oblivion of sorts. The recommended dosage was two teaspoons. Half a bottle would reduce me to a stupor within an hour. But better to face what was to come like that, and not like this. I ripped off the top and forced the syrup down. I staggered to an armchair to watch the minutes pass.

At four o'clock that afternoon I found myself, overnight bag in hand, sitting in the waiting room of one of London's more fashionable mental homes. Nowadays they politely call them clinics. The seats were of brown leather, the parquet flooring shiny and the receptionist, who stared at me from behind an enormous bunch of flowers, unnervingly healthy-looking. I didn't fancy the look of the place.

The Night Nurse had blunted my nerves. Even so, the wait seemed interminable. I was so weary.

Luckily, I didn't have to sign in. I thought at the time that this was a sympathetic gesture, a chance to enter the establishment with dignity rather than be forced to admit that I couldn't write legibly that day. Later I found that no one signs in: radical chic in the nuthouse. They've already checked your credit rating.

My room was small and white. The single bed was narrow, the wardrobe functional and ugly. I sat down on the bed and managed to light a cigarette. The bedspread was burnt orange, so was the one picture. I wondered vaguely which came first: the bedspreads or the pictures? Did they find a job lot of orange pictures or a job lot of orange bed-spreads?

A nurse came into the room to take an inventory of my possessions and to help me unpack. This was not entirely altruistic; her prime motive was to discover whether there was any booze secreted about my person or in my bags.

We wrote out – or rather, she wrote and I dictated – a list of my belongings. On paper they seemed woefully inadequate and I started to cry. This can't be happening to me.

Another nurse arrived to take down my medical details. Wallowing in Night Nurse and self-pity I failed to grasp the importance of whether I had had chickenpox at the age of seven or the age of eight. I wasn't drunk in those days. It was all too awful to comprehend. My dreaded nightmare was here.

'The vast shipwreck of my life's esteem'; John Clare's extraordinary metaphor came into my mind as I lay there, watching the cigarette smoke hang in the dying rays of the afternoon sun. The poet was describing his feelings when he was committed to the Northampton Asylum. I was glad he had used the word 'vast'. That was what it felt like, vast, and all-embracing.

If I could just have dropped this burden for a minute . . . but the merciful sea of the bottle was not available. In some ways it was a relief not to have to pretend any more; to acknowledge that this demon was beyond my control. It had always seemed so important to make a stand against things that were less per-fect than they should be; issues that were spiritually false, emotions that produced neither heartbreak nor ecstasy, physical qualities that fell far short of natural beauty; pale blue cardigans and the tepid, convenient morality of the middle class.

I realised that I had not slept properly for days. Scotch-induced sleep is about as refreshing as a lukewarm shower.

My legs were covered with bruises, evidence of a drunk's progress through chairs and tables, of falling down steps and out of beds.

Evidence too of sexual encounters with strangers? I couldn't remember – and I certainly didn't want to. Twenty-four hours earlier I'd been on a plane, and eight days earlier I'd been on another plane. What the hell had happened in between?

I work as a freelance journalist and occasional magazine editor, and my work has taken me all round the world. The peripatetic life has suited me, fulfilling both a love of travel and an inability to stay happily in one place. This time I'd been bound for Cyprus, to help start a Middle Eastern weekly TV guide. The project was pioneered and financed by another restless journalist. His love of foreign parts was equal only to his love of new ventures. I'd met Tony in Kuwait and the concept of the magazine had been cooked up one drunken evening. Everyone agreed it was a brilliant idea. A couple of years had passed. Tony had been in Bahrain, Saudi Arabia and now in Cyprus. I had been in London. He telephoned one day to say that the magazine was ready to publish. Did I want to come to Cyprus and edit it for the first two months of its life? I was pleased and flattered that he considered me crucial to his venture, and said I would come.

I was glad to be going. My sense of aimlessness was being magnified by the booze – or was it the other way round? My relationship with William was secure, but I wasn't in love. I suspected that I was staying with him more out of apathy than true commitment, a feeling that brought not only guilt but tremendous restlessness. I thought about moving out several times, but always put off the decision. There were some obvious advantages; we got on well, he understood and tolerated me. Weakened by drinker's paranoia, my affection for myself was wearing thin. Who else, I would wonder, would put up with the drunken excesses? Who else would love me? I was thirty years old, unmarried and I drank far too much.

But never mind, I thought, as I sipped a whisky and soda in the departure lounge. Two months of sunshine and hard work would help straighten me out. I thought gleefully about the affairs which were bound to occur; then felt guilty about William. I pushed the worries to one side and jaunted down the long walkway to the plane.

I have always loved flying. The knowledge that no one can reach you for the next few hours to tell you they love you or hate you is delicious. Planes provide a wonderful forum for fantasies, and I've elaborated tremendous stories to my neighbours on many flights. I've been an explorer of the forgotten quarter of the Arabian desert, a film producer on her way to premieres. When the plot of my own life has been sufficiently interesting I've been myself. Aboard an almost empty 747 home from New York, I joined the mile-high club.

The event, hazy in the extreme, was uncomfortable. But, like the gun-toting cowboy, I notched it up and managed with typical skill to whitewash the more gruesome details. I've also got very drunk on planes, though from this point of view the journey to Cyprus passed uneventfully.

Still, by six p.m. on the day I arrived in Cyprus, I was drunk. There was no particular reason. Granted, the sun was hot, it was good to see my old friends again, it was good to be out of England. But as excuses for getting drunk these were pretty insubstantial.

So, I was drunk on day one. I stayed more or less drunk till day eight. Even to me, a bender of such proportions was outrageous. I had never been drunk on such a scale before.

There were patches of sobriety; times characterised by the hangover and my struggle to hold on to sanity. I remember Tony sitting with his arm around me saying, 'What's the matter, what's wrong? Why are you so unhappy?' and replying, 'Have I blown it completely? Can I still go on working here?' I still wanted to go on drinking, and I needed somebody to say that it was all right, that I was still in control.

Another day I met Sybil, a friend from school, in the cramped lift on the way to the seventh floor of a downtown Nicosia apartment block. We were both attending a diplomatic party in honour of a departing *chargé d'affaires*. Desperately in need of a drink, I just managed to ration my intake to two camparis and embarked on a bizarre series of reminiscences. We had once shared a cubicle in one of England's most illustrious colleges. With worldly sophistication, we agreed that the days of thick green underpants and first periods were thankfully remote. Early the following morning I awoke to find a stranger in my bed. A little later I lost the left shoe of a favourite pair of cream sandals, which I had bought to wear to my mother's funeral.

In the office I idly shuffled press clippings from one pile to another in an attempt to look busy. I tried to pretend that life was fine, which it was until about noon, after which it was generally necessary to go home to bed. I felt so ill, so ashamed of having been drunk every day when I woke up, that there didn't seem to be anything to do but to go and get drunk again. Most nights I would wake at about five in the morning. Nicosia would be coming to life, the cries of the cockerels mingling with the backfiring of exhausts.

Am I going mad? I would wonder as I struggled out of bed to look for another drink, my head splitting and my body racked with waves of nausea. Shakily holding a bottle and preparing to choke the liquor down, I would recoil from the obvious madness of the act. But knowing that it would ultimately make me feel worse, and that the relief was only temporary, did not make me stop. Just one more, I would say to myself. Just to get back to sleep. Then I'll stop.

But I didn't. When my friends saw that kindness and tolerance were having no effect, they drove me to the sea for one briefly happy day. But the sun and salt water failed as well. We reached home at seven o'clock and by nine I had passed out. It was finally decided that I had better go home.

No one had the time or the inclination to babysit a thirty-year-old lush. We left for the airport late, and there was only just time to buy a half of vodka from the duty-free shop. I scrambled to my seat, hearing my friends' warning as I left them: 'Don't have anything to drink on the plane.' I ordered not just a glass but a whole can of tomato juice and then added the vodka, discreetly, from my bag.

When the alcoholic cage starts to close, most people, and I was no exception, establish rules they will not break. I had vowed I would not actually lose a job as a result of drinking too much. In the past there had been a number of other rules. Not to get drunk in public, not to get drunk at my father's house, never to drink in the mornings; the list was long. One by one these had been broken. I was so far gone that I had been ignoring the fact that, of late, my work was not going well. Sometimes days would pass when I felt too ill to do anything at all.

But losing this job? That fell right into the forbidden territory, and for the time being vodka was the only way to escape the mental penalties. I knew what would probably follow: a clinic and the possible end of my drinking days. I'd thought about the possibility often; usually when wallowing in morning-after misery. The idea had filled me with terror. Later, I was to wonder if I had subconsciously induced the Cyprus bender, so as to force myself to change. Cyprus, three thousand miles away and remote from home, was the perfect stage for the last scene of my long and tragic farce.

Withdrawal symptoms. Agonising. Everywhere hurts: head, eyes, teeth, breasts, stomach, limbs. I was shivering with cold but I could feel my hair sodden with sweat. My throat was dry, blocked somehow. It was as if I had been trying to swallow a stone and it had lodged. The physical assault was total – far worse than anything I'd ever gone through before. So this must be death. But I knew there was one way out, such a simple one. Spirits, any kind of spirits. Three inches of Scotch and the nerve-ends would stop screaming. At any rate they always had in the past. At least the enveloping terror would leave me; the mental anguish, the permanent panic, was worse even than the torment in my body. The symptoms of withdrawing from heroin addiction are supposed to be the ultimate hell on earth. I'd been through that and now I knew it wasn't true. And then I'd been lying on the concrete floor of an Asian jail.

This time I was in luxury and here was a kindly nurse with four enormous pills in a sterilised cup. I knew they were no substitute for Scotch before I swallowed them. An hour later I had proved it. I was still weary unto death but I was also still awake. The unremitting panic was still there, perched on my shoulder like a vulture. It was eating me, and glorying in the feast.

So this was the madness John Clare knew, there was nothing else it could be. Poor John Clare. What he needed was a large Scotch. That's what I needed, just one, and then just one more.

TWO

In a manner of speaking she'd been dependent on whisky since she was twelve. Long before she had so much as sniffed the stuff it had been providing the basis for her education. Her father's evening tipple was rarely more than a glass of sherry, as befitted an ex-military man with his eye on pensions and securities. In retrospect, his gamble with the liquor was as much at odds with his character as her own predicament was with her respectable beginnings.

Charles had left the army in 1956, cursing the fact that his own education – Bradfield public school followed by Sandhurst – had equipped him for nothing commercial. His two daughters must have the best that money could buy, however, and a chance meeting in 1955 provided the funds.

At a recruiting conference in Cambridge, Charles had been approached by someone whose face he dimly recognised, but whose name he could not place. 'Good to see you old boy,' the man said, pumping Charles's hand warmly. 'I'm so grateful for what you did for me back in 1946, I'm going to give you a tip.' The date coincided with Charles's period as secretary to the general staff in Vienna, a position from which to hand out favours. 'Whisky, old chap. It's a giveaway. Buy it at three weeks old, either grain or malt, then sell it in three years. Cream off a big profit.'

It was like backing a horse: Glenfiddich in the 3.30. It came in, at long odds. The pay-off sent Rosie to Cheltenham Ladies' College, and Charles was always the first to explain how he had afforded such a luxury in an age of austerity.

Rosie was born Rosel Marie Boycott on 13 May 1951, in St Helier, Jersey. Her mother, Betty, was Jersey born, of a French Breton family which had lived on the island for nearly two centuries.

Rosel was the younger of two sisters; Collette Lavinia had been born in Oxford in 1945.

At the time of Rosie's birth Charles was a major in the Suffolk Regiment. The Boycotts, their two daughters and a variety of nannies were on the move till 1956 when an expected promotion failed to come Charles's way and he decided to enter civilian life. He was then forty, Betty thirty-nine.

Their last army home had been a rambling piece of Victoriana set in a large square garden in Bury St Edmunds barracks. Space compensated for the lack of charm. They exchanged it for one which offered neither, a small house hovering uncertainly between the quaint village of Old Harlow and the sprawling mass of the New Town, built to absorb the post-war boom.

Charles's entry into civvy street was no easy one. The fact that similar difficulties were being encountered by countless other ex-servicemen didn't make much difference. He studied accountancy in the evenings and by day worked at various jobs, one of which was selling sheets in Selfridges. Later there was a transfer to the Christmas present department, where amid the tinsel and gold baubles he'd welcome his wife and daughters on their infrequent trips to London.

He passed his accountancy exams and went to work for Reads, the Liverpool-based metal-box company. His promotion was bewilderingly fast. Within four months he was made head of the open can division. The machines, he was fond of saying, made open cans faster than bren guns fire bullets. A new Ford went with the job. Rosie started riding lessons. But the success was not to last. In the early summer of 1960 Courtauld's took over the company. They checked the list of employees and decided that a recently retired army officer was no man for the high-powered task of distributing unadorned tin cans to dogfood manufacturers, soup makers and the like. The letter, announcing his dismissal and requesting the return of the car the following Monday, arrived in the Harlow house one Friday. Betty opened it although it was marked confidential. Charles was in Liverpool.

The car upset her most. Suddenly there were no more trips to the seaside, no more picnics in the country. Charles returned to London to look for work, walking the city streets all day rather than stay home in Harlow.

Betty returned to work as an underpaid, overworked social worker for the local council. Before the war she had worked in the East End, after graduating from Bedford College with a degree in social sciences. When Charles found work as an accountant in a travel agency in South Kensington, Betty had hopes of skiing holidays, but Charles was deskbound. Free holidays were not part of the package.

Money, or the lack of it, impinged on Rosie's life for the first time. The riding lessons still went on, but she sensed her parents', in particular her mother's, resentment towards those richer than themselves. Betty was brilliant at making do on nothing, at cobbling together pretty frocks out of clothes passed on by friends. But an air of martyrdom went with the busy needles. Whereas Collette grew up to save automatically, Rosie grew into an extravagance mixed with respect for those with money.

Collette remembers standing on the landing of the small twenties house, holding on to the banisters, listening to the arguments which raged from the living room below. Would the family be together tomorrow, she would wonder, until sleepiness overcame worry and took her back to bed. Like all children, they wanted their parents in sharp focus, with labels correctly and firmly attached. They were puzzled by Betty's irritations, now thrown into relief by the chaos of Charles's career. Rosie missed her early memories of her rustling mother, perfumed and silken, coming into her room to kiss her goodnight before going to military balls.

There was a sense of pretending in Harlow. There was the fairy story about a mouse which lived in London, invented by Charles to amuse Rosie. He'd cup his hands, exclaiming that the mouse was tickling his palms, telling of the mouse's latest exploits in the capital. More seriously, Charles and Betty were trying to live an upper middle-class life in a middle-class suburb. They clinked sherry glasses with unconvincing bonhomie in the homes of their richer friends, while inhabiting their own, slightly shabby property.

It was a relief to move again. In 1961, shortly before Rosie's tenth birthday, Charles shifted the family across England to Shropshire. He was going to work as an account-ant in a small but thriving Ludlow firm which specialised in light agricultural machinery. Rosie was not sorry to leave her Harlow school. Collette was at boarding school in Bath. Everyone was pleased. The pay was better, the job secure.

Mrs Freeman, the headmistress of Rosie's prep school, had

none of the airs of a lady. To her, knowledge was foremost. On the strength of examination results Rosie was made head of the school within a year. She did well at sports. Mrs Freeman listened patiently to Rosie's father's queries about her next school.

'Cheltenham Ladies' College,' she said, unhesitatingly.

Cheltenham, one of the most expensive private girls' schools in England, was divided into twelve houses, each of sixty to seventy girls, located in a variety of side streets within a mile's walk of the main building, which hovered like a giant gothic bug behind the promenade. There was a dignified and scholastic air about the long corridors, tiled in black and white marble, and about the great hall, which rose to three balconies' height.

Rosie had done well in her entrance examination and was placed in a class a year above her age. Intellectually, the accolade was meaningless; socially, the instant promotion was disastrous.

Every girl needed a best friend. Best friends served many purposes and were not dissimilar to marriages of convenience. Best friends went to church with you on Sundays. You sat next to your best friend on school outings, and danced with her at least twice on Saturday evenings, when the gramophone would thump out the 'Paul Jones' and 'Dashing White Sergeant' and the odd Viennese waltz, and all the girls in the house, clad in their mufti outfits and regulation brown flat buttondown shoes, would cavort together under the watchful eye of the housemistress.

As well as a best friend, it was necessary to acquire a 'pash'. Pashes were what Cheltenham Ladies called crushes; the reverse of the fagging system in boys' schools.

The junior would choose her pash from among members

of the fifth or sixth form, write her a note, requesting the honour and so on and so forth, and then clean her shoes, pump up her bike tyres, fetch her jars of peanut butter from the shop, offer her sweets and hope to hell that she'd dance with you once on Saturday night. Preferably a waltz, if that could be arranged.

Rosie, coming late into her year of fifteen thirteen-year-olds, had little choice in either matter. The best friend was forced upon her. Three days after the start of term, a fat Cypriot struggled into her cubicle and announced that she was to be the occupant of the spare bed.

'Well, we'd better be best friends then, hadn't we?' said Rosie, who had been awaiting Sybil's arrival with a mixture of longing and dread. She was terrified that Sybil might turn out to be some sort of Mediterranean lemon.

'God, it's cold here,' said Sybil, as she began unpacking her copious suitcases. Heavens, she had such a lot of mufti, thought Rosie, gazing at Sybil's dresses, which were rapidly taking over the allocated wardrobe space. Her own two blue dresses looked inadequate beside such expensive splendour.

But if Sybil and Rosie were an odd couple, then Rosie and her pash made far stranger bedfellows. The reason why Virginia Christmas was the only pash available was simple. Christmas was the most disorganised person in the house.

But she was beautiful; tall and dark, with a strong body and large breasts. She was always bottom of her class in academic subjects, yet Rosie had overheard an art master say that she was the only girl in the school who could paint, and not just paint, he added, but paint damn well with real originality and style.

Christmas looked terrific on the hockey field and even better playing lacrosse. Her hair always fell out of its ponytail, and despite the injunctions of the games mistress, she'd stride in, waving her lax stick, terrorising opponents who stood in numbed silence before this veritable valkyrie. But, while delicate with her brush and deft with her hockey stick, she was all left feet when it came to dancing.

On the first Saturday night after Christmas had accepted Rosie's offer to pash for her, Rosie sent a note requesting the first waltz. This was a custom, a stately courtship, and even if they didn't have dance cards, the routine was strictly adhered to. Christmas floundered in just before the waltz was due to be played. Rosie, standing there in a corner, was suffering all the agonies of a wallflower.

'Sorry I'm late,' gasped Xmas, as she was sometimes known. She placed her arm on Rosie's left shoulder at the same time as Rosie placed hers on Christmas's right. Impasse. Oh God, who was meant to be the man in this situation? Rosie waited vainly for Xmas to make some sort of decisive move, but she seemed oblivious.

Apparently she'd never waltzed before. They teetered round the floor, Xmas humming snatches of 'Blue Suede Shoes' and holding the show on the road by virtue of her great stature and total lack of interest.

But if the social life at Cheltenham was torture it was nothing compared with the classroom. From the top of her class, Rosie began a slide to the bottom. 'Her work is poor and she has made no effort to improve it,' said Mr Richards of Maths. She made 'headway' in music, whereas in science she was producing work that was 'barely satisfactory'.

'I hate it there,' she sobbed to her father one grim, rainy night, as they drove back to Cheltenham from Ludlow. She was usually sick in the car, partly from nerves, partly as a delaying action.

'But you have some nice friends?' he said anxiously.

'Yes, I do have some friends,' Rosie agreed. 'But it's not that, it's that they think I'm so stupid.'

'Don't let anyone ever tell you that,' he said firmly, stopping the car and taking his daughter's face into his hands. 'You're not stupid, no one with eyes like yours could ever be stupid.'

They drove on in silence, Rosie clutching a small parcel containing a jar of honey from the bees in the garden back home, plus a new jumper that her mother had knitted for her.

The Boycotts were now installed in their new home. The date they moved remains memorable because of a world-shaking event which had occurred the day before. Rosie had been sitting with sixty others in the dining room, having just said grace and preparing to eat the Friday offering from the kitchens, when the housemistress had rung the little bell she kept beside her place.

'Girls,' she said, her fleshy lips wobbling with emotion, and her eyes misting over behind their thick glasses, 'I have something to tell you. The President of the United States has been shot and killed this afternoon.' She paused. No one moved.

'Now, I don't want any of you to be upset, but this is the most serious thing that has happened since the last war.' Everyone began to look not only upset but scared too. 'Of course, it probably won't have any effect on any of us and we'll just go on as normal, same old way with the same old spirit, but I want you all to be quiet for a moment and remember the President and his wife and children. Pray for them now, in their hour of need.'

Rosie bent her head, watching the gravy congeal into cold rivers across her plate.

*

'God, is this how you do it?' said Kate. She was sitting on the piano stool in Music Room 3, her legs apart. The Tampax hovered between her thighs.

Snoopy Cooper, sitting on another music stool, demonstrated skilfully. 'Move 'em in, move 'em out, Rawhide,' she yelled by way of encouragement.

'Success. Your turn,' said Kate, standing up and wiggling her legs to accustom her body to the new presence.

The door opened. 'What are you girls doing?' The wretched, loud tones of the duty mistress.

Rosie scrambled back to her feet, pulling down her green skirt and groping frantically for her green knickers which were twisted round her knees.

'This is disgusting, disgusting; I should report you. Oh dear, I just don't know what to do.'

The three teenagers hung their heads. Miss Webber spurted on, finally running out of steam and annoyance and departing the music room with a stern toss of her head and a last word of warning about immoral behaviour.

'She's a fat one to talk,' said Kate, scrambling up on top of the piano. Rosie considered them both her best friends. The Cypriot lemon had long since been dumped, and though they still walked together to church on Sundays their state of best friendship went little further.

'That woman was here again this morning,' said Snoopy, 'I went out through the rose garden, on the way to breakfast, pretending that I'd dropped something there yesterday, and do you know, Adams was taking photos of Webber standing behind a giant yellow rosebush; Web was grinning her silly head off, and Adams looked so bloody pleased with herself.'

'Do you think they actually spend the night in the same bed?' asked Rosie.

'Of course they do,' scoffed Kate, 'they're lesbians.' She pronounced the word with satisfaction; it had taken some research to discover it.

'But what do they do?' persisted Rosie, sufficiently curious to confess her ignorance to Kate.

'Oh well, I don't exactly know,' said Kate, 'touch each other there' – she pointed – 'kiss each other. It all sounds pretty boring to me.'

'It's disgusting,' said Snoopy. Rosie nodded, imagining the pair of them rolled up together in carnal embrace and shuddering at the thought of all that loose skin wobbling together. 'They're both so old, too,' added Snoopy. 'The head really ought to sack them. I mean, they can't go on doing those knicker checks like that.'

Knicker checks and vest checks were the two most humiliating experiences of school life; sporadic, unforeseen and always resulting in further black marks, these checks were designed to find out if the girls were wearing vests and regulation green knickers over white under ones. In front of both Webber and, lately, of Adams you had to pull up your skirt and then open your blouse to reveal the vest.

To be caught out without the cumbersome garments meant Web making a note of it in her book and a long flog back through the corridors to the dorm to dress correctly. Since Adams had become a firm fixture around the house, the knicker checks had increased.

'How far did you let him go?' Snoopy was sitting on the edge of her bed, helping her unpack. It was the start of another term, a new year at Cheltenham. The long, glorious summer vacation was over and it was the start of life in the fifth.

Rosie blushed. 'Well, I met someone, he's called James. He's really interesting, he's just going to Cambridge this term.'

'Well come on, out with it,' prodded Snoopy. 'Who is he, where did you meet him, is he good-looking?'

'He's got very long fingernails,' Rosie replied, hesitantly. She was not sure what to say. James had unlocked something. 'He went below the waist,' she said, finally.

'I did it too,' Snoopy confided in turn. 'So did Kate.' Rosie breathed a sigh of relief. She hadn't gone too far, then, she was still in line with her friends and they could continue to feel morally superior to Boshoff, who had, only the hols before, allowed some student at the university where her father taught to take off all her clothes. When Boshoff died of a heroin overdose at the age of twenty-four, Rosie was to remember feeling sorry that she had been so censorious. Not that it would have made any difference.

The three of them all planned to leave after O-levels. Kate and Snoopy's parents were in favour of the scheme; Charles and Betty were not. The prospect of Cheltenham without her friends seemed gloomy. 'What would you do?' raged her father. 'You've got to stay there and take your A-levels.' A-levels? Rosie was worried about not getting any O-levels, let alone any As. French had been abandoned; she was so bad that there wasn't any point in continuing, or so the mistress told her. At the time, she'd received this news with joy, but later she was furious.

She passed five O-levels but no amount of persuasion made her father change his mind. She returned to face the first year of the sixth. Passed over for prefectship, and the privileges that went with it – a study, a fire on which to toast muffins, the right to go shopping alone on the Prom – she curled up, rebelliously, in the large study with the younger girls and started courses in A-level biology and English. She asked to take A-level maths, but the Master laughed her out of the room. English and biology as an A-level combination was for flops. It was neither arts nor science, unsuitable training for any university course.

Towards the end of the year, which had passed slowly and depressingly, she was summoned to the headmistress's office for an interview. Was she to be expelled for her poor academic work, she wondered, as she waited outside the imposing door?

'You're not happy here?' said the head.

A surprising start, better than anticipated.

Rosie shrugged. 'Well, I like the school.'

'Yes, but you're not doing well, are you?'

'No.'

'Do you think you would have been happier at another school?'

'I don't know. It's not that I'm unhappy, it's that I've done so badly in class.'

'Yes.' The head flicked through copies of reports. 'Why? You did so well in your CE. You're obviously a clever girl. Is Cheltenham too large, do you find it swamping?' Downstairs in the library the elite of the upper sixth were sitting their Oxbridge entrances.

'What do you want to do?'

'Go to university,' replied Rosie.

The head pursed her lips. 'Well, I don't like to be pessimistic, but you won't, not the way you're going on now.'

There was silence. Rosie's education, which had cost her parents so much, seemed to be reaching the end of the line. Her sister Collette, whose schooling had been comparatively cheap, had passed her A-levels with excellent grades and was now attending the London School of Economics.

'Perhaps you ought to go somewhere else to finish your A-levels? What do your parents think?'

'I think they want me to stay here. Maybe they'd change their minds.

She was filled with a gloomy sense of failure. She would have preferred to have been expelled in a storm of anger and retribution. The head's understanding attitude made matters worse. But she was right. Rosie had no future at Cheltenham.

She left at the end of the summer term of 1967.

THREE

I awoke unwillingly from my drugged sleep. A nurse was sitting on the end of the bed.

'How do you feel?'

My head ached, my mouth tasted foul. 'Awful,' I mumbled. I rubbed my eyes. The sun was pouring through the orange curtains. Another warm summer's day.

The nurse, whose name was Carol, poured a glass of water and handed me five pills. Three of yesterday's white slugs and two red vitamins.

'They're hemenevrin,' she said, in answer to my look. 'A sort of booze substitute which helps the withdrawals. I'll be back later.'

She left the room, her neat white nurse's coat fitting her snugly.

I can walk out of here tomorrow, I thought, trying to fight the fear, but I knew that it was not going to be so easy. I wobbled out of bed and went to the bathroom. The striplight above the mirror did not reveal a pretty sight. I've never thought I was beautiful. Lately, suffering endless hangovers, I'd felt downright ugly most of the time.

My eyes are my best feature. That morning they looked as though they belonged to someone else. There were bloodshot veins running in streaks across the whites. Even the pupils looked wrong; the blue seemed murky. I couldn't bear to look at them any more, or the dry, flaking skin. I felt iller than I could ever remember.

I didn't want to go out of the room – at least it was quiet and secret – but I couldn't stay there all day.

'Jesus, why me? why me?' I muttered over and over again. Drunks: alcoholics: people of no future, and no hope. I'm better than this, I have to be, I thought. Could it all be a mistake?

I went back over what I could remember of the last ten days, recalling moments when I could have turned down drinks – you shouldn't have had that one, that's the one that caused all the trouble. Rewriting reality to assuage my guilt, warping the truth to convince myself that there was always another chance. And till now there always was.

I opened the window, breathed in some fresh air and felt a little better. I tried to see the plusses in the situation. Aside from my boyfriend and my father everyone thought I was in Cyprus. All well and good. Past benders had always been resolved by a bargain. A promise to go easy; even, as in the case of a ghastly four-day spree during the run-up to my thirtieth birthday earlier in the summer, a promise to lay off the booze for two months.

I had solved that one by laying off for a day, then sneaking beers during the next week, then by going to New York, then by not telling my boyfriend, who had been away during that particular debacle, that the doctor had told me not to drink.

I found myself plotting an escape plan – my buzzing head had devised a timetable already. Three or maybe four days in the clinic, then back to Cyprus if they would have me, or else off to Devon or somesuch place where I could pretend to be away in Cyprus and roll back into London around the end of September with everything under control. It might work. So I had better go along with other people's plans for me – starting now. That meant, I realised with a bout of nausea, getting up and out of that room. I returned to the bathroom to put on some make-up, which did little to improve the saggy skin under my eyes or the puffiness induced by tears. But it was the best that could be done. I tied my hair back into a ponytail, then let it loose again. It was dirty but at least obscured my features that way.

My room was the second one along the neon-lit corridor. There were six rooms on the floor, which constituted the alcoholic unit of the clinic. Next to room one was the sitting room. Opposite that was the nursing station. I passed it, receiving a cheery and surprised wave from Carol. She did not expect to see me up. I pushed open the door of the sitting room and confronted the people who were to be my companions for the next few days.

My God, I thought, I'm in the wrong place. The four people sitting on the fat orange chairs looked well, healthy – utterly normal. Cups cluttered the table, the air was thick with cigarette smoke. I sat down on the only available chair.

'How do you feel?' asked a dark-haired, middle-aged woman.

'Awful.' I looked round the room. There was the dark-haired woman, whom I later discovered was called Anne. An elderly man, with distinguished greying hair, slightly balding over his crown, glasses, ruddy nose, gentle smile; long fingers which tapped nervously on his knees when he wasn't smoking. His name was Taylor. A younger man, not much older than me. Tall, well built, with a slightly round face. Blue-green eyes, an engaging smile, brownish beard.

Fanciable. His name was Brian and he was American. A quiet, chubby-cheeked Malay, whose eyes were partially concealed behind thick pebble glasses. Raju's brown-skinned cheeks were flecked with split capillaries – the alcoholic's mark of Cain.

The door opened to admit the doctor. He was small, wearing a seedy mustard-coloured suit. His long fingers raked back his hair, which kept falling untidily across his heavily lined face. He could have been forty-five or twenty years older. He sank down into a chair and hitched his right foot on to his knee.

'Well hallo, everybody,' he said cheerfully, and turned to me. 'You're . . .'

I supplied my name.

'Yes, yes, Rosie. How are you?'

I felt like screaming. Couldn't anyone ask anything else, wasn't it obvious that I felt like hell?

'I feel fine,' I replied as steadily as I could.

His eyebrows shot up, as he turned to the others. 'Well, yesterday we were talking about getting into situations where we're liable to drink, going into the off-licence for cigarettes when we could go to the newsagents, and so on.'

I listened to the talk swing back and forth. Anne and Brian were vocal. Raju and Taylor chipped in the odd remark. The effort of getting up was beginning to tell, and I was finding it hard to concentrate. I felt the odd one out, the only one who was a real drunk, isolated by the mad world I had built for myself.

The doctor turned to me again.

'Do you feel like joining in?' he asked.

I struggled out of my miserable reverie and attempted to look bright.

'What do you do?' asked Anne.

'I'm a journalist. I blew a job . . . got drunk for eight days, couldn't get off the plane on Tuesday, and here I am.' Everyone looked sympathetic. 'I drink in benders. Sometimes it's all fine and I drink very little then suddenly I'll drink far too much and be drunk for a day, sometimes more.'

'How long have you been drinking?' asked the doctor.

'What do you mean?' I asked. 'Out of control or just drinking?'

'Just drinking,' he said.

'Well, I suppose since I was about seventeen. I'm thirty now.'

'That's how I drink,' said Anne, sitting forward on her chair. 'Fine for a while and then it all goes wrong.'

'Do you think you're an alcoholic?' asked Brian.

'Well . . . I've got a problem,' I admitted, 'but I'm sure that it's one that I can beat. Other people can.'

The group gave each other significant looks, which irritated me because I failed, at that point, to understand their implication.

'I'm just so angry with myself,' I added.

'Listen,' said Brian, 'if you see it in terms of a war, then realise that there's only one way you'll ever win; by giving it up!'

'Yes, I suppose so,' I said, with no conviction. The hangover settled leadenly. I was exhausted and depressed, too apathetic even to fake a smile.

The doctor called the session to an end and I went back to my room. Carol came in after me, with more fat white pills for me to swallow.

'Were all of them alcoholics?' I asked her. 'It doesn't seem possible.'

She laughed. 'Yes, they still are! Talk to them, they've all been drinking for years, there's no difference between you and them except a matter of time.'

I crawled back into bed. The sudden possibility that I wasn't the only person who had lived with this madness gave me a sense of hope. More to the point, they looked OK, even nice. They didn't seem to be in any doubt about their alcoholism, nor about the way to beat it. Were they defeatists or realists? I didn't know. But, they'd all been drunk, fallen over in public, lost hours of time to blackouts fucked up and been stupid like me. Almost immediately I began to suspect the spark of hope; I was so convinced that I was the only person alive with this problem. Alcoholics were down and out winos, not nice girls like me.

I fell into an uneasy sleep and didn't wake until the room was once again full of shadows. Curiously, I felt safe. There was an odd sense of belonging to that ugly little room, to the cheap wardrobe, above all, a sense of belonging in some way to all the other people. I fought down the feeling, and the sudden wish to give in, to return to the nursery and be looked after. I was, after all, tough, grown up, responsible. I had a problem with drink, no big deal, half the people I knew had problems with drink. I could hear laughter from down the corridor.

I rolled away from the sound. Suddenly I just wanted to curl up into a ball and let go.

In 1936 Scott Fitzgerald wrote:

Of course all life is a process of breaking down, but blows that do the dramatic side of the work – the big sudden blows that come, or seem to come, from the outside, the ones you remember and blame things on – and in moments of weakness, tell your friends about, don't show their effect all at once. There is another sort of blow that comes from within – that you don't feel until it's too late to do anything about it, until you realise with finality that in some regard you will never be as good a man again. The first sort seem to happen quick – the second kind happen almost without your knowing it but is realised suddenly indeed.

The crackup I experienced over the next three days was of the second kind. An enormous welling of emotion which I could not stem. Scenes of drunkenness, of failure, of idiocy, of madness, rolled through my mind like a picture-show. Echoing voices – my father on the telephone saying, 'Darling, can't you stop?' My father standing beside my bed in the country saying, 'If you don't stop you'll lose everything – looks, brains, no man will ever want you.' My boyfriend's look of despair, hardening into one of anger.

I thought at one stage that I might be having the DTs, but I knew that it wasn't so. These were my own inner visions. The guilt I felt was shattering, the pain enormous. I was a failure as a woman, as a human being, as a spiritual entity.

On the morning after my second night in the clinic, the doctor came to my room for his first private session. I'd been sobbing for forty-eight hours and I looked a wreck. He smiled and sat down on the armchair. I perched on the edge of the bed. The day was warm and I wasn't wearing tights; I was past caring about the bruises.

'I feel so fucking angry,' I said in answer to his opening question. 'Why did this have to happen to me? Why didn't it happen to my sister, or my father? What's wrong with me? Is it because I don't have any willpower?'

'No,' he replied very slowly. 'Can you think back to where it began?'

Yes I could. 'I remember a night in New York in 1975 when my boyfriend of the time, a guy called John, had gone off with another woman. I knew he was going and I knew why. I just thought, fuck it, I'll get drunk. Nothing wrong with that,' I added defensively.

'How many times have you drunk to escape like that?'

I didn't want to answer; the constant repetition of drunkenness had become an inescapable fact. I wanted this man to fix me, not probe me. I wanted to be someone who could drink, without the shakes, without the guilt. 'A lot,' I conceded. 'But there's usually a reason.'

He looked at me quizzically. 'Do you think there's a good reason for someone of thirty to end up here after admitting to being drunk in Cyprus for eight days? That's not living, is it?'

'What do I do?' I asked him, knowing full well what his answer was going to be.

'There's only one thing. You have to give up.'

'I can't,' I said angrily, 'how would I cope, I'd have to admit that I can't handle it . . . have to go to parties without booze, have to have people knowing that I can't drink, because I'm an . . . I'm . . . well because . . .'

'Because you're an alcoholic,' he finished for me. I nodded my head, then started to walk around the room.

'Start at the beginning . . . where were you born?' This was better. I've always revelled in talking about my past, since it has some good moments. He took scrawly notes in an erratic and spidery hand.

'So you feel that your father dominated you?'

'Well, I always felt he wanted a boy, but that isn't much of a reason to explain this, is it?'

He shook his head ruefully. 'No, it isn't. We never really know the reason. I'll see you tomorrow,' he said finally. We'd reached my twelfth year.

Tomorrow, God. How many tomorrows were there going to be locked in this prison cell? In the kitchen making coffee, I started to cry again. Carol came and put her arm around my shoulder. 'Let it out,' she said, hugging me, 'you'll feel better.' I went back to my room, my shoulders heaving, and began to think of suicide.

That will really upset them, a nasty little voice inside me said, and the movie started, like movies of the past, of me standing beside my parents' graves, stoically fighting the tears and being congratulated for my bravery. Well, this time let it be me. I could always do it. The almighty seemed to have punished me enough as it was, the hellfires could not be any worse; no one would miss me, and everyone would feel guilty.

I felt so near the bottom of the heap that there seemed to be only one direction – down, and out.

I went off to have lunch, creeping down to the dining room, my face towards the floor, oblivious to the attempted jocularity of the other patients.

That I had a conscience I did not doubt, where else did the guilt come from? But I had sheltered myself in ambivalence and compromise for so long that it was hard to pinpoint how much was real guilt, and how much was self-dramatisation.

Drinking manufactured its own commotion, its own confusion. One of the clichés about alcoholics is that they can't stand boredom, or an even pace in their lives. Before I began to drink, I solved the problem by always being on the move. I'd move countries, jobs, and boyfriends at fantastic speed. For a certain number of months, the new venture was OK, satisfying my need for the unexpected, staving off the necessity to confront myself. Once that palled, drinking threw chaos into my life, becoming in the process its own inbuilt excuse to do nothing. If I had got violently drunk the night before, then I couldn't reasonably be expected to do much the next day. Of late this was becoming a repetitive scenario.

William came to visit that night. He was quietly sympathetic but I felt the gap between us yawn. He brought with him the outside world, wearing it round him like a cloak. He was free to come and go, to drive his car, enter a bar, meet a friend. I was confined, imprisoned by my own madness. My news concerned the patients and the menu, a sharp contrast to his jocular patter.

I was glad when he left. The TV blinked in the corner of the room, but I was hardly watching. His sympathy had somehow jolted my negativity. How long is it since you trusted someone? I wondered. How long since you went to a party and walked in with your head high, confident you wouldn't end up drunk by the end of the evening? How long has it been for him? Always watchful, always wondering if he would come home and find you passed out on the floor?

I'm too frightened to die, I don't even want to die, I thought sadly. Sad because dying would have been the easiest thing, the quickest way out of the guilt and confusion.

In the corridor someone laughed; deep and heartfelt. On the pavement outside my window I heard two drunks returning from the pub, breaking into song, then dropping a bottle. Their curses echoed with the sound of the tinkling glass. I'd taken my life for granted for so long and tested its durability so often, pushing sanity and endurance to the limits in order to prove my existence. Now there were no externals, only the quiet rise and fall of my breath, the warmth of my skin.

FOUR

A decade earlier she had been more daring. During the season of psychedelics, LSD had provided a non-stop joust with God. The more scared you became, the more you felt you had survived, and the more you trusted that the gods were on your side. Rosie liked the sense of survival, though she was never sure she really liked taking acid. But the drug was part of social macho and to have refused would have been cowardly, a much worse prospect.

She was nineteen when she decided, at the beginning of 1970, that her university career (a brief two terms, minus two weeks, at Kent University, studying pure maths) was over. Her friends in their third year were trying to solve their finals problems with psychedelic revision aids. Acid, like liquor to the alcoholic, provided excuses and diversions. Sometimes even clarity of vision, but Rosie wasn't comfortable with what she saw in those panoramic moments.

She had left Cheltenham in the summer of 1967. Rosie's father proposed a year at home, taking her A-levels through correspondence. Rosie had no choice: she skated through the exams after a year of unremitting bleakness. She'd breakfast with her parents and then, after Charles went to work, sit

33

down at a card table in the spare room and study textbooks until lunch: two hours of the same in the afternoon: clock off at tea time. At the time it seemed dull and tedious, later it seemed weird.

She had isolation but no privacy. None of the girlish communion which sixteen-year-olds need, and at the same time a sense that her every move was watched and assessed. She felt like a crazed relative, exiled upstairs, out of the way of the rest of the household. She read novels when she was meant to be working, long absorbing fantasies like *The Lord of the Rings*, and she'd hide the book on her lap, afraid her mother might come in, yet conscious of how stupid it all was.

As a reward, or so it seemed, for the endurance test, Charles and Betty let her go to London in the summer of 1968 to work for the Cheltenham Ladies' College Settlement, St Hilda's East. St Hilda's was a charitable institute, funded by the college. Numerous old girls did 'their social-work bits' in the run-down building near Brick Lane, in London's East End. Some even lived there for short periods, working in the neighbourhood, upper-class adjuncts to the social services, nice ladies who could be relied upon to rush to slum tenements and jollify suicidal women.

It was mid-July when she and her friend Julia, the daughter of some family friends, turned up on the doorstep of the East End building. Both sets of parents had been sceptical but could not refuse a request based on the desire to do good.

And they both wanted to. Julia was by then studying for her A-levels at a college in Oxfordshire. Her year there had turned her from pony-club supporter to flower-power radical. She was kicking against her parents' wish that she go to cookery school, preferring the headiness of the sixties, of rock-and-roll, of Marcuse and the anti-war protest. Both she and Rosie revelled naively in the idea of getting in with the poor, believing that people with no money were somehow more real.

'What can you do?' asked the imperious middle-aged woman, whose neatly coiffed hair and manicured hands suggested that she didn't partake of too much of the rough stuff herself.

'We want to help. We'll do anything. Visit old people, help with playschools, deliver meals on wheels.'

'How old are you?'

'We're both seventeen,' answered Julia.

'Too young. You can't work here, you can't even stay here.'

'Let's go to the local church,' suggested Julia, 'they must need people like us.' An Australian Methodist minister, with flowing red hair, straggly beard and wild Rasputin eyes, offered them camp beds in his chapel. In return he put them to work cleaning up after meths drinkers in the crypt below the church. They scrubbed, cleaned, unpacked louse-filled suitcases, and sorted out boxes of clothes which were sent up daily from the commuter belt. The suits, designed for paunches used to eating three-course lunches at Simpsons, fitted the shrunken bodies of the emaciated clients like rags on scarecrows.

Then, though not in the East End, Julia came up with Adolpho, her Peruvian revolutionary. Adolpho's social and ideological soul lived further west – in the Troubadour Café off the Earl's Court Road.

He spent his nights in a murky basement in Tufnell Park surrounded by pictures of Mao Tse Tung and Che Guevara. Adolpho aped Che in his dress. Certainly Rosie and Julia found that the dead revolutionary held far more appeal than their meths drinkers.

ROSIE BOYCOTT

In the week before the 27 October 1968 Anti-Vietnam march on Grosvenor Square, the *Daily Express* ran a full-scale feature entitled 'The leading performers and their not all supporting cast.' Adolpho ranked as one of the four ambitious understudies to the twenty-five-year-old Tariq Ali.

'Dearest comrades,' Adolpho said one night in the Troubadour, as they squeezed together on a wooden bench, peering at each other through the flickering gasps of a candle stuck in an old bottle of Mateus Rosé, 'it is our duty to get organised. The world is entering a new era; the era of complete collapse of imperialism and the victory of the people.' At first Rosie thought that Adolpho spoke like a bulletin board because he was foreign. By now she realised that he thought that way too.

Julia, detecting irreverence, kicked her under the table. Her look was one of triumph and excitement.

'Our great Latin American hero – Guevara – is with us in spirit. We must fight a pitched battle until final victory. And it will be ours, my dear comrades.' Adolpho leaned forward, gazing at each of them in turn, but it was always hard to tell at which since he never took off his dark glasses. They clasped hands, thumbs upwards.

'Money doesn't mean anything,' Julia said one night when they were sitting under the altar, each on her own camp bed, wearing short nighties. Rosie was trying to fry a banana skin over a candle flame. Someone had said that you could get high smoking the result. Since she hadn't smoked any dope, and the revolutionaries weren't into it, bananas seemed like a good alternative. But the skins always fell apart before you could try the experiment. Neither of them drank much and were critical of what they saw as the older generation's dependence on their nightly tipple.

Rosie agreed. 'These people here, they're so much more real than everyone back home. They need us. Don't you agree?'

'Yes, and isn't that wonderful?'

Julia got up and changed their one record over; the vicar had installed a gramophone for use at the Tuesday youth club. 'They call me mellow yellow . . .' Donovan's words thumped into the lofty ceiling while the banana skin fell apart into sooty dust on the tiled floor. No highs from those ashes.

There was a sense of being part of history that summer. 1968 burgeoned with events from every corner of the globe. In France, the students revolted at the Sorbonne, in Czechoslovakia the Russians invaded, in Vietnam atrocities were uncovered which fuelled the anti-war movement. In America Martin Luther King and Bobby Kennedy were shot. Nixon was elected president. The Beatles had been to Rishikesh to study under the Maharishi in 1967 – a move which united eastern metaphysics and radical politics. The Yippies rained dollar bills on to the New York Stock Exchange, in an attempt to say that brown rice and Marxism could, all expectations to the contrary, walk hand in hand. Chicago in August 1968 focused their energies against the government, personified by Mayor Daley. In London the influence of American youth culture was felt through poetry, arts, politics and most especially through music.

After one summer in the East End, Rosie moved back to London to go to a crammer school in Victoria. She had a rented flat, which she shared with a girl from Ludlow who used to go to pony-club camps with her, and she had an allowance from her parents of twelve pounds a week. Her father paid the rent.

The flat was in Earl's Court, just around the corner from the Troubadour, but she didn't go there any more. The revolution, as far as she was concerned, had now moved to the Round House at Chalk Farm, heralded by journalists as London's answer to Haight-Ashbury. Right through Friday night and Saturday night she'd dance to the music of Joe Cocker, The Doors, Jefferson Airplane, the Who and countless other bands. Pepped up on blues, clad in one of her grandmother's old shawls which she'd converted into a jacket, its long fringe hanging down almost to her knees, she'd dance till dawn.

Here she smoked her first dope. 'It's far out isn't it?' Noel said, handing her the fat cigarette.

'Yes,' she agreed, praying for the much-heralded distortion of reality to clamp down, for the colours to start exploding. But the revolving purple spotlights remained the same and her feet still hit the ground every time she moved. Noel sensed her consternation: 'You've got to keep at it.' She did – soon she saw herself as an active member of the drug scene.

'Wanna come to my place later?' Dave the manager asked. Rosie nodded nervously. It was already five in the morning, mid-October, the night was winding up. The floor was covered with cigarette ends, Rufus Harris and Caroline Coon were clearing away the Release stall, and Jeff Dexter the DJ had just put 'All Night Long' on to the stereo.

'If only the music would keep on playing, if only I could dance with you, if only I could keep on singing, all night long, all night long . . .' The hippies mouthed the Airplane's words to themselves, reluctant to leave the party.

There was unspoken camaraderie, a sense of belonging to a world which was far outside anything their parents had dreamed of, held together by a love of music, of dope, of each other.

Rosie made her way to the door, looking for the blue Saab.

She was nervous, though the loss of her virginity had been carefully planned. Dave appeared on the stairs, splendid in blue velvet. His hair reached his shoulders and his fashionable Zapata moustache drooped down over the edges of his lips; hazel eyes twinkled provocatively behind black-framed glasses. Her stomach turned over; God, he was good-looking. God, I pray he doesn't realise that I've never done it before.

Dave flicked the stereo and music flooded the car. They drove through the streets of Chalk Farm, under the harsh orange street-lights. She looked at a group of hippies, wandering along towards King's Cross, their arms linked, then looked at Dave. He whistled under his breath as he spun the car expertly through the bends; she was overwhelmed with a sense of self-importance.

He shared a flat in the Gloucester Road with the Pretty Things. She was impressed as she took in his beeper phone, stereo and four-poster double bed. She realised she hadn't opened her mouth since they'd left. What to say? What to do? Utter panic. Should she take off her clothes? Or his. Dave threw off his jacket, put 'Light My Fire' on the stereo and started rolling a joint, oblivious to her nerves.

The eagerly anticipated act was a flop. Expecting drama and romance, something earth-shattering, she found only a dull aggravation. Having nothing to compare it with, she had no way of making comparisons. But she mostly wondered if she, herself, had been satisfactory, if she had managed to conceal the fact of her virginity and appear worldly and sophisticated between the fashionable purple sheets.

Dave certainly made no complaints, but neither did he refer to her sexual prowess. The following morning, creeping along the Sunday morning streets, she had felt decidedly changed and resolved not to go home to Shropshire for a few weeks as the change must surely be noticeable. Had she bled, she wondered? There had been no chance to inspect the sheets that morning since Dave was still in bed. She hadn't been able to tell whether the dampness between her legs came from blood or semen and the room had still been dark when she had left. Still, at least he hadn't been able to see her without her eye make-up.

Rosie was attending an expensive London A-level college. Academically, it was a farce. She went to movies with her maths teacher and her British Constitution teacher did not care whether or not she came to class. She did less scholastic work than she had done during the year at home, and in the summer of 1969 did not even show up to sit her exams.

The flat she lived in in Earl's Court had transformed itself into jumble-sale hippydom. Food (pâté, turkey wings and caviar) was ripped off from the supermarkets and her allowance went on drugs: acid, grass and speed. She drank champagne; the only alcohol she touched. Her friends were middle-class kids whose common denominator was their parents' wealth and willingness to set them up in London. They planned a trip to the south of France. Rosie offered to rent the villa and make the arrangements, ensuring, by doing this, that she would be at the nerve centre of the group. Through the classified ad pages of The Times she found a six-bedroomed villa in a small village above Vence. The £100 for rent, they all assured each other, would be easily covered by selling dope to the rich clientele of St Tropez and Cannes.

She told her father she was going camping with Jill (Snoopy) Cooper. Old school friends always added their respectability. Charles spent hours planning their itinerary and amassing their camping equipment. Both she and Snoopy felt guilty because none of it would be used, but their guilt was soon forgotten once they reached France. Rosie had failed her driving test twice but within fifty miles of Calais she'd taken the wheel of Snoopy's Mini. Snoopy sat in the back recovering from the effects of the acid they'd dropped on the cross-Channel ferry.

If the acid hadn't been stolen out of her room at the start of the third week, the month might have passed in an orgy of champagne-soaked peaches, nights on the terrace under the lemon trees, and days on the sun-sparkled beaches. The finances were working fine due to regular orders from three St Tropez restaurateurs. The dope was flown in from London once or twice a week.

As it was, a situation that was already unstable due to the copious drug intake of all the participants deteriorated rapidly into paranoid chaos. Rosie, officially in charge of the house in the week that the acid went missing, was expected to account for its disappearance. She couldn't. In London the address of the villa had been liberally passed around, and each day the phone would ring from some coastal bar announcing the presence of yet one more drifter heading towards Spain, Italy or just coming for the ride. The six bedrooms were always full; some nights there would be people sleeping on the sofas, or in the hammock.

Rosie was fairly certain who the culprit was. A curly headed old-Etonian with a hefty triple-barrelled name who made his living squiring middle-aged American women around St Tropez. He arrived at the villa for a two-day stay;

in between, he said, gigoloing for a Minneapolis heiress and the arrival of a woman from the West Coast.

By the time she discovered that the 100 tabs of pure white lightning were no longer hidden in her underwear, he had already left. Bill, who was in charge of the dealing operation, had just turned twenty. He was tall and skinny and his drug-hammered brain cells were only capable of grasping one idea at a time. But when he got it, he never let go. She met him off the London plane that afternoon; he was returning from a two-day trip to acquire further smoking pleasures for the St Tropez restaurants. He railed and bitched and accused her of selling it herself, or of throwing it away in a fit of stoned madness. Her innocent protest only hardened his conviction of her guilt and Rosie quickly realised that rational arguments meant nothing to a mind as responsive as soup. Cutting her losses, she packed in a hurry. Her last memory of Bill was the sight of his long body bent over the garbage bag, sifting through the rubbish like a prospector panning a river of fool's gold.

Back home she received the predictable news that she had failed her A-levels. The real story of the quasi-camping holiday was still under wraps, but rumours about life in the London flat had reached Ludlow.

Incensed by her A-level failure, Charles sent her to a small, intensive crammer in Leicestershire. The fees were £300 a term. Rosie was expelled on the twentieth day. 'A bad influence,' the headmaster told Betty and Charles when they arrived to pick her up.

She was eighteen, legally an adult since the Representation of the People Act had been passed earlier in the year, and she despaired. In the face of her parents' anguish, all the alternative creeds – who cares about exams, about degrees, they don't mean anything any more – fell apart. Rebellion was no longer fun and she felt dumb and frightened.

Just before Christmas she moved into digs with a retired maths teacher and worked her way through two terms of the Shrewsbury Technical College's A-level classes.

The mystique of America had grown to enormous proportions. It was a country where everything was possible; involved where England was detached; enterprising rather than conformist.

In the summer of 1970 Charles and Betty gave her a Greyhound bus ticket and, in the company of a local vicar's son and a schoolfriend of his, she set off for a three-month trip. The ticket, like the trip to the East End, seemed like a good behaviour reward. Who could come to harm in the old school settlement? Who could come to harm with the vicar's son?

With *On the Road* in her rucksack they hitched to San Francisco, arriving on the west coast on 7 August, the day that Angela Davis, then twenty-six, went underground following the shoot-out in the Marin County jail.

Haight-Ashbury was dingier and scruffier than she had expected. 'It's over now,' someone said to her, 'everyone goes to the Golden Gate Park nowadays.' She was sad to feel she'd missed something, but in the park the music was loud and insistent.

In *On the Road* when Kerouac is nearing Denver for the first time, and dreaming of his encounter with the fabled mile-high city, he says that he imagined that he would be in their eyes 'strange and ragged and like the Prophet who has walked across the dark land to bring the word, and the only word I had was "Wow".' That was it exactly. Rosie's first sight of Denver was from the back of an old Chevvy driven by two erratic but charming dope-dealers who had been on a trip to Kansas to collect some grass from a five-acre field they just happened to know about. The fresh leaves dried quickly on the hot metal nearest to the engine and they were all stoned on the fumes as the flat miles raced by.

The Magic Bus had already taken to the road, the counter-culture was throwing up its myriad lifestyles faster than the rest of the world could absorb. It was a perfect moment to be young.

Her A-level results came through via a telegram, on a windswept morning in Cape Cod at the end of August. She was staying in a beach house belonging to a boy waiting to go to Oxford on a Rhodes scholarship. She'd met him in the middle of the Salt Lake Desert, while she and her friend Charlie had been hitching rides west. Hunter was also hitching; he was already in the car when they clambered in, dusty and terrified following an encounter with a gun-toting, hard-drinking cowboy who'd tried to strand the pair on a little desert tor called Rattlesnake Mountain.

The day before they had gone with him to lunch with J. K. Galbraith. Hunter was helping to organise William Sloane Coffin's election to the Senate (he was then Dean of Harvard Theology College). Galbraith had agreed to speak at a rally to be held in a few weeks' time. The economist's retreat house was reached after driving for miles through the New Hampshire woods, already starting to turn into their autumn hues. After lunch Mrs Galbraith had questioned her about England, confessing her great dislike of the Cambridge University system of forbidding women to sit at the high table. She had been there for a visit.

'What did you do in the evenings then?' Rosie asked.

'Sat in my room. I wouldn't have minded, except it was my honeymoon.'

'You did well,' said Hunter, looking over her shoulder. He'd brought the cable down from the house to the water's edge, where Rosie was paddling through the waves, screwing her toes down into the sand and feeling the grains work their way up between them. He kicked off his shoes and joined her. It was early, and sunlight was pouring across the sea.

'You going to go to university then?' he said.

'I suppose so, but now that I can, now that it's no hassle, well, I don't know. The fun's gone out of it. I mean if I can do this –' and she looked at the grade As and her father's congratulatory message 'then I know I can probably get a good degree and then what? Can you really see me in spectacles, teaching pure maths?'

Hunter grinned.

'God knows what you'll do. I know you're going to do something. But you're right – you'd look fucking lousy in spectacles.'

The Kent University campus perched on the side of the hills to the north of Canterbury. The residential halls, clinging to the escarpment, afforded long views over the town and valley. The winds were bitter.

She was irked with her own smug sense of superiority; disappointed with the provincial feeling of the university. What she had done seemed to set her apart from her fellow students, even from the third years who had invited her to share a huge ramshackle old Queen Anne vicarage with them.

Now, facing their finals and drowning in LSD, they all looked so frightened. Eyes large and staring, like trapped animals looking for escape. She was frightened of the fears that acid always uncovered, the feeling of never belonging, the restlessness which kept saying Move. Would it be lack of staying power to go, or cowardice to stay?

She didn't know. Being her age at that moment in time meant being young without guidelines. And though she was the first to use the freedom, and all that it offered, the pill, the music, the nights when you didn't go to sleep, the lack of discipline, it could be hard operating without maps. Too much freedom can daunt even the bravest, and the lack of limits – that unheard whisper which said, 'Go on, now you can do anything' – was a double-edged challenge. Running to, or running from? It could have been either.

She arrived in London in the spring of 1970. She had no job, nowhere to live and no money. She hadn't even told her parents of her decision to leave, fearing that she would be talked out of it.

Three days later, she was facing another uncomfortable night on the sofa of some distant girlfriends. The doorbell rang. 'I've locked myself out of my flat.' The words sounded down the hallway. 'Can I crash on your sofa?'

'Someone's already there.' Cassandra's tones were apologetic. 'But I'm going to be out all night, so you can have my bed.'

Rosie looked up to greet the visitor. He was dark and energetic, slightly sweaty as though he'd been running to get a bus. His Jewishness was unmistakable. He wore glasses, faded jeans, grubby sneakers, and his belly protruded over his belt, threatening to burst the buttons of his blue shirt. His fingernails, like hers, were bitten to the quick.

'Hi, I'm Jonathon.' He sat down beside her and then immediately got up and announced he was going to bed. She tried to engage him in conversation and poured him some wine. He worked, she soon discovered, for London's alternative weekly guide *Time Out*, and supplemented his income by dealing a little grass. Cassandra and her friends were his customers. Before *Time Out* he'd worked for *Frendz*, before that for *Rolling Stone*. He was twenty-three, an Oxford graduate. She moved in with him two days later.

FIVE

In the dining room at breakfast time a woman walked up to a table occupied by two elderly men and upturned her breakfast tray in front of them. Coffee and egg yolk ran across the table. A nurse took the woman's arm and led her away. A Chinese cookboy appeared carrying a pail and cloth. The silence was slowly filled by chatter.

'Jesus, bloody loony,' said Brian.

'Does that happen often?' I asked, grinding my sixth cigarette of the morning on to the edge of a saucer. Taylor looked up over the top of his *Times*.

'They're all perfectly barmy, if you ask me,' he said and went back to his newspaper.

It was my fourth day in the clinic. My self-obsession was lifting slowly, leaving a strange airy sense of emptiness. I was not feeling particularly bright, or gay, or happy, nor was I feeling particularly unhappy. I felt I had been in the clinic for weeks, not just four days. Emotional crises always warp time and prolong moments so that you forget the edges of days and the natural markers within them.

The alcoholics always sat at the same table. Unlike most other patients, the schizos, depressives and kleptomaniacs, the boozers were taken off drugs as fast as possible.

Hemenevrin was usually prescribed for four or five days. It depended on what state you had arrived in. My state on arrival was pretty bad; not as bad as some (I wasn't incontinent, and I could still walk and conduct conversations) but I'd taken a lot of liquor on board in the preceding few days. Boozing is classed as an illness, but not as a mental illness; another important distinction, apart from the lack of drugs, which made the boozers hang out together and pass rude remarks about the other patients. It was also true that after a few days, once the shakes subsided, we all felt better than we had done in ages.

'Pity you missed Abdullah,' said Brian with a grin.

'Who?' I asked.

'Oh, an Arab who could only go to sleep in the elevator. He would commandeer it whenever he could, lie on the floor and keep his foot on the button. I guess he missed being on a camel!'

Breakfast lasted from eight-thirty to nine a.m. and was followed by the daily community meeting.

That morning the subject under discussion was the patients' party. 'Well, what do you all think?' asked the head of occupational therapy. Silence. A fat man called Andy turned his back on the speaker, swivelling buttocks which hung over the side of the seat like joints of mutton. It turned out he was only waiting to announce his contribution to the festivities.

'I'll ask my friend Nikki Lauda to come and talk about racing cars.'

A sigh went round the room. Everyone fidgeted, not from embarrassment but from the boredom of hearing him embark on one of his racing-driver fantasies. He lived in them most of the time. Soon I got used to them and, like everyone else, would discuss the scars he suffered in his last race as if they and his dream races were real. He would point to his white, fat legs and say that the way they had healed so well was a miracle.

'Now, Andy,' said a member of staff, 'let's be serious, the party is in three weeks and we don't want a repeat of the last time.'

I wondered what that meant.

A very black African who was certifiably violent, and had a personal nurse-cum-bodyguard, leapt to his feet. 'I got a far-out idea. Let's have a bar.' He raced across the room to the huge colour TV. 'We could put it here.'

'Sit down,' ordered a nurse. 'Now, you know we can't have a bar at the party, since we don't allow drink in the clinic. There are people here . . .' He didn't finish the sentence. The truth was that the occupational therapists were all a little frightened of the drunks. We were all fit and well, on the whole bright, and far from enthusiastic about playing party games meant to divert lunatics.

'We'll serve wine,' suggested a fat Qatari, 'that's not alcoholic.' The staff looked depressed. No one said anything. People began getting to their feet, although the nurses were still talking about the party. Another clinic day had begun.

From the outside it is an unobtrusive building. You pay highly for the exterior discretion. Inside it's a bit like a ship. You go upstairs to the dining room, even further upstairs to the rooftop balcony. The inside corridors have no windows and are permanently lit by harsh strip-lighting. Our floor was the upper ground, which meant we were just above street level. The windows of our rooms only opened six inches upwards or downwards, thus preventing patients sneaking out for a quick one at a pub called the Chelsea Potter, which was tantalisingly situated across the street.

Alcoholism is no longer classed as a mental illness, but is described as an illness; not because it can be caught, like a virus, but because it has an observable set of symptoms. Articles about alcoholism in popular magazines always set out a series of questions, and end with the remarks, 'If you say yes to any two or three of the above then you have a drink problem.' If you are drinking in the morning; drinking to run away from something frightening; drinking when you're already drunk; having memory blackouts and so on, then that is not normal drinking. On the other hand it may not mean that you are necessarily alcoholic.

The definitions of alcoholism are as varied and numerous as the doctors who have devoted their lives to studying the subject. My doctor was a believer in the works and studies of Jellinek, in whose honour the unit I was currently residing in was named. Loss of control due to drinking, on a regular basis, means you're alcoholic. As a medical definition, it's a good one. I've known people who can drink half a bottle of Scotch a day and not come to any apparent mental harm. They may get a bit slurry, but their behaviour is not anti-social, they don't pass out like flies who've suddenly been squirted with Black Flag and their inner calm does not degenerate into alcoholic paranoia. They are, however, harming their bodies.

Over what is a 'safe' amount to drink, there is also endless debate. Women with smaller bodies and smaller livers, can drink far less. But people's constitutions vary and what can poison one can be tolerable to another.

Alcohol itself is ether. Chemists call it ethyl alcohol and what we drink is ether with flavourings for taste. Ether reduces the activities of the nervous system, and in small quantities this creates the 'high', since your inhibitions are lifted. You get sexier, happier, funnier and so on. I know the magic of the first few drinks as well as anyone. After the first few, when the alcohol cuts deeper into the brain, your judgment becomes severely impaired, senses numb, stumbling starts because you are cutting off the motor controls which govern your body. As judgment goes, belligerence, anger and lies may emerge. Finally you can numb the brain so much that you pass out. You also have blackouts.

Blackouts are the only piece of irretrievable human memory known to man. You can subject an alcoholic to sodium pentathol, to hypnosis, to any of the tricks which are supposed to bring back deeply buried thoughts. No luck. Later in my stay in the clinic, I met an American doctor who worked for the US Navy. Alcoholic pilots were his speciality. He had treated men who could remember leaving their hotels in London's Gloucester Road at nine in the morning, and the next thing they could remember was walking into another hotel in Manhattan. Three hundred lives in their hands in between and 3,000 miles at 30,000 feet. No joke.

The body, as well as the mind, suffers from alcohol excess through liver disease, pancreatitis, heart disease, gastric inflammation, malnutrition and brain damage. Most are reversible if you stop in time, though each on its own can kill if left to run riot with constant supplies of booze. There is no escaping the fact that alcoholism is a fatal disease. Quite how many fatalities it actually causes is impossible to pinpoint, since a respectable city gent who dies of heart failure at his desk is going to be recorded as leaving this planet as a result of a heart attack. His widow is not going to want a doctor to stick on his death certificate that his premature death was caused by copious quantities of alcohol which had weakened his heart, built up fatty deposits around it and caused that fatal seizure.

No alcoholic will survive to end his days naturally. It may be a car accident, it may be cirrhosis, it may be internal haemorrhaging due to the wearing down of the skin surrounding the oesophagal veins until they become so worn that they literally burst open and flood your blood right into the wrong places: stomach, lungs and life.

Day patients often joined the group sessions. Later on, during my fourth day in the clinic, a middle-aged blonde, wearing a bright red polyester suit, came hesitantly into the room.

'Anne,' she cried, her prematurely lined face breaking into a smile.

'Shelagh!' Anne leapt up from her seat and they embraced.

'What are you doing here?' they both asked simultaneously.

'I've been here for two weeks. It's really working this time,' said Anne.

Shelagh looked at her friend encouragingly. 'Great,' she said, 'I'm checking in tomorrow.' The two women had met in another clinic in London. This was my first introduction to the phenomenon of clinic-hopping. The boozer tries one after the other, in the hope of finding some cure, and always seems to end up relapsing. The concept was grossly depressing, but it also had its funny side.

The doctor came in. 'Hello there, Shelagh,' he said and smiled brightly at her. 'You're coming in tomorrow?'

Shelagh looked glum. 'Andrew can't stand it any more. The kids are in a state. The gardener found ten empty vodka bottles in the potting shed.'

Her hands were shaking. She twisted her fingers together in her lap.

'I had a disaster in the house, too. I passed out and when I came to I'd forgotten where I'd hidden the bottle. The maid came to do the washing and when she turned on the machine there was this awful noise. I'd hidden the vodka in there. It wrecked the kids' clothes and Andrew says we've got to have a new washing machine.'

The doctor looked at the floor. Shelagh had been his patient for two years and success, so far, was elusive. 'How long did you stay off this time?' he asked her gently.

'Under a week. I can't seem to manage it. Andrew's threatening to leave me. I feel so useless.'

'But what about the children?' asked Brian. 'Aren't they an incentive to stay sober?'

'They don't need me,' she said sadly, 'neither does Andrew. No one does. I've tried having a maid, and not having a maid, so that I have something to do, then I find I can't even make the effort to make the bed in the morning.'

She looked tragic and frightened. She was overweight, badly dressed for someone with a great deal of money and always wore the same pair of plastic, imitation patent-leather black shoes. Her tights usually had a ladder in them. She bit her fingernails. But her hair was always immaculate.

'Do you have to go out, entertain?' Brian asked.

'No, Andrew doesn't ask people to the house any more . . . he daren't. But I never drink in public.'

'Same as you, Anne, though not you, Rosie,' said the doctor. A difference between the generations: older women only drank in private, younger ones got drunk sometimes, at least, in public.

Very few marriages survive alcoholism. It's a hard statistic that whereas only one in ten alcoholic husbands are left by their wives, nine out of ten husbands eventually leave their alcoholic wives. Taylor coughed gently. 'I can't imagine what I would do if my wife was drunk all the time.'

'My wife left me because I drank,' said Brian. 'Well, it was one of the reasons.'

'I suppose the man I really loved left me because of the booze,' I added. I hadn't confronted that fact before, only suspected it, and immediately shut it out.

'Pauline, my wife,' said Raju to Shelagh, 'nearly left, but then she started going to Al-Anon and somehow got me to go too.'

'Well, what are you doing here?' Shelagh snapped back.

'Impulse!' The word came out staccato. It was Raju's favourite word, and his only explanation to account for his presence in a booze clinic after being off the stuff for one year.

'No such thing,' retorted Shelagh, who was recovering from her bout of self-pity.

There was a silence.

'How was the year without booze?' I asked Raju.

'OK,' he said. Raju worked as an anaesthetist in a West-country hospital, so his alcoholism was a potential killer not only to himself, but to others too.

'How did you cope with going to parties?' I asked.

'OK,' he replied again. The question was silly anyway. Raju and I had nothing in common, bar the booze.

'Does the fact that you're asking about going to parties mean that you're starting to see that you'll have to give up drink?'

Brian turned towards me. I shrugged, noncommittally.

'Do you yet admit that your life has been fucked by booze?'

I nodded.

'And you want it to go on?'

'No, of course not,' I said crossly. 'Why would I be here if . . .'

'How many times have you tried to stop?' asked the doctor.

'None. Well, that's not really true. I've tried cutting down,' I added.

'And it hasn't worked,' interrupted Anne.

'Sometimes, yes, sometimes it has,' I muddled on, defensively.

Every drunk is different. It took Anne half a bottle of sherry to pass out, it took Brian a couple of bottles of vodka. What we had in common was an addiction to booze, and a sense of worthlessness in our lives. No one could pinpoint the magic line where we stopped being 'social drinkers' and became alcoholic, but we all publicly or secretly knew that we were there. Our lives were in a mess, were being run by the bottle. That doesn't mean being drunk all the time, either. In my case, I would go for long stretches, sometimes weeks, sometimes months, drinking normally. At least, that's how it appeared. I wasn't drinking normally, because I would be anxious near lunchtime, anxious around six-thirty p.m., anxious to make sure there was always wine for dinner. But in terms of quantity, I was actually drinking no more than William. Except at times. Loneliness, misery, a sense of no purpose to my life would come rushing up and I knew the answer. Drunkenness was a shield against pain, against the failure of too many dreams, against a sense of spiritual confusion. But what had started out as a protection racket, my third mad lady (the drinking me) taking care of the inner baby, was no longer working. Now it was no longer possible to see what problems stemmed from booze and what were problems in themselves.

I remembered endless visits to a Harley Street shrink, who probed, at great expense, into reasons for my drinking. He thought, and many people do, that if he could ever crack the reason, then the booze problem would disappear. 'See if you can manage to have more orgasms,' he'd once said. 'Did you see your father in the bath when you were a baby?' He thought that if I got fucked better then I'd stop drinking. I'd discuss this problem with him quite seriously, but for only one reason: it kept the conversation away from my growing dependence on alcohol. By the time I got up to leave his office, he'd smile, I'd smile and then I'd scamper to the off-licence or the pub and have a drink. My weekly visits to the shrink were a sanction to drink.

I snapped out of my reverie to find the doctor asking me a question.

'I'm trying to get you all to write your life stories,' he said. 'No one has bothered to do it so far, but since you're a journalist maybe you can sit down and write something, or take notes, and then tell us.'

William brought my typewriter into the clinic that night. He had been a faithful visitor, but I was finding it hard to deal with any visits. I was reverting to a childlike state: accepting help for the first time in my life made me vulnerable, shaky and shy. The growing friendship between me and my fellow patients was becoming increasingly valuable. We were finding out each other's habits; who liked which TV programmes; who had sugar in their tea; which newspapers people liked to read.

The absurdities of the other patients (and of ourselves) presented an absorbing soap opera. The clinic, like it or not, was fast becoming my home. That night, I carefully cleaned off my eye make-up and applied moisturiser to my face. It's absurd, I thought, but I don't want to be anywhere else until . . . until when? I didn't know the answer. It wasn't like checking into a hotel. You arrived only when you had no alternative.

Six

The offices of *Frendz* magazine spanned two floors of a run-down terrace at the top of the Portobello Road. On one Saturday in April, just before Rosie's twentieth birthday, the street was busier than usual. The day was warm and the jokers and pranksters with beads, bells and mantras were rifling through the tatty bargains and baubles which bowed the stalls lining the street. Underfoot, oranges squelched in the gutter.

The resident man-with-a-monkey-dressed-in-a-tee-shirt-and-red-trousers was taking Polaroids of his pet perched on the shoulders of foreign tourists. Local hippies snickered.

Jerome was staring gloomily at the accounts book. They were broke: there was not enough to pay the print bill. Little Tony, the office's teenage factotum, came into the room, his hand clasped firmly round the wrist of a nervous red-haired woman. She looked about forty and her clothes were ragged and dusty.

'This is Daphne – she wants to give us some money,' Tony announced in triumph. 'I met her out on the street and I've been telling her about the paper. She says she'd like to help.'

Everyone brightened. Pat, the advertising rep, fetched a chair. Daphne opened her large handbag, which was dirty white but had started life in Bond Street. The notes inside were equally dirty, stuffed in like old Kleenex.

'Ten, fifteen, thirty-five, forty-five, fifty, how much do you want?' She paused at four hundred and twenty.

'Well . . .'Jerome hesitated. 'Are you sure? It's a lot of money . . .'

'I don't have anything to do with it. You see I won't be here very long . . . and I've been a bad girl. Five hundred.'

She closed her bag. 'Do you mind if I stay here a while?' she asked.

'No, luv, stay as long as you like,' Pat said. 'Where do you live?'

It was the reversal of normal etiquette. Take the money, then ask questions.

'Tony, can you fetch my bed?' Daphne asked.

Tony was always pale; somehow he went even paler. 'You mean that old set of springs?'

He reappeared dragging the bedsprings, scattering particles of rust over the worn carpet.

'Where would you like it?' he asked, like a Harrods man delivering a new kingsize. She waved towards a narrow space on the floor under the window, where the sun cast warm shadows.

Daphne stood up, peeling off her cotton dress. She was naked underneath, and her breasts drooped and flopped like half-inflated balloons. Everyone stood up nervously and moved towards the back room. She lay down, eyes shut, impervious to the sharp wires digging into her thin buttocks.

Pat picked up the money. 'She's a right bloody loony,' she said, once they were all safely out of earshot.

'We can have an issue out by this time next week,' said

Jerome, settling himself at the small desk, and reaching for a planning board.

Since she couldn't type, Rosie had immediately acquired the status of an editor. Jonathon had got her the job through the conventions of the old boy network. The system worked as well for hippies as for civil servants. The current editor of *Frendz*, Jerome Burne, had been an Oxford friend of Jonathon's.

He'd welcomed Rosie on to the staff, asking no questions about her qualifications. Instead, he sent her off with the office tape-recorder to interview John Lennon and Yoko Ono about Yoko's poetry book, *Grapefruit*. The book had been disastrously reviewed. Privately, Rosie thought it incomprehensible.

The interview, which took place in the Apple headquarters, had been an ordeal of nerves. Rosie had never used a tape-recorder before. While thinking up the next question, she kept glancing at the machine, checking to see that the spool was still winding. She was anxiously trying to think of angles which would shed new light on the superstars, but the combination of her nerves, their presence and the possible unreliability of the machine resulted in an interview of benign blandness.

Jonathon was working for *Time Out*, dealing dope to supplement his income and to provide an ongoing supply of marijuana. Rosie had already met his partner, David.

In 1969, Julia and Rosie had got to know two Cambridge graduates, one a writer, the other a painter, who lived in a small narrow mews house behind the cinema in Westbourne Grove. Both young men had lots of money. Their house was luxurious in comparison to the tacky basements that she and Julia were used to. They were also witty and highbrow. Rosie's metaphors were then confined to what she'd picked up in the Troubadour Café and the Middle Earth club; drugs, psychedelia and a smattering of lefty rhetoric; jaunty street chat.

The artistic references which David and his friend Jerry bandied about were impressive. They paired off. Julia with David, Rosie with Jerry. He was strangely magnetic. She never thought of him as good-looking. His face, even at twenty-two, was gnarled, misshapen by the tensions which hovered beneath the surface. His eyes were small, and a brilliant blue. Like his face his hands were wrinkled, prematurely old. Rosie remembered looking at his palms and thinking, these are the hands of an old man. His hair was Afro, blond, wiry and springy like Scottish heather.

They tumbled into bed while Jerry murmured endearments which seemed straight out of another century: high-blown, romantic stuff. They'd concluded, somewhere in the middle of the night, that fate must have brought them together and that possibly they'd met in some previous lifetime. The sentiments matched the instant passion.

The next morning, Jerry, bare-chested, was standing in front of his easel, dabbing colour with erratic small strokes. His mood had changed. When he saw she was awake, he came and sat on the end of the bed. 'Listen . . .' he said hesitantly, 'about last night. About the things we said. Well, I've got a girlfriend . . . someone called Lucy. I don't want to sound heavy, but that was heavy stuff we were getting into.'

'That's OK,' Rosie replied breezily, jumping out of bed and pulling on her clothes. 'It's cool.'

She did understand, but she didn't think it cool. She was disappointed. Jealous of Lucy for a fleeting moment. But her hip image was important, so she waved goodbye and expected never to see him again. It wouldn't have been the only such casual encounter.

She didn't expect to see David again either. So she was surprised when Jonathon introduced his partner. David hadn't changed. He was still aesthetically slender, still struggling to write. Jonathon's dark, earthy cynicism contrasted sharply with his romanticism. Drugs, David thought, were valid only as consciousness expanders and he viewed Jonathon's ability to get wholly, and often untidily, out of it, with distaste. Where David liked Zen and brown rice, Jonathon liked Raymond Chandler and steak. David drank Chinese tea and an occasional glass of champagne; Jonathon copious quantities of the latest Australian ale, Fosters. They were hopeless dealers for different reasons: David because he thought that selling drugs went badly with his artistic aspirations. He let Jonathon know that he was too good for it, like a Victorian gentleman forced into trade. Jonathon was simply terrified of getting caught.

David and Jerry were still friends. Jerry was now living with Lucy and when Rosie and he met again neither of them referred to the two-year-old one-night stand, but they were pleased to see each other.

A room was vacant in Lucy's house and she and Jonathon, tired of the dosshouse they were living in, moved in immediately, along with their waterbed which they had acquired for nothing; courtesy of an American company which was trying to launch its wet-dream fantasy into Britain. And where better to begin than with the underground magazine staff?

Like Daphne, Donald walked into the *Frendz* office on a particularly desperate day. He didn't bring five-pound notes but expertise. The accounts books were in arrears, and IBM were threatening to repossess the typesetter for non-payment of rent. The cash flow was erratic. No one on the staff knew how to keep the books. Donald was a dropped-out forty-year-old Scottish accountant and a numbers wizard. The accounts were in order in a week. Jerome nicknamed him Donald O'Cash.

'Why are you doing this?' he said to Rosie and Jerome at the dawn end of a long night spent pasting up an issue. 'Do you mean all this . . . the overthrow of society, off the pigs . . .?'

'Everything is changing, Donald,' Jerome said, 'things aren't going to be the same. Look at you . . . you're here.' Donald nodded, then grinned. 'Yes, but I've made my money . . . I've worked for years. I want to relax, go and live in a commune. But you, you've been to universities, you're smart. Isn't there anything better than this?'

The latest edition was devoted to lengthy coverage of the rock world, an interview with Jennie Dean, 'New York's Supergroupie', full reports on the prices of dope, an investigation into why the 1971 Reading Festival was such a disaster (the police? the site? the rain? the faulty PA system? the greed of the hip capitalist entrepreneurs?), and an article written by a trainee teacher condemning the system's method of educating the educators. Among the small ads in the personal column was the following:

'I got this idea for scoring a village or three and maybe a fishing fleet in the north of Scotland. It might work – but it needs people. Do you have childbearing potential?'

'I suppose I'd think you were less mad if I thought that you genuinely just wanted to advance your careers,' O'Cash went on, 'learn about papers, but then sometimes, well, you all seem crackers. Like that madman, Farquharson. Jesus, where do they come from?'

Farquharson had first come to their attention after the Isle of Wight Festival. *The Frendz* festival news-sheet reported that: 'The author, Robin Farquharson, freaked out and scared bystanders. He was quickly ejected from the *Frendz* tent and just as quickly returned on the hood of a taxi shouting, "Right On, Right On." He was beaten and taken to St John's by Security men. He was later removed in a Land Rover as no one could get it together for an ambulance.'

The legendary author had arrived in the Portobello Road offices the day before. Shouts below the window had caught their attention. Outside a tall, wild-looking hairy man was fighting with a cab driver. Breaking free of the driver's arm, he'd run up the office stairs.

'I've just sold this building,' he panted, 'you can all retire. I know how to destroy the banking system of the country. Everyone must open six accounts and then transfer their overdrafts from one to the other, increasing them all the time. We'll bring the pigs down in a few months. It's easy . . .'

'Yes, Farquharson was crazy,' Jerome admitted. 'But not everyone is. The people who write to us from communes for instance, they meant it, they're living in a different way.'

'I know,' said O'Cash. 'I'm going to join that person who writes from his communal farm in Ireland. But I won't go yet.' He added, 'I'll keep on keeping your accounts in order.'

Rosie's only contribution to Jonathon's dope dealing business was the use of her car for transport. He had always refused to learn to drive and had an aversion to all things mechanical, reckoning that what he didn't know he couldn't fuck up. His contribution at home had been to build bookshelves and a wooden surround for the waterbed. The shelves – stuffed with free items that fell into their laps daily – collapsed and the waterbed sprang a leak. A nail had worked loose and gouged the latex.

Jerry and Lucy, whose bedroom was immediately below, had begun pounding the ceiling at six in the morning when Jerry had been woken up by the steady drips.

'Water, everywhere, all over my paints.' Jerry stamped around the kitchen, like a spoilt child. They'd been living there for about three months and Rosie had already concluded that she'd had a lucky break. Jerry was hard to live with. He spent a lot of time in the bath playing with a duck, entirely indifferent to people coming in to pee or shave.

Later that morning, Jonathon went into the bathroom to shave. Jerry harangued him from the tub.

'You hate me, don't you?'

'No, I don't,' replied Jonathon.

'Well, Rosie does.'

'No she doesn't.' Jonathon cursed as he nicked his skin and dabbed at the blood with a tissue.

'She's angry about the rhino . . . thinks I cut it up.'

'She doesn't,' Jonathon retorted. 'Stop going on about it. We don't know who cut up the rhino.' Rosie had had a rubber rhino which had disappeared. She'd found it cut into small pieces in the garbage can. At the time she'd assumed it was Jerry; he was the only person who possessed scalpels and he regularly cut up his canvases. But he'd denied it and she'd dropped the subject. It seemed silly to make a fuss about a rubber rhino.

'Anyway, we're away for the weekend,' Jonathon said. 'No water, no rhinos, no fuss. OK?'

Jerry nodded and pushed his bath duck around in the soap suds.

They collected a new waterbed from the wholesalers and set off for Glastonbury, where a four-day midsummer pop festival was in progress. Rosie had to write about it for the

paper and she was looking forward to the Somerset countryside, listening to the assortment of bands. Jonathon was
not so sure. He loathed the country and insisted that green
fields made him insecure. A concrete child. Their last country
weekend, one organised by Rosie and Jerome, had gone
badly.

A regular letterwriter to *Frendz* had been urging the two
editors to come to stay on his commune. In April they had
agreed to go. The weather had been foul; the hippie's directions less than perfect. Eleven o'clock at night found them all
out of the car, in sheeting rain and pitch dark, trying to push
the reluctant vehicle out of two feet of mud. Jonathon held a
copy of *Frendz* over his head and the coloured inks ran in
streaks down his cheeks. Through his misery he shouted that
his fears had been justified.

When they found the commune, it was past midnight. The
small stone house stood in open country, shutters banging in
the wind. They were all dying for a drink. Round the open
fire, the five commune members huddled together against
the cold, drinking tea.

Jonathon asked for wine. 'We don't drink,' replied their
host, regarding him with distaste.

'Well, food then.' A bowl of brown rice duly appeared.
They crouched in front of the fire. Rosie stifled laughter at
Jonathon's dismay. He was counting the minutes to when
he could leave this macrobiotic haven and get back to the
city, the sidewalks and the rat race.

He hated Glastonbury even more, confronted as he was by
no less than 8,000 peace and love devotees. He spent most of
the weekend drunkenly propping up the press enclosure,
eyeing the latter-day Jesus Christs with disdain. Unlike Rosie
he wasn't impressed that the organiser had sold his family

gun collection to raise the necessary capital. He complained bitterly about the open plan lavatory.

England was experiencing an economic boom, and nothing was too good for those selling kids' culture. Every day the postman would deliver parcels of books from publishing companies for review, records, and invitations to press parties which were unrivalled in their lavishness and conspicuous cost. The papers were almost wholly supported by the consumer society they claimed to rebel against, but financially the counterculture was missing the boat.

Efficiency had been thrown out along with the rest of the establishment ethic. It was cool to be untogether, 'uptight' to be businesslike. Superstition had replaced suspicion. Hippies were wonderfully gullible.

Reading the Sergeant Pepper album cover upside down would, they said, reveal the secret number of the Beatles. By chance the insignificant numbers led callers to the *Guardian* night newsdesk, which took calls from worldwide asking about John and Paul's health. It was also a handy number to call if you were broke, they claimed. Everyone knew how free John and Paul were with their cash.

Laid back meant losing out, and the hippy philosophy, which eschewed commercialism, paved the way for the culture's own extinction. Maintaining that work was abolished because now all work was play, was romantic in the extreme. When the Establishment saw the commercial potential in the new lifestyle – health food, country-style furniture, clothes – and produced Terence Conran and Laura Ashley, the hippies thought it a good joke. Especially laughable was the news that the cigarette companies had already taken out patents on the brands of dope they intended to sell when marijuana was legalised, as everyone confidently expected it would be. Closer to home, the rock bands who began playing on the Portobello Road were now owned by the large record companies.

All the evidence from the sixties that Britain was becoming a classless society – epitomised by Ted Heath's rise to Tory power started to collapse.

Jerry and Lucy tagged along with Rosie and Jonathon to some of the larger promotional parties: rock band shindigs where the booze flowed and everybody could walk off with half a dozen free albums which could then be sold at record stores. Jerry had dragged Jonathon down to the Tate one day and, smoking a surreptitious joint, had sat him down in front of the great red Rothkos and explained to his reluctant listener how Rothko had one day taken off his neat formal grey suit, folded it over a chair and then slashed his wrists and watched himself bleed to death.

'God, I'm bored with his obsessions,' Jonathon remarked later in the day, while struggling to fit into his black velvet suit which was rapidly becoming too tight for his expanding stomach. They were off to yet another party, to be held at Pete Townshend's house in Surrey. The promised gluttony threatened to burst the suit, but by four in the morning, staggering drunkenly home along the King's Road, singing to the morning sparrows, they were past caring.

In the autumn of 1971, *Frendz* produced a woman's issue. The male staff thought it a good idea; it meant a two-week holiday, and anyway, since the publication of Germaine Greer's *The Female Eunuch*, the issue of women's politics could not be ignored.

Rosie coordinated the issue, since she knew the mechanics of laying out the pages. In between the regular articles were features about emergent female sexuality, equal pay demands, abortion, and the plight of the working-class woman.

The underground press had an ambivalent attitude towards women. 'You can fuck anytime, but ask a girl to make Ovaltine?' *Oz* editor Richard Neville was quoted as saying. He was almost right. Going to bed, or, as the cliché had it, getting laid on the back copies, was expected. To refuse was both old-fashioned and hypocritical in a culture promoting free love.

In 1969 *International Times*, Britain's oldest underground paper, was condemning the Miss World competition in its editorials. Safe territory for the men of the underground. Mecca and Miss World were neat symbols of big business, capitalism and plastic living. The editors could sigh complacently because they weren't subjecting their girlfriends to parading in swimsuits round the Albert Hall. But they weren't encouraging them to become editors or reporters either.

In itself the woman's issue of *Frendz* was no great triumph, but the timing was right. The *Oz* trial was over, and the three editors, charged with conspiracy to corrupt public morals, had been sentenced. In the three-day public outcry following Judge Argyle's verdict, the sentence had been suspended. Jonathon and Rosie had burnt an effigy of the judge on the steps of the Old Bailey. In the ensuing mêlée the long hair of a *Frendz* reporter had tangled with a policeman's buttons. A picture in a popular tabloid depicted the scene, captioned 'The Wailing Wall of Weirdies'. Later Rosie heard that the sub-editor had been promoted for his witty line.

After the trial, Marsha Rowe, who was working on *Ink*, the weekly paper set up by Richard Neville, Andrew Fisher and Ed Victor to rival magazines like the *New Statesman*, and helping with the *Oz* trial defence, invited Rosie to a series of meetings which she and Richard Neville's girlfriend, Louise Ferrier, were organising. Later she was to say that it was the *Oz* trial which had woken her and Louise up to the peculiar fix women were placed in by the counterculture.

During the trial Neville had responded to the accusation that his magazine was part of a community 'without love' by saying that, on the contrary, '*Oz* was against guilt and repression and was trying to redefine love, broaden it, extend it and revitalise it, so it could be a force of release, and not one of entrapment.'

'That may be true for men,' Marsha commented, 'but it isn't true for women.'

She was a glorified secretary at *Ink*, doing a great deal of everything but missing the limelight which fell on the editors. She was then twenty-eight, very pretty with a thick mop of dark hair which curled around a pixie face.

By 1970 feminism was becoming fashionable, so it would have been reasonable to expect Neville's book, *Playpower*, to mention it. But the closest the index came to mentioning women's liberation was the 'Female Fuckability Test', referring to a feature in *Screw*, the New York sex tabloid. Germaine Greer rated two credits; one under acknowledgments 'for having assisted the author', the other as the author of a piece entitled 'Lady Love Your Cunt', in *Suck*, a Paris imitation of *Screw*.

The long summer ground into winter uncertainties. Jonathon edited *Oz* for five issues – a court order had banned the editors from returning to work on the paper – but the sparkle had died. *Frendz* sales dropped and the tenuous connections which had held the underground together started to snap. Group structures of more specialist interest emerged: communes, the music business, the left wing and women.

Donald O'Cash set off to live in a commune in Ireland. Jonathon's guest editorship of *Oz* came to an end and he sat back, terrified, wondering what the hell to do. 1971 turned into 1972 and they were broke.

Their second waterbed had sprung a leak.

They saw little of Jerry and Lucy. Occasionally, when all four were at home together, they'd go out to eat and their friendship would reassert itself over the wine. Jerry always paid. He was unfailingly generous with his money, though Rosie sometimes suspected that he used it to buy friendships. He was having an affair with a nineteen-year-old model whose face regularly appeared on the fashion pages of magazines like *Honey* and *19*. He made little attempt to conceal the fact from Lucy, who alternated between sobbing and stoicism. Like Rosie, she found it easy to advocate free love for other people, but almost impossible to deal with it personally, and she confessed her envy of Jonathon's dogged adoration. 'Would you mind if Jonathon went off with someone?' she asked.

'Yes,' Rosie answered, feeling honest. 'I'd hate it.'

Then Jerry's father died. For some months he'd been talking about the Oedipal fantasy he had about his mother, who was twenty years his father's junior, slim, sexy and provocative. At first the idea had been intriguing, and they compared parental relationships, but interest soon waned. Not for Jerry. He told his father over dinner at their country house in Norfolk that he'd always wanted to sleep with his mother. That night his father had a coronary. Jerry rang up Lucy, waking her at five in the morning, incoherent with grief. She took Rosie and Jonathan out to lunch the following day and asked their advice.

'I suppose he'll be guilty as hell,' Jonathon said, rather jauntily.

Lucy frowned. 'Of course he will be. Wouldn't you?'

'Academic my dear, totally academic,' he replied.

Their concern was superficial. Jerry's role in his father's death though at one time a ripe subject for a three-volume novel – was afforded no more than a couple of minutes' discussion. They slipped it in, anecdotally, between the news of someone's pregnancy and the business of rolling the seventh joint. It didn't even cross anyone's mind – least of all Lucy's – to suggest that he ought to have professional help, since their current feeling about analysis was that it helped people adjust to a sick society rather than questioning the society itself. More harm than good.

Jerry came back to London chastened and subdued. He showered Lucy with flowers, gave up the model and returned to work. In the wastepaper basket in the bathroom Rosie found a letter he'd thrown away from a West End gallery offering to show his work. She wondered why he never took up the offer but gave the matter little thought. She'd been to her first meeting of the women from the underground press and feminism was proving a total preoccupation . . .

The meeting had begun calmly enough. Twenty women, wearing bright, colourful clothes. When had she last been in a room full of women? School, presumably.

'I expected to be encouraged to write and to edit. Instead all I do is type.'

'I do research, some of the background writing, but do I ever get a by-line?'

'I hate being called a chick . . . I've tried to get that word stopped in the paper, but I'm laughed at.'

They became more animated. Someone talked about the horrors of her illegal abortion, which brought the conversation to sex, and sexual satisfaction.

'I'm too embarrassed to say what I like in bed. I'm not even sure what I want. But how to ask? I'm too scared of being thought whorish.' It was very personal and self-revealing, almost shocking. But no one was ego-tripping or telling anyone to shut up.

A young woman with pretty fair hair spoke for the first time. 'I hate to admit it, but I've never had an orgasm.' The response was wholly sympathetic. Rosie shuddered. As far as she knew she'd never had one either, but despite the openness she was too scared to speak. Exposing herself would mean exposing Jonathon and she couldn't bring herself to do that.

She had assumed that if men enjoyed sleeping with her, then it was all right. She didn't know what her needs were, let alone how to express them. Aware of endless times when a man would roll off her, leaving behind a strange tightness in her belly, she'd nevertheless conclude that if he seemed happy and came back for more, it must mean she was sexually together. Now she was hearing that not only could she expect more, she ought to demand more. But wasn't it wanton to ask for something so personally gratifying? It was far less scary to worry about pollution.

'But you don't have orgasms vaginally, you know.' The speaker was in her thirties. 'Have you read *The Myth of Vaginal Orgasm* by Anne Koedt? It goes further than Masters and Johnson. Men have suppressed it. They don't want to deal with the idea that the penis is only necessary for reproduction. It's revolutionary. Don't you see, it unites the personal and the political for the first time. Being stuck at the kitchen sink, or getting less money . . . that's related to our sexuality. We're being kept down all the way – in bed, in the office, everywhere . . .'

Rosie walked back home through the cold winter night. The miners' strike had caused power cuts and there were no streetlights, but she was tingling inside. How could she not have thought of all this before? She knew, by some miracle, she'd been lucky. As the younger of two girls, with no brotherly shadow, she'd been encouraged to work at school. That it had been something of a disaster, didn't seem relevant then. She'd never learnt to type, so no one could dump that kind of work on her. Out of all the women in that room, she realised that she was the only one who had a wholly editorial job on an underground magazine. And she'd never had an abortion.

When her childhood dreams of excelling in athletics or showjumping had become slightly more practical, she'd formulated three goals, or anti-goals: never to have an abortion: never to get divorced; and to go round the world by the time she was twenty-five.

I'm a child of the pill age, she thought. Going to the gynaecologist the morning after losing her virginity had been automatic. But it wasn't, she realised; nearly every other woman at that meeting had had an abortion.

It was too simple to ascribe her foresight to the times. A friend of hers from school had already lost one of her Fallopian tubes as a result of an ectopic pregnancy.

All the women at the meetings knew that there was a huge gap between what their lives were about and what they read, between the cushioned world of the women's weeklies and the reality of inequality and feminine conditioning. And though, afterwards, no one was quite sure whose suggestion it was to start a new magazine, the support was unanimous.

By the end of the third meeting, Marsha and Rosie had emerged as the two most willing and able to undertake the project. Both were filled with giddy enthusiasm.

If in 1970 Neville could ignore feminism in his book on the underground, by 1972 no one could. Raising money in such a climate proved easier than they had anticipated, though they both quaked with fear when their credentials were laid on the line. Marsha had worked on Australian *Vogue*, on *Oz* and briefly on *Ink*. Rosie had worked for *Frenz* for a little less than a year and was still a few months short of her twenty-first birthday. But their temperaments, for the time being, meshed well. Marsha was solidly feminist. She joined a consciousness-raising group, attended the political meetings and versed herself in the law affecting the rights of women. Rosie went to a few meetings and a large number of parties and talked the whole idea up to anyone who would listen in the hope that they'd forget her age and inexperience and come over with the cash.

They set their targets low and estimated that the magazine, which at Claud Cockburn's suggestion they called *Spare Rib*, could be launched on £3,000. 'You're mad,' Richard Neville said to Marsha. 'You'll never do it on that, you'll be bankrupt in a month and never have a chance to really work it out. You've got to wait till you have at least £10,000.'

But by then it was too late. The magazine had been started back to front; their first act had been to contact a distributor and promise him copies by mid-June, for publication on Midsummer's Day. Then they had told a printer the same thing. They went to every possible financial source, accepting investments ranging from £10 to £500. Rosie had even dragged Marsha, protesting strongly, to see a rich Arab in Park Lane whom her friend Cassandra had once patronised for handouts. The meeting was a disaster; the first indication of their political differences. Rosie thought it was fine to accept money from any source, Marsha saw limits to which even such a good cause should stoop. The Arab decided, eventually, not to invest.

At the beginning of March 1972 they moved into a two-roomed office off Carnaby Street in Soho. The premises had just been vacated by an up-and-coming designer, who left behind rush matting and canary coloured walls. *Ink*, founded on cash and goodwill a year earlier, had just declared bankruptcy. Marsha acquired desks and filing cabinets from their offices before the liquidators moved in to divide the spoils.

The music was dying for the underground press. Jonathon, unable to make a living from the faltering papers, started writing features for a tit-and-bum monthly called *Knave*.

Rosie hated his work and was publicly embarrassed to talk about it. Jonathan resented her growing involvement in the movement. He was left out, and in the hope of resuscitating their limp affair suggested they move house. Rosie agreed. Jerry's behaviour had long since ceased to amuse and the flat they found was both pretty and affordable. But as *Spare Rib* gathered momentum, she was home less and less. They lost touch with Lucy and Jerry.

Four years were to pass before Rosie heard the full story. In the spring of 1973 Jerry had suddenly flown to the West Indies with a teenage model. Stripping off his clothes one day he'd run through the streets of a predominantly black town, shouting that he was the Messiah, a saviour of the coloured race, come to free them from the burden of white oppression. He'd been shipped home in a straitjacket. His mother, like his friends, was unwilling to face the fact he might be seriously disturbed. She refunded his bank account. Lucy took him back. A year later she gave birth to their son.

They moved to Wales, renting an isolated cottage. One snowy morning shortly after Christmas 1974, an engineer called at the house in answer to a request to fix the telephone. Jerry, naked bar a pair of underpants, opened the door, an axe in his hand, and threatened to kill the man if he didn't leave. When the police came, they found Lucy's dismembered body lying in pools of blood on the kitchen floor. The baby, unchanged and filthy, was crying in hunger and fear from an upstairs room.

Like Jonathon, Rosie was horrified by the brutality, the waste, and her close call. Twist fate a few turns and she could have been lying on that Welsh cottage floor. Lucy's death seemed so arbitrary. Craziness had been encouraged in the years when she knew Jerry. He came from a respectable home, was thoroughly one of the old school. His eccentricity was part of his arty exterior. Knowing she had been close to someone prepared to play God with someone else's life was awesome. Jerry was diagnosed as a schizophrenic and sent to Broadmoor. The doctors registered the role of LSD in his transformation.

'He changed after taking it,' one old acquaintance was reported to have said. But how far was his crack-up the result of drugs? Rosie and Jonathon took as much LSD and neither emerged with ideas distorted into acid grandiloquence. Scaremongering fantasies about LSD were rarely true. The idea that sanity lay on the other side of madness was widely prevalent and accounted for most people's experiments with the so-called pharmaceutical miracles. But very few people were stranded in the middle, leaping off buildings to prove they could fly.

David, Jonathon's one-time partner, stayed in touch with Jerry after he went to Broadmoor. By the mid 1970s David had become a successful novelist and he and his wife Sarah had been among the last visitors to the lonely Welsh retreat.

Jerry's behaviour, he recalled, was growing steadily weirder. The week before the murder the cottage had been squalid; Lucy was making cream cheese in the bath, and no one looked as though they had washed for weeks.

Jerry was having an affair with a girl called Sunshine, a devotee of Aleister Crowley. Through Crowley's influence Jerry saw Lucy as a witch who should be destroyed.

In Broadmoor, David said, Jerry went through an initial period of rage, convinced that what he had done was right, but over the years remorse, bewilderment and regret took over, plus an aversion to sex and drugs.

Both David and Sarah had sensed a disaster brewing on that last visit to Wales. 'But we thought it would be the break-up of the relationship . . . that degree of violence was unthinkable. Jerry had always played up his eccentricity. Lucy, with her upper-crust background, was like a moth drawn to the flame. She was unlucky. They were casualties of an era . . . what more can you say?'

Only, it would seem, that life always breeds victims and Lucy and Jerry were two of them. In the hop-along world of the early seventies, given their wealth and backgrounds, it didn't seem that way. In another level of society they might have lived to old age, their wackiness concealed behind suburban net curtains.

For Jerry and Lucy, in a society which encouraged outrageousness, the outcome was disaster. For others, though, the doors opened not on to Jerry's hell but on to something far more constructive. At the start of the seventies, if you had talent, style and a sense of the extreme, then barriers could be broken. If you were young and especially if you were female – then the sky was the limit.

SEVEN

On my ninth day in the clinic I read my life story to the group. I was terribly nervous, and when I had finished I waited anxiously for comments. I felt naked and vulnerable. Everyone now knew more about me than I knew about them.

'If I was an editor, I'd take a red pencil to a lot of that rubbish,' said a fat American called David, who had come in for the day. I was hurt, but said nothing. 'Sounds like you're on a suicide mission,' he added.

'I'm not. I don't think I ever was,' I retorted crossly. He stirred himself in his chair, his fat belly falling over the top of his trousers. He was repulsive. (Two days later he collapsed, drunk, in the Hilton bar and was committed to a National Health hospital. I felt faintly victorious about this but disliked myself for being mean.)

'Do you hate standing still, not being at the top of the heap?' asked Anne.

'Yes,' I said, 'that's true. It's always been a case of if I couldn't be best then I'd be worst. It was when I wasn't being either that I couldn't stand it. I'm great in a crisis,' I added sarcastically.

'How did you have the nerve to do those things when you were so young?' asked Shelagh.

'I didn't think about "nerve" or "risk",' I replied, 'I was there and things were there and I wanted to do them.'

'Suicide mission!' David burped back into the conversation. I began to suspect that he was still drunk from the night before, or possibly from odd drinks on the way to the clinic. 'No, you're really wrong about that,' I said, 'I've never been on a suicide mission. I've thought about it – who hasn't? – it's always felt like something that I, and only I have control of. I could use it if I wanted. It's always made me feel safe. Do you understand?' I addressed the question to Anne, who nodded.

'Don't you see that everything I was doing was just a way of proving that I was alive ... greedy for living I suppose, greedy for experience.'

'What do you think, Brian?' asked the doctor. 'Judging from what I know about you, I'd have thought you'd have a lot to say. You've been through the drug scene like Rosie has?'

Brian shrugged, then yawned. 'I've heard a lot of stories like it. And what a dumb way to see the world. Dying men, gaol cells. Did you ever see the Taj Mahal?'

'No,' I replied, puzzled by his reactions, hurt by his dismissiveness and, I was forced to admit, piqued that I hadn't managed to awaken his interest.

'It seems to me,' commented Anne, 'that you've spent most of your life getting what you think you want and then chucking it all away.'

'Yes.' The observation was near the bone. Did I lack staying power, did that in turn mean that I lacked willpower? The changes in my life had not always happened through my choice. Often enough, I'd been forcibly chucked away.

The group session was way over time and everyone was

hungry. The doctor stood up to go, then turned and looked at me. 'You didn't notice something,' he said, 'there was one thing you didn't mention in all that.'

'What's that?'

'Well, you didn't say anything about being angry, resentful, cross, anything about how you were going to carry on trying to beat the booze battle in your own terms, in fact you were indirectly acknowledging what booze had done to you.'

I made my way to the dining room. It was true, I suddenly wasn't angry any more. Confrontation with the facts, with other drunks, had somehow evaporated the anger.

'I'm an alcoholic . . .' I said it to myself slowly. 'I've got blue eyes.' Would I complain if I were a diabetic? Yes, I would, but not for long.

We were sitting at lunch. David was still cracking jokes about how he'd like to get at my story with a red pencil. He was becoming very tiresome. I reckoned he probably had a bottle hidden in the copious pockets of his garish check golfing jacket. What did we have in common, I wondered, beyond the fact that booze had run riot through our lives?

The alcoholic personality; the phrase had come up in many disucssions. Was an alcoholic personality a mad one or a very sane one which had allowed a particular drug to get out of control? I was by then nine days away from my last drink, four days away from my last hemenevrin, and the only drug I'd been taking was a sleeping pill at night. My mind and body were as near to being drug-free as they'd been in several years. I certainly didn't feel mad, but even to myself I had behaved insanely.

Shelagh, trying to diet and slowly eating lettuce and tomatoes, turned to me and said, 'Are you really not angry any more?'

'No. I'm not sure what I feel, but it isn't anger.'

What had we in common? Books on alcoholism invariably point to such characteristics as impatience, a low sense of pain, a sense of futility about life, lack of a father figure in men when they were young (no one has yet made this observation about women), certain physical characteristics, like a low production of control hormones, and a generally addictive personality (it is true that most alcoholics bite their nails and smoke).

When you judge a person, you base your judgment on their actions; how they react to certain events, what they say, what they manifestly believe in and talk about.

The practising alcoholic presents a baffling mass of evidence. Someone perfectly capable of controlling their drink, of having three drinks and saying no to the fourth, looks at the drunk and sees only his lack of control. Any normally decent person who suddenly starts shouting or throwing the furniture around is dubbed a weak-willed nut. Maybe we were 'weak-willed' over drink, but not otherwise.

Shelagh had been married young to a man who was a millionaire several times over by the time he was forty. She came from a working-class background. Her will, both to live and to beat the system (smuggling booze into the clinic, for instance), knew no bounds.

Anne's husband had died and left her a struggling little business in South London. Single-handedly she'd built it up into a thriving concern. It was unfortunate that the profits were being literally soaked up in clinics. Anne had been in five times by the time I met her that August – and I'm only talking about one year.

Brian was the son of a titled European ambassador. He'd left a pampered home to make it on his own. By his own account he'd been earning almost a quarter of a million bucks a year on the American Stock Market. Before his retirement Taylor had been a director of a large company. Raju had made his way from the jungles of Malaya to his job as an anaesthetist.

Doctors also point to the immaturity of the alcoholic, but the immaturity is a symptom rather than a cause of alcoholism. Drowning yourself in drink prevents the natural process of living through ups and downs, learning to take life in your stride. When the alcoholic stops drinking, this immaturity catches up on him. A simple example in my case was the fact that I never cried unless I was drunk.

The business of marshalling self-control had been the best I could do, and it was only when I was half cut that the tears would come. Several months after leaving the clinic, I suddenly found myself in the grip of depression. I cried like a baby. I realised after two and a half days, roughly a year and a half after my mother had died, that I was finally letting my natural grief for her untimely death surface. When you're in the habit of seizing the bottle every time your equanimity is threatened, normal emotions don't get a look in.

Alcoholics are also described as self-indulgent, self-centred, insecure and sexually confused. A little of each trait was present in all of us. We all needed to be loved and accepted. We were all looking for some meaning to our lives. In a biography of AA's founder, Bill Wilson, he is described as a child stretching his hands towards the sky saying, 'I want, I want.' I understand that feeling; I spent all my twenties doing the same. My search for spiritual peace and understanding took me first to drugs, then to drink. I thought that the near-psychedelic state which hard drinking produces might somehow reveal the answer.

I was always making bargains with God. Riding motor-bikes over the Himalayas, flirting with dangerous drugs, taking giant physical risks, were all attempts to test the strength and durability of life itself. Turning downwards into drink was the answer when the answers failed to come. I couldn't see that my survival was the answer in itself. There was no sin in seeking solace from a wasteland.

Group therapy for alcoholics works because, even though we could never satisfactorily articulate the reasons for our drinking, we all empathised. I understood Anne when she said 'I couldn't stop' on a level which someone who has never had a problem saying 'no' ever could. We were growing close to each other; just how close and how mutually responsible was brought to light on the evening of the day I read my life story.

It was Thursday, a day when the drunks were supposed to attend the local Alcoholics Anonymous meeting which was held in the church hall over the road. The location was superb; opposite a nut-house, and adjacent to one of London's most famous pubs. Carol had come down to the dining room just after supper to remind us to attend.

'Good for your souls,' she said with a laugh.

Taylor stubbed out his cigarette and stood up.

'Well, who's coming?'

'I've had booze up to here,' said Anne, 'I really feel like going to bed.'

Taylor looked at me, I looked at Shelagh, and Shelagh looked at the floor.

'Come on, you can't let him go alone,' said Carol. 'What are you doing, Brian?'

Brian said he was going to the movies.

'Oh,' asked Carol. 'Did you tell the doctor?'

'No,' he replied firmly, 'Angie and I are going to the movies and that's that. The film starts in ten minutes and I'll be back by eleven o'clock.'

Carol shrugged. She didn't approve of Brian's relationship with the rich American from the third floor, who had had a serious nervous breakdown. All sexual relationships between the inmates were frowned on. In the touchy, vulnerable state induced by intensive psychotherapeutic treatment, it's natural to seek comfort and physical love. But the relationships, based largely on insecurity, always spell trouble; over-dependence, over-involvement, overboard.

In the end, Taylor set off for the meeting alone.

There was no air-conditioning in the clinic and the stuffy atmosphere drove most of us on to the roof in the evenings. I loved the view of the Chelsea rooftops, but the physical closeness of so much normality – washing hanging on lines, half-seen TVs through open curtains, barbecues burning on smart patios – only emphasised the distance between institutional life and the rest of the world.

Anne, Shelagh and I took our coffee on to the roof terrace and settled ourselves at one of the wrought-iron tables squatting on the bilious astro turf. The sun was setting across the jumble of chimneys.

We were joined briefly by the youngest inmate. Kim was the product of an unsuccessful mixed marriage between an eccentric British woman, who wore ermine on hot days and painted her nails green, and a Middle Eastern businessman. They lived alternately in Arabia, Beverly Hills and a house by the sea in Sussex. Kim, an only child, had been packed off to a swanky girls' school and expelled at the age of fifteen. The reason, she was never slow to reveal, was that she had scrawled 'god is dead' and 'god sucks' and other profanities all over her school Bible.

She was dark and vivacious and bursting with sexual energy. She was also a pain in the arse, since she would find any banality hilarious and laugh hysterically in an attempt to entice others on to her confused and lonely wavelength. At the age of fifteen she had no place in the clinic. That night she stayed for ten minutes, then left to look for Andy, who had been walking round the clinic earlier in the day wearing a grey asbestos fire-suit in preparation for his next race with Nikki Lauda. His flabby body looked as though it had been poured into the suit like runny cement.

At about nine-thirty, after the sun had dipped below the rooftops leaving the sky shot with violent reds and purples, Kim came bounding up on the roof, closely pursued by Andy, who had exchanged his suit for a pair of dirty shorts.

'I've got to tell you . . .' he stuttered, 'at least I think I should tell you, it seems to be the right thing to do, don't you agree Kim? that they ought to know, about this, well, it might be important . . .'

'Oh, get on with it, Andy,' snapped Shelagh.

'I've just seen Taylor going into the Potter,' he burst out.

'What?' said Anne and I in unison. 'You can't have, he's at an AA meeting.'

'It was him, I know,' he insisted, 'I was so worried that I followed him in there and watched him go to the bar, order something, drink it and order something else. Then I left.'

I felt miserable and said so. Shelagh looked surprised and told me sharply not to be so naive, but her sharpness was only a mask for the fact that she was upset too. We waited up on the roof, wondering when Taylor would return, hoping Brian would come straight back from the movies.

We didn't wait long. Taylor came sauntering on to the roof, hands in his pockets, shoulders thrown back in a debonair, man-about-town attitude.

'Evening all,' he said in mocking tones. He stood by the wall gazing out over the rooftops and started to whistle. It was all a certain giveaway. He wasn't in any sense drunk but those two stiff shorts had changed him. For the first time I started to understand, because I was seeing it in someone else, how William could always look at me and say, without hesitation and with constant accuracy, 'You've had a drink.' I would think I looked, acted and behaved totally normally; as in fact Taylor was doing right now, to anyone who didn't know him. Yet the change was undeniable; the gaiety was slightly forced, the control mechanisms were working hard to ensure concealment of his relapse. 'How was the meeting?' asked Anne, as Taylor pulled up a chair and sat down at the table.

'Fine,' he replied quickly. After a short pause he added: 'I saw Cynthia there.' He was referring to an AA member who regularly visited the clinic to give pep talks to the patients. 'She asked where you all were. Said to tell you that you were all being jolly lazy and she expects to see you tomorrow.'

The wind picked up and the unmistakable smell of vodka drifted through the air. Boozers have the notion that vodka doesn't smell on the breath; it does.

No one knew what to say. To challenge him seemed an invasion of his privacy; yet not to seemed an abdication of responsibility. We all hoped Brian would return: maybe, man to man, Taylor would talk. The night turned completely black. The odd sounds of drunken revellers, leaving the Potter, going in and out of Wedgies and other clubs, pierced the air. Taxis and cars made their way up the King's Road, single sounds now, in the night, as opposed to the solid hum of daytime.

Taylor stood up and wished everyone goodnight. He strode off, his shoes making small squeaks on the astro turf.

We all got up to go to bed, still uncertain as to what to do.

Half an hour later I heard Brian walking down the corridor. I got up and went to his room.

'Listen,' I said, 'Taylor went to the Potter tonight and had a few drinks. Andy saw him.' I told him how Taylor had behaved on the roof.

'Did you say anything?' Brian was lying on his bed. Socks, shoes, expensive shirts were scattered in profusion around his room, interspersed with copies of *Time* and *Newsweek* and endless photography mags. The maid had long since given up.

'No,' I replied, perching on the edge of his bed after throwing a few magazines on the floor. I suddenly longed to leap into that bed, to tumble into the embrace of strong arms, and lose myself in someone else's flesh.

'Will you talk to him in the morning?'

Brian said he would, though he admitted he didn't know what good it would do. But, like me, I could sense he felt the betrayal of trust that Taylor's trip to the Potter meant to the group as a whole. I said goodnight and went back to my room. I was bewildered and my body was tingling. I remembered the unbelievable urge for sex that had hit me after giving up heroin. Hindus would explain it as the sudden release of the power of the seventh chakra, the one located under your coccyx, repressed by the opiates, and once freed, literally raring to go.

I seemed to be having the same feeling now. Three days earlier I had been back to the flat to pick up some clothes.

William and I had had a quiet and miserable cup of tea. Quiet, because I didn't know what to say; miserable, because memories of events that had transpired in that flat hit me like a pail of cold water. I'd been edgy too, because I didn't like straying far from the safety of the clinic. But I had picked up my vibrator, which had burned its way through a significant number of batteries while I'd been in that sexy, unfulfilled state of semi-drunkenness; orgasms filled the void and temporarily took me away from my surroundings. It had been a long time since I'd had an orgasm while actually making love. I'd been too afraid to let go, to surrender myself. I was frightened of that moment, and felt that if I let it happen something would take me over. Considering that I was periodically abandoning all elements of control to booze, this was fairly twisted thinking. But I had come to think of orgasms as things I would 'give' people, as a sign of trust in them; it had nothing to do with whether they were good or bad in bed. So what had been going on for years was skilful faking; speedy screws and the knowledge that the vibrator could do the job quite adequately, if a little coldly.

I got it out of the drawer and threw my body from passivity to abandon and back to sanity again in a matter of moments. The Chinese call masturbation the disease of mating with ghosts. Exactly.

By ten-thirty the following morning everyone knew about Taylor's relapse and Taylor knew that we all knew.

'Why did you do it?' asked the doctor when he began the group session.

'I'd rather not talk about it in public,' Taylor answered stiffly.

The doctor paused. He would have to try another tack. Taylor was not someone who could be approached head-on.

There was a new face among the group that morning.

Mid-forties, beautiful, with classic lines connecting aquiline nose, full mouth and widely spaced deep-set hazel eyes. Blonde hair swept in a curve across her forehead, falling in a thick swoop to her shoulders. The beauty had clearly been ravaged by booze, the unmistakable little veins visible even through the make-up, the eyes tired, not shining. But she must have been stunning when she was twenty.

Sylvie was in the clinic for a 'rest'. She'd been told it would be a good idea to attend a few alcoholic group meetings. The doctor had met her before.

'How's your husband?' he asked.

'Oh, fine. I'm not though. He just doesn't care . . . he goes off with young women, leaves me alone, expects me to organise dinners for him. All the usual shit.'

The doctor looked amused. 'How does he feel about your drinking?'

'Too busy to notice,' she said with a wan smile.

'But he must see you drunk sometimes,' said Anne, assuming, correctly, that Sylvie wouldn't be in the room at all unless the problem was acute.

'Well, I suppose he does *notice*. Actually,' she looked around the room, summing up the faces to decide whether they were trustworthy or not. 'Actually, he's been going to Al-Anon meetings, and he's been locking up the drink.'

'What you mean,' said Taylor, suddenly deciding to overcome his embarrassment and join in, 'is that he notices, but you think he doesn't care. He must care, you wouldn't be here otherwise.'

She nodded. She was the only one in the room who didn't know about the events of the night before.

'No, he just wants to get rid of me. Put me somewhere out of the way.'

Taylor could not fathom it. Who would want to get rid of Sylvie, who looked like Garbo with voice and figure to match? He started slowly to prod her with questions, drawing out little details of neglect and abuse, of a disintegrating marriage and a lousy sex life.

'Do you want to give up the booze?' he asked her.

'No,' she said, then grinned and added, 'it's an incurable disease, at least that's what I've been told, so I figure I'm incurable!'

Taylor pursed his lips and touched his fingertips together, resting the praying hands on his chin.

'I suppose I think the same.'

We all watched and waited; which way would this go? Was Sylvie's blunt confession going to nudge Taylor into talking? He cleared his throat.

'I had that drink last night because I damn well wanted it. I was fed up with that AA meeting, fed up with this place, with being treated like a child, with being old and thinking of my life, whatever's left of it, without the booze.

'I'm sorry.' He looked round the room. 'I know how you all feel. I can tell from your faces. You think that I've let you down, that I've given up.

'I don't think I really started. You're all younger, you've got more to throw away than I have. I don't want to spend my days with nothing to do. I know, because I've learnt enough here, what will happen if I really start drinking again. I'm going to end up ill again, and I won't be able to play golf. But I've been weighing it up. I just think I'm too old to learn a whole new way to live. I feel guilty about going to the Potter, but not because I had a drink. I feel guilty towards all of you. I've never had friends like all of you in this room. That's the worst part of it.'

I'd been staring down at my fingernails while he was talking. I was too embarrassed to meet his eyes, to see this gentle,
proud old man drawing out of himself words and sentiments
which, to his generation, were things that you did not confess
in public. I looked up when he stopped speaking and noticed
his eyes watering.

He stood up. 'I think I'll go to my room now.'

EIGHT

The first issue of *Spare Rib* went to press on Rosie's twenty-first birthday. The black-and-white cover showed a picture of two women with no make-up, laughing and jaunty. In contrast to the glamour magazines it represented a new ideal; sisterhood, friendship, partnership.

Inside were features on the suffragettes; the battered wives' refuge centre which was, over the years, to turn its founder Erin Pizzey into a media star; a discussion about women's unease about the shape of their breasts; a story on the forthcoming law to allow vasectomies on the National Health; street pictures showing the types of jeans all ages were wearing; a beauty article on the importance of clean skin; praise from Juliet Mitchell (author of *Women's Estate*) for Joan Didion's *Play it as it Lays*; directly from America a column by Lillian Roxon, the Australian journalist, who said that no one in New York would ever call anyone Miz; a short piece on a new abortion referral centre in Liverpool.

Rosie's twenty-first birthday party went on till five in the morning. Seventy people squeezed into the flat, drank and smoked dope, tried to dance in the limited space and generally got wasted. The cast was impressive. Rosie was staggered when Germaine Greer arrived. Uninvited because Rosie had been too nervous to ask her, but there nonetheless.

Jonathon prowled between the living room and the kitchen, serving up the huge plates of chopped chicken livers which he'd made for the occasion. 'I'm turning into your slave,' he said angrily when they coincided by the kitchen sink.

On the stairway, Marsha sat on the top step, hugging her knees and sobbing. 'I'm pregnant,' she whispered to Rosie, her brown eyes swimming. 'I'm going to have to have an abortion.' The party was temporarily forgotten while they downed a litre bottle of wine. There was no question of having the child, only the ghastly business of figuring out when and where to get rid of it.

'We're always alone when it comes to this,' she said, 'Jonathon may be neurotic but at least you've got him.'

Five weeks later there was another party: *Spare Rib*'s official launch. A group of gay liberationists, dressed in clown outfits with smudgy make-up, stormed in uninvited. 'You're selling out,' they said to Rosie. 'Your magazine is straight and bourgeois. You're all rip-offs.'

She lost her temper and yelled at them to get out. Jonathon and two other friends manhandled the colourful band into the street.

The correspondent from the *Spectator* witnessed the mêlée. In his column the following week he reported that he'd seen a large lady shouting, 'Get out of my party, you cunt,' at a harmless gay liberationist. Rosie took more objection to being described as large than to the misquoting.

The publicity was extensive and favourable. The first two issues sold out, and the two editors found themselves working round the clock to keep pace with the mail and with the enquiries. They were buoyed by the enthusiasm and the heartfelt letters of thanks they received. Erica Jong and Ingrid Bengis, both in England to celebrate publication of their books, visited the office and drank with them in their local pub. Their operation was fast becoming a focus and a barometer. But at home it was a different story.

Jonathon was still working for *Knave*, bashing out articles entitled 'Knickers Through the Ages' and 'Sex on Horseback'. On the rare occasions when Rosie was at home, she was usually working and their arguments were bitter.

'Can't you do anything but that bloody magazine?' Jonathon asked crossly one night, when she'd started editing an article immediately after finishing dinner.

'No, I can't, it's important . . . far more important than that rubbish you write. It's so bloody embarrassing to have you doing that while I'm trying to run a feminist magazine.'

'Jesus, you're selfish,' he shouted. 'Do you think I like doing this? Do you think I like being your answering service? Or trailing along to smart parties with you, knowing people only want to know you, and couldn't give a fuck about me.'

'I'm sorry,' she said, not really meaning it, but wanting to duck the confrontation. 'Things will get better.'

But, she thought, if it hadn't been for Jonathon she'd never have had the job on *Frendz* in the first place. Wouldn't have started this magazine now. What had she given him? And how much do you owe a person anyway? She didn't really know any more if she loved him. She still needed him and hated herself for her dependence.

By October Jonathon was beaten, despairing of ever finding work he liked in England. He packed his bags and moved to New York. He was then twenty-four and haunted by the sixties credo that everyone who was going to be successful would have made it by the age of twenty-five. Rosie's example was ego-bruising. In his role as her Svengali, he was now watching his labours bear fruit. He didn't like it.

She was glad when he left. In many ways the situation was ideal; there was a boyfriend, albeit three thousand miles away, to stave off any fears about finding a man. On the other hand she no longer had to compromise between her work and her home life.

While they lived together, Rosie cooked. But not because Jonathon didn't offer or because he couldn't cook. It was just unbearable to watch him in the kitchen, actually to witness the role reversal which she claimed to advocate. In one sense, it made her insecure, in another it made her resentful. She couldn't equate masculinity with the sight of Jonathon with a shopping bag, and was irritated with her own traditionalism.

In November she went to New York to visit him. The trip was a disaster in terms of their relationship, a success in terms of meetings with women from *MS* and other New York feminists. The gap between them widened and when he returned home in January Rosie told him that she no longer wanted to live with him. The parting was messy and ugly.

Rosie moved to a tiny room in a friend's house in Shepherd's Bush. Marsha left at Christmas for a long-over-due visit to Australia. She hadn't been home for five years. The magazine, for the time being, was left in Rosie's hands and she was glad. The political differences between the two editors were beginning to emerge, small samples of an incompatibility which was later to prove insurmountable.

'The fiction is not feminist, the cookery isn't either, the fashion is ridiculous . . . none of this has anything to do with the movement,' Marsha had said one day. By 'not feminist' Rosie understood her to mean unpolitical, though it was often hard to know. In the attempt to be politically correct reality was often warped; real women did wear make-up and worry about their love-lives.

'Yes, but it sells,' Rosie answered. *Spare Rib*'s fiction was of high quality: Fay Weldon, Edna O'Brien, Eva Figes, Margaret Drabble and John Berger had all contributed stories.

'You don't know that, do you? We're producing a hotch-potch, it isn't one thing or the other. The trouble with you, Rosie, is that you don't care enough. You never go to feminist groups, never study.'

'Well, we do that teaching job,' she answered, referring to the night classes on male/female relationships that they taught at a West London adult education centre.

'That's just for your own personal glory and for the money.'

'Damn it, Marsha, that's not bloody fair. I don't like giving up endless evenings to sit in a dirty old classroom,' Rosie said angrily – and defensively, because Marsha's accusations weren't far wide of the mark.

'That's only because you go out all the time. You're always at trendy parties. You only stayed for two days at the women's conference.'

Rosie blushed. She hadn't told Marsha the real reason why she had left the women's conference in Manchester earlier that year. On the Sunday morning she had dutifully rung Jonathon to find out how he was. Duty had turned to anguish when he mumbled, through a heavy hangover, that he'd been to bed with a girl the night before after a press party in Claridges to celebrate a band who'd made a record called *Fuck You*. Standing in the phone booth in the lobby of some technical college, stuffing coins into the slot and watching the denim-clad feminists sitting in small huddles on the brown vinyl benches, she'd almost cried with jealousy. 'I'm coming home . . . right now.' Jonathon sounded amazed and nervous. He started to protest.

She slammed down the phone and exited through the swing doors, without bothering to tell Marsha she was leaving. On the train she rehearsed Jonathon's goodbye scene. Would he have packed by the time she arrived? But when the train drew into Euston, there he was, contrite at the ticket barrier. Anger and annoyance at her own pathetic behaviour quickly ousted the panic and she bitched at him all the way home, wondering what excuse she could offer for leaving Manchester so abruptly. Flu would have to do, as usual. Ten years were to pass before she told Marsha the truth.

'We're going to wreck this paper if we take all this stuff out of it,' Rosie countered. 'You can't deny that we have a good time . . . but we're not letting that get a look-in. If we just left the news section, or extended that type of stuff right through, then it would look like nothing good ever happened. Feminism isn't supposed to be miserable. What the hell is the point of liberation if it isn't fun?'

'Not everyone has as good a time as you do . . .'

'OK, I wear make-up, so do you, and I buy clothes, and I like them, and I like parties and I like men, and you like all these things too . . . you can't pretend that they don't exist.'

'Oh, go and work for *Vogue* then.'

Rosie laughed. 'God, this is ridiculous . . . you have to see it.'

Marsha started laughing too. 'Come on,' she said, 'I'll buy you a drink . . .'

They were sustained by a romantic notion of sisterhood; an idea that being women together, working together and acknowledging their deep friendship, would somehow be enough. So when the political differences emerged, they both felt betrayed. Both, in their way, unconsciously widened the split. As Rosie partied more, transferring her social life away from the office and the movement, so Marsha channelled her energies deeper. She went to four women's studies groups a week, and railed at Rosie for avoiding the hard work. Rosie, in her turn, found the role of the socialite hard to give up. They clung so firmly to the concept of sisterhood that it was impossible to feel detached, to acknowledge their differences. An argument about the wording of an introduction could turn, easily, into a veiled argument about their relative lifestyles. So when Marsha would say, critically, that Rosie didn't understand something because she didn't bother to study, Rosie would answer by saying that Marsha was losing touch with the outside world.

They knew that others wanted to jump on to the liberation bandwagon. The power of the youth culture in recent years had become so obvious that the cannier over-thirties, whom Jerry Rubin had memorably insisted must never be trusted, were always careful to keep one foot on the right side of the fence.

Some were undistinguished and not above writing child-ishly seductive letters to Marsha and Rosie after they'd appeared on a TV programme or had their picture in the papers. But there was a smaller and far more influential group of hangers-on; luminaries of the liberal arts establish-ment who were easy to recognise by their dogged attendance at every party. Their hair was shorter, their jeans too tight, but their chequebooks were solid. Michael White, Christopher Logue, the Tynans, the late Clive Goodwin were among those responsible for funding *Spare Rib*.

In America, Timothy Leary, Richard Alpert (Ram Dass), Allen Ginsberg and other survivors of the beat generation not only associated themselves with the youth movement, but in some areas took it over. They became the philosopher kings. In England John Mortimer became the legal guru after the *Oz* trial. Others, such as Ken Tynan, Michael White, Feliks Topolski, George Melly and Chrisopher Logue, lent their expertise in a variety of ways; premises for parties, know-how, publicity, and cash. Logue gave a poem for use in *Spare Rib*'s first issue.

Until the rise of the underground they had been at the forefront of the sexual revolution. But by the end of the sixties Jimmy Porter's casual promiscuity in *Look Back in Anger* and Billy Liar's fantasies, once the pinnacles of sexual adventure, had been overtaken. The daughters of the Angry Young Men of the fifties, though not running around in lacy tights and black silk underwear, had a wholly different attitude to sex. The guilt lifted, the pill available, they worried about it less and seemed to enjoy it more. Middle-aged men found it irresistible.

The result was mutual exploitation. Rosie knew that the older men who asked her out did so, for the large part, because of what she represented. They believed that the only way to keep her coming back was to provide sexual fantasies which would be in keeping with their own avant-garde stance. The Angry Young Men had become Dirty Old Men. So she ended up getting tied up to a hotwater pipe and covered in butter, drinking champagne with three others in a marble bath in Amsterdam, and, once, beating someone's lilywhite back with an old horsewhip.

None of it lasted, despite the laughs, because no one's heart was really in it. She was aware of the paradox; wanting to please men and to be thought attractive, but wanting too not to be considered in a sexual light alone. Suddenly withdrawing her favours was one way, albeit old-fashioned, of staying ahead of the game.

The newly emergent feminists were upsetting tradition. Outwardly they were independent, unresponsive to traditional courtship and flattery. But Rosie knew that going dutch in a restaurant, or choosing the venue, were shallow stabs at deep-rooted chauvinism. She was as frightened of her independence as any other woman, and never suggested dates for fear of rejection, never suggested sex for the same reason. Everybody worried like hell about everyone else's orgasms. It was often simpler to fake it, leaving macho pride intact. Asking still seemed pushy. She still bowed to superior male knowledge in worldly matters, and was as vulnerable as anyone to the implication that she was only a woman, and therefore didn't know. It was hard work not letting her insecurity show.

The Left was just as hard to deal with. Marsha started seeing a Marxist film-maker. Her reasoning, at least, was sound. Leftwingers should have more sympathy towards women. But while Francis openly encouraged her career, he loathed it when she talked to another man. Ultimately, like Jonathon, he was jealous of her success.

Ken Tynan, too, viewed feminism with suspicion. He tolerated his wife Kathleen's interests and invited the feminists to his parties. Rosie watched Cagney's *White Heat* perched on the end of a sofa next to Ava Gardner. Later, though, Tynan's face went bright red as he condemned feminism for its triviality.

But Tynan, unlike many of his friends, never made passes. Marsha said after one party that Ken had given her a drink and studiously looked above and beyond her. 'As though I wasn't there.'

In 1970 he was quoted as saying that 'a century and a half ago there were no knickers and girls read the Bible, now they wear impenetrable body stockings and read *Portnoy's Complaint'*.

The new feminists, with *The Story of O* rather than *Portnoy's Complaint*, were tantalising to the latter day Don Juans.

An American friend gave Marsha early proofs of *The Story of O* just before she left England for a holiday with Germaine Greer in Italy. Germaine pounced on the story and after skimming through it asked Marsha for her opinion. 'Boring,' she replied carefully, unsure how to react. 'Good,' said Germaine, her response based on the current feminist belief that masochism could never provide genuine sexual pleasure. It was another ten years before Marsha and Rosie admitted to the book's eroticism.

Kate Millet rang one day to say that she was in London raising money for Michael X, the black power leader on trial in Trinidad for the murder of an English girl.

Marsha and Rosie went to Millet's meeting out of curiosity rather than sympathy. Michael X had left a lousy reputation behind him in London. Funds donated to his movement had apparently been diverted into stereos, leopardskin car rugs and white women.

Millet was sitting on a kitchen stool, her thin fierce face peering out beneath copious black hair.

She was angry. 'The English don't want to help, they aren't interested in the plight of this man who is going to die unless we can prove his innocence.'

'But is he innocent?' Rosie asked.

'Does that matter?' Millet responded. 'He's a man fighting for his life against a system. It's our duty to help.'

'Have you got any idea what he did in England?' Rosie

persisted, 'conning people for money and then using it all for himself?'

Millet waved her hands in the air, brushing aside the objections. 'It doesn't make him a murderer.'

'No, but someone killed her, someone buried her body in that garden.' Rosie thought she was crazy.

'But she made me feel guilty,' Marsha said, as they left.

'Me, too. I suppose we'd better help with the press conference.' In the end, they did, but hardly anyone turned up.

In Trinidad Michael X was hanged.

'I've written an article about bisexuality.' The woman standing in front of her desk held the pages out to Rosie. 'I thought *Spare Rib* might be interested.'

She was dark, with long thick hair twisted into ringlets. Her skin was like a child's and she had beautiful hands.

'I'd like to read it,' Rosie said. 'Are you . . . bisexual yourself?' It seemed an embarrassingly personal question.

'Oh yes,' she answered candidly, adding, 'my name's Sue.'

Spare Rib had, to date, published little material about sex. Their Christmas issue for 1972 had included a long article about the myth of the vaginal orgasm. In keeping with the festive spirit, the December cover had shown a woman, supposedly in the ecstatic throes of orgasm, arms flung backwards, mouth slightly open. The photographer had spent hours with the girl, a mutual friend, trying to achieve the correct look. Rosie wasn't certain, but she suspected that none of the women involved in the photography session had ever had an orgasm. However, they improvised as best they could. Underneath ran a cover line saying: 'Orgasm: have one yourself for Christmas.'

The staff themselves were, at the beginning of 1973 at

least, middle-class, white and heterosexual, though they knew a number of women who were now openly living with other women. Rosie had mixed feelings. She could understand why someone could get so fed up with trying to have an equal, caring relationship with a man that they turned to women, accepting the apparent safety that the relationship might offer. But though it seemed daring to defy convention to that degree, it also seemed passive; opting out of the fray, like underground exiles who went to live in the country and grew veg, made jam and reared goats.

And are they really in love, she would wonder, do they get a kick out of looking good for each other, and what the hell can it be like in bed? Passion, romance . . . I can't believe it.

'Yes, we'd like to publish your article,' she said to Sue over the phone a couple of days later. 'There are a few changes. Could we meet for a drink, sometime later this week, after work?'

The drink turned into dinner. One of the greatest delights of starting *Spare Rib* was spending evenings with women, going out to dinner, to the movies or the theatre and enjoying it; no longer thinking it a failure to be out with a woman, like two teamed-up wallflowers.

'Have you ever had an affair with a woman?' Sue asked. She was then twenty-eight, an exile from New Zealand. She made films and was then working on a documentary about a transsexual, which was to scoop a number of awards at film festivals the following year.

'No.'

'Ever think about it?'

'Who hasn't? It's a political topic now.'

'I don't feel political about my bisexuality,' Sue answered. 'I'm not trying to say that I don't want anything to do with men . . . but it does make you less vulnerable, less dependent, and it gives you a clearer idea of what you are trying to get out of a relationship.'

'What do you mean?'

'Well, if you can have a relationship that is undependent, unneurotic and unjealous, then that is what you start to look for with men.'

When Rosie's curiosity finally got the better of her and they went to bed together, she was predictably struck by the warmth and softness of Sue's body. The act was friendly rather than passionate, a curious dissolving of roles as they touched each other's sexual organs. Breasts were kind to the touch in an artistic rather than erotic way. She was mildly aroused. So this is what women feel like, she thought, pleased to feel the absence of post-coital frets, but aware, nonetheless, that she didn't naturally incline that way. Men found it fascinating: soon joining a threesome was expected. To refuse was as old-fashioned as refusing sex altogether.

Her affair with Sue was the first experience that she didn't share in detail with the rest of the staff. Aware that her reasons were not strictly political, she felt flippant in the face of *Spare Rib*'s growing feminism. Wanting to confess to this new radical chicness, yet nervous of the criticisms, she stayed silent. As a consequence she felt her magazine work turn into a mere job, rather than a whole way of life.

Marsha returned from Australia in the spring and was immediately stricken with a bad attack of measles. She was in bed for nearly three weeks, disturbed at what she thought she saw happening. 'I think we ought to run the magazine as a collective . . . I've been thinking about it while I've been home. We can't go on with this élitist structure.'

'They don't work,' Rosie replied. She was sitting on the end of Marsha's bed in her Notting Hill flat. 'Inevitably it means the lowest common denominator, not the highest.'

'You're afraid you'll lose your power,' Marsha countered. 'You've liked not having me here, haven't you?'

'In some ways, yes, I have,' Rosie replied, sounding angry to cover up the nervousness, 'but that's got nothing to do with not wanting a collective. It's hopeless when ten people make decisions.'

'We'll never be a feminist magazine while we have a hierarchy . . . *Spare Rib*'s just like any male magazine without the men . . .'

There was no meeting point between them, though Rosie admitted, privately, that part of Marsha's argument was true; she didn't want to relinquish her role as the youngest magazine editor in London.

Three weeks later Marsha announced that she wanted to resign from Virago. Virago was the publishing company which they had started with Carmen Callil, a freelance publishing PR, who had supported the magazine with monthly advertisements and constant advice and encouragement. Carmen had approached them at the end of 1972 with the idea of a woman's publishing company, solely devoted to women's books, run in a professional way and with solid distribution and financial backing. Carmen, who carried the bulk of the workload, had persuaded another newly formed publishing company, Quartet, to take on Virago as a subsidiary. Marsha's and Rosie's main contribution had been to drum up support for her and counterattack criticism that the thirty-four-year-old Australian was using the movement simply to advance her own career.

'Why?' Rosie asked. 'You can't just walk out of it like that.'

'Yes, I can, and I will,' Marsha retorted. 'Virago is only an ego-trip for Carmen . . . and for you, for that matter. I can't bear working with those men at Quartet and I don't want to be associated with something as obviously sexist . . . and I've written to Carmen to tell her.'

Carmen was glad that she had resigned. 'I couldn't take her sanctimoniousness,' she said to Rosie in the pub. Carmen was small and dark-haired, efficient in a way that no one from the underground, and few from the women's move- ment, ever were. The quality didn't embarrass her, nor did she regard it as male and therefore suspicious. They had first evolved the idea of Virago in the pub and the meetings had continued there out of habit. 'She always makes me feel that I'm in the wrong.' Privately, Rosie agreed with Carmen, but publicly she didn't say so.

Marsha did make her feel inadequate as a feminist, so, by implication, inadequate as a woman. Her frivolity, instead of being fun, was ridiculous in Marsha's eyes. 'I'm glad that she's left,' Carmen went on. 'I don't like working with the men at Quartet either, but for the moment, well, there isn't a choice. The moment there is, I'll take it. Believe me.' Rosie grinned. Carmen's determination was infectious.

One of the things that immediately attracted her to John was the fact that he had nothing to do with any of this. He didn't know the difference between a liberationist and a liberal and he didn't give a hoot. His unapologetic whackiness bypassed questions of political correctness, or swinger status. He wasn't trying to establish his place in the feminist hierarchy, nor was he tortured with guilt.

Some American friends brought him to dinner. 'You'll like him,' Jay had said on the phone. 'He's been around . . . John

Steinbeck's son . . . he blew the story about the GIs and dope in Vietnam.'

Her immediate impression wasn't favourable. His face was too tough, and his jaw, hidden under a beard, seemed heavy and bullish. A scar ran round his nose, resulting in a lip of skin above the right nostril. He wore round gold-framed glasses. He wasn't much taller than she was, and his heavy brown boots, out of keeping on the summer's night, completed the impression of someone who lacked grace and lightness. Later, when his face was almost as familiar as her own, she was to puzzle over this impression, recalling its accuracy but unable to remember quite why she had seen him this way.

But she envied his life; he'd tucked adventures and experiences under his belt the way other people collect labels from fancy hotels. He combined irreverence with a deep spiritual hunger. Life, to him, was to be pushed and prodded, but simultaneously revered. She was fascinated and intrigued.

He'd been in Paris to attend the Vietnam peace talks, though that fact was more of an excuse for a trip to Europe than a burning necessity. He'd been drafted to Vietnam when he was eighteen, in 1965, and had stayed on when his military service was through. Stayed on, he said, because he loved the country and the people. He had a terrible weakness for oriental women and oriental life. With friends he'd founded a news agency called Dispatches which broke the story of the Tiger Cages. For two years he'd lived on an island in the Mekong, the disciple of a silent Buddhist monk called Dau Doa. He had a child by a woman who had run off to study transcendental meditation in the Balearic Islands. Rosie found it all wonderfully romantic.

He slipped into her life without demanding any changes in it, as self-contained as his suitcase, and as mobile.

'Do you want to go to the country for the weekend?' she said. 'Some friends of mine are away and we can borrow their cottage.' John produced the acid over breakfast on Saturday morning; the day was clear, hot and cloudless. The strong scent of roses drifted in through the cottage window. Rosie hadn't taken any acid for almost two years, since the Glastonbury festival. But it was offered like a challenge; half a dare and half a way of saying, I want to know more about you, so let's see how you function under a couple of thousand mikes of heavy psychedelics.

She swallowed it with her tea, and sat in the garden, watching the honey bees crawl down the rose petals, their furry front feet scooping out the nectar.

'You're frightened,' he said later. They were lying on thick grass, minutely examining its rich fabric. Sunlight was exploding behind her eyes. 'And you know why?'

She shook her head.

'You don't have anywhere to go in your head, and you can't stop running. It's all transitory, ephemeral. Like this.' He broke off a blade of grass and crushed it between two fingers. 'You're not in touch with anything spiritual, with anything that's really creative.'

'Where do you go?' she said. She'd looked at herself in a mirror often enough on trips to know that she did look scared.

'I know it won't last,' he said, 'you hope it will. Two minutes ago is gone like twenty years, or two hundred years. You can't hold on to anything, even yourself.'

She shivered.

'You're holding on to so many things; to your magazine, to your reputation, and for what? Just to maintain your ego – but egos aren't solid, they're only your creation.'

He sat back on the grass and started to play his shake-hatsi, a large Japanese flute.

'I wonder if I can get those cows to pay any attention?' He grinned, and wandered off across the field towards the Friesian herd. The cows jostled around him. The pied piper, Rosie thought, watching the black and white animals dissolve and reappear, like a polkadot dress spinning in a tumble dryer.

On the way back to London the following day, they stopped for lunch in a country pub.

'I love you,' John said, somewhere between the main course and the cheese. He can't mean it, she thought, why me, what's there to love. He didn't seem to expect an answer.

'What was it like being your father's son?' she asked as they pulled on to the motorway towards London. 'Were you friends?'

'We were before he died. He liked *In Touch*, my book. He read the galleys when he was in hospital. Before that, we'd not got on so well. You know he came out to Vietnam to write that book *America and the Americans*? He sold out with that book. Betrayed the trust of people who loved him . . . and he really did have the common touch in his writing. He got to people's hearts with books like *The Pearl*.

'And then, there he was saying in that book that the war was a good thing for "our boys". He knew he was wrong. His friends, like Bellow, they told him he was wrong, but he never publicly said it. So when he read *In Touch*, I think he realised that I was saying the right thing. I really miss him.'

'What about your mother – your real mother, not your stepmother in New York?'

'I haven't seen her for years. Neither has Thom my brother. She's in Arizona now, lives alone. Thom and I went between the two homes. Summer camp every year. I used to hate school so much that I'd take lots of codeine in the morning and then curl up in the cupboard and go to sleep for as long as possible.'

'Jesus, what a weird way to grow up.'

He laughed. 'No weirder than some.' His arm rested on her shoulders as comfortably as an old scarf.

He moved in a few weeks later, when his hostess's mother arrived from America.

'It's amazing to meet someone – a girl – who can drink as much as I do.' John was musing into his Scotch, late one evening after a party where they'd already drunk enough to ensure a good night's sleep. She grinned and took his acknowledgment of the fact that she could drink like the boys as a compliment. And it was true, she did take pride in her head for drink.

'You've been a lot nicer,' Marsha said to her one day in the office. 'John must be good for you.'

If suddenly not caring so much about the fate of the magazine was good, then he was good for her, though she was amazed by the change in her feelings, by the transference of her dreams. She camouflaged her jealousy when he flirted with other women, and pretended she didn't care that he sometimes wanted other women in their bed. (It's all right, isn't it? I always come in you.) She knew that this acceptance was one of the attributes that he found attractive. So she faked it, knowing, all the time that her deceit would ultimately backfire.

The final decision to run *Spare Rib* as a collective was taken during a long morning meeting.

'I don't agree, but it looks as though I have no option,'

Rosie said finally, thinking about other jobs and mentally checking over the two rather lucrative offers that had recently been made. She stacked them against crumbling pride.

'Don't you see, while we run this as a hierarchy, then no one else ever gets a look in. We just have to put up with you and Marsha competing with each other – well, not Marsha any more,' Marion, the advertising manager, said. 'It was OK to start with, you were the only ones who knew about magazines, but now we all know as much as you do. Listen, Rosie, remember what you used to say about the underground press, about how women were still kept down . . . doing advertising, production, it's the same bloody thing here.'

They allocated office days to each member of staff, making it one person's responsibility to answer the phone, open the mail, clean up, see visitors and go to the bank for the wages if Friday was your office day. Editorial meetings were wholly collective, although the staff still retained areas of responsibility. Rosie was in charge of the news. Marsha of the features; but each suggestion and item came under the communal microscope at the weekly meetings. In the seven-way discussion, the items of lighter interest, the ones which Rosie generally considered ballsier and funnier, were usually dropped for the more serious stuff, which stood up to the feminist critique. The cookery, fashion, beauty were phased out. No personality, Rosie thought gloomily. Though politically more correct the magazine was undeniably duller.

On 6 October 1973, Yom Kippur, combined Syrian and Egyptian forces invaded Israel. By the time a ceasefire was called on the 22nd, the balance of power in the Middle East had irrevocably altered. Oil meant politics, meant power.

On the tenth day of the war the phone rang at home.

'Jesus, great,' said John, when he put the receiver down. 'That's Steve, my old buddy, he's on his way to the Middle East, filming the war for NBC. He's coming to stay for a day or two en route.'

Rosie had heard about Steve. He'd been in Vietnam (at the same time as John), a teacher in the peace corps. His wife, Crystal, had left him for John and had borne John's only child. She was now remarried. 'We've both lost her now,' John commented, while he waited for Steve to arrive. 'It'll be so good to see him again without that cloud.'

Steve was thin, dark and in his early thirties. His face was lightly dusted with freckles and when he smiled he resembled a benevolent water rat, with a sharp nose, shrewd twinkly eyes and lightly pursed lips. His chuckle was low and melodic.

'God you look great,' they both said simultaneously.

'When I last saw you . . .' Steve cocked his head at his friend. 'Stumbling on to the plane to Hong Kong, smacked out of your mind, Jesus you were thin, you looked like an old water-carrier.'

'And that was some trip,' John was chortling. 'I took the grass in to HK compressed in my ticket, so that when they searched me and my stuff, I just held on to it all the time, along with my passport papers. Even held on to it when I was starkers.'

'You're fucking crazy. God it's good to see you again, mad man.'

'Come on, dump your stuff, I'm taking you down to the pub.'

Pub closing time passed and Rosie went to bed. She was woken up later, sometime towards dawn when the dim grey light was starting to glimmer behind the white bedroom curtains. John was lying beside her, his body heaving with sobs.

'What is it?' she muttered, struggling out of deep sleep. 'Darling, what's the matter?'

'He's dying. He's got cancer. He's going to die in a few months. He's my friend and he's going to die. Oh God . . .' He hugged her till her ribs jarred, trying to haul comfort out of flesh that was whole and undiseased.

What do I say, thought Rosie the next morning. Sorry seems horribly inadequate, but I can't just ignore it, can't ignore someone's life like a bad case of acne. Can't say, it'll be all right because it won't, and there aren't any platitudes, at least not in my book, not in my upbringing, which tell me how to deal with this. But it was Steve who pre-empted the situation.

'John told you, I suppose,' he said. Rosie was standing by the stove, watching the kettle boil. John was asleep. Steve was sitting at the kitchen table. 'Yes . . . I'm . . .'

'I'm sorry to dump it on you,' he interjected. 'It feels an imposition to come somewhere when you're dying. Impolite. Dragging around this useless body, making people feel embarrassed. No one knows what to say.'

'Does it hurt?' she said, pouring the boiling water over the coffee grains, watching them bubble and pus like sores.

'No, not yet. They took out a chunk of intestine and it hurt before that. I feel really well; actually, I can't believe it . . . I'm going to have radium treatment, chemotherapy, the works, may even get better. I'm far too young to go . . . It could all be just a rotten joke on a cosmic scale.'

The planned two-day stopover in London turned into a week and the news flashed over the radio that the war was over.

Steve found a doctor and began courses in chemotherapy and radiation treatment, and worked on his last ambition; a filmscript about his love-affair with a Vietnamese hooker called Twiggy.

'She named herself after the model, but she was far better looking,' Steve said. He'd lived with Twiggy in Saigon after Crystal's departure. The story was poignant; Twiggy's attempts to ape western women, and the hours she spent reading French fashion magazines, worrying about the shape of her body, her nose and her breasts, seeing their Asianness as a failing, were a reminder of how much women everywhere tried to conform to artificial ideals.

John and Steve both assumed that Rosie was going to Asia with them. They could have been talking about a trip to Wales, for all the fuss that was made. John and Jay Landesman had formed an agency while John had been in London. The motto of CAL (Creative Artists Limited) was 'We'll take the sting out of success and put the fun back into failure'. Their one successful project had been finding a backer for the film. Steve decided to go to Paris for Christmas, Rosie was taking John down to Shropshire to join their family Christmas. Her sister Collette was coming from Denmark with her husband Alan and heaven only knew how long it would be before they would all be home for Christmas again.

Leaving *Spare Rib* also entailed minimal fuss, which was both a relief and a sadness. They don't really care whether I stay or go, she thought, as she packed up her desk, filed papers, and wrote out the phone numbers from her book which other members of the staff might need in the months to come. She hugged Marsha after a quiet farewell drink. There wasn't much left for them to say. They sat there, like two ex-lovers meeting to try and find what they once saw in each other.

NINE

I woke up the following morning in a deep depression. For the last few days just the fact of feeling well had been enough to make me jump eagerly out of bed.

Taylor's trip to the Potter made me aware of what I was up against. Aware, too, of the fact that I'd been hiding behind the group, involving myself in clinic affairs and forgetting, temporarily, just why I was there. I realised that I hadn't even begun to peel the orange; only scrape at the zest. I was in a nut-house and I hadn't got there by accident.

Taylor's pronouncement had sounded like a personal death-sentence, passed with full knowledge. 'Alcoholism is a fatal illness,' are the opening words of an American book called *I'll Stop Tomorrow*. I'd been reading it two days earlier. A fatal illness, one which you don't choose to have, but nevertheless one which only you can cure.

No magic stuff like penicillin, no instant cures, no transplants. It would be no good, I realised, to wear my alcoholism like an old overcoat, it had to be far more than that. It had to become part of me, like my nose, my hands and my pear-shaped arse. Being in the bug house at the age of thirty was serious, but not the end of the world. Coming out of the bughouse and finding my self back in one again a few months later was a different story. I was tolerant towards myself in terms of becoming an alcoholic, but what now? The world will give you lots of chances, but how many can you give yourself?

What it boiled down to was simple; I was on my own. It was a terrifying idea, but exhilarating at the same time.

Few women are ever brought up to feel that they are entirely on their own. I was certainly no exception. Although my upbringing had not been so archaic as to assume that I would be my father's daughter until I was my husband's wife, I had relied on the idea that something, somewhere would bail me out. When the going got rough, there was always an airline ticket, a job, an article to write, a meal, a shoulder to cry on. I'd been avoiding responsibility for myself all my life; politics, movements, gurus, a long list of boyfriends, whichever way, always someone or something.

In the nuthouse, I'd reacted in the same way. I'd found external events on which to pin my traumas and emotions. I'd carried on changing shape to fit into circumstances in the easiest possible way. But I was responsible for being a drunk. I was responsible for carrying on being a drunk or not, and that meant that I was also responsible for the rest; my happiness, my financial security, my ability to give as well as take.

I suddenly felt an enormous sense of urgency. This business was life and death. I needed facts, knowledge.

Taylor said he planned to go home after the coming weekend. He was brittle and defensive. Inevitably, the subject of relapses amongst recovered, or recovering, alcoholics came up at the next group. The doctor turned first to Raju, who had stayed off booze for a year.

'Impulse,' he replied.

'What do you mean, impulse?' I asked. 'Nothing can be

that unpremeditated, especially when you know you've got a booze problem.'

'Well,' he said, 'I was driving back from the hospital. I was happy. I saw a liquor store. I stopped the car. Got out. Bought a bottle of Scotch. Then drove home. I didn't drink it straight away.'

'Well then, it wasn't an impulse,' I said. I was needling him, almost rude in my urge to try and understand exactly what had gone on in his mind when he slipped over the hill.

'No, not to drink when I finally did.'

'Well?'

'It was an impulse to buy the bottle.'

'So why didn't you throw it away when you got home, instead of sitting looking at it?'

'I had a bath.'

I was lost. What had the bath to do with this?

'After the bath, I thought, I'll have one. Then I had two. Then I had another. Then I don't remember any more.'

'Surely, though, it doesn't have to be like that?' said Brian, addressing the doctor. All alcoholics don't have one drink and then necessarily go right on into a binge?'

'For me,' said Anne, 'it's because I feel so guilty about having had the first drink that I think, well, what the hell, and have a whole lot more. Before I ever had any treatment, I often used to be able to have one drink, or two, then stop. After having treatment, learning how out of hand it all becomes and how quickly it all happens, I think I let it happen, it's an excuse in itself.'

This was terrifying; but more interesting than pursuing Raju and his impulse.

'You mean that you're actually losing confidence as a result of having therapy?' I asked.

'No,' she said, 'it's not confidence I'm losing. It's guilt that's growing. I keep on throwing everything away that I've gained by being in the clinic. It's crazy, because like Raju I go and buy a bottle on an impulse. Almost as though I like to have it around so that I know I could get soused if I wanted to. Then once I've got it, I find that I'm drawn to it, like towards a snake or anything that you find really horrid, and then I'm there. The first drink makes me more cheerful for a while. Then I start to feel guilty. So I have another.'

There was a pause. The doctor cleared his throat. He said, 'It's more likely when you are tired, hungry, miserable, lonely, thirsty.'

'But you're talking about leading a magic life,' I said. 'All those things are going to happen to you often.'

'Oh yes,' he answered, 'but it's a question of minimising the risks. Don't go and buy your cigarettes in the off-licence. Go to the newsagent. If you're tired, have a rest. If you're lonely, get on the phone and call someone. Try to make life happier instead of wallowing in misery. Put temptation out of the way.'

There was a logic in all this, but it did not spell out the kind of life I wanted to lead. I had no intention of changing my world when I left the clinic. All my friends drank. There would be booze at home. There would be dinner parties to give, parties to go to. Temptation, in other words, round every corner. Giving up heroin, in retrospect, seemed like a cinch; it is not, after all, common currency at most fashionable dinner tables.

'Surely the important thing to remember,' I said, 'when you have a craving for a drink, is that the craving is psychological. There's nothing physical in it.'

'Did you read that?' asked the doctor.

'No,' I said, 'but it's true, isn't it? I know that if I suddenly craved a drink now it wouldn't be anything in my body. So, if it's in my head and I think about that, then that must make a difference.' I looked at Taylor, who was staring out of the window. 'Well, Taylor?'

'Oh, I don't know. I just felt so fed up.'

'I suppose I wanted to see what it would be like,' said Raju.

Poor excuses, I thought, sensing somehow they were all hiding something from me, covering up for themselves in some way. Later on I was to discover for myself how apt Raju's words actually were.

Institutional life was beginning to tell.

Clinics suit people who have been to boarding school or in the army. Without one of those disciplines early on in life, I suspect that such places are a lot harder to handle. The regression to childhood, and then racing at speed back through the years trying to fill in the gaps created by the booze, produces infantile humour and manic impulses to upset applecarts, provided they are not your own. Brian and I, who seemed to share a sense of humour and mischief, found the opportunities for practical jokes irresistible.

We set off the fire alarm, sent fake messages, changed notices on the agenda board, and laughed uproariously at the minor confusions we caused. We laughed, too, at the feeblest of jokes.

Brian had once been so drunk in Paris that, driving at top speed through a crowded street-market, he'd hooked a woman's shopping bag on to his door handle. Too scared to stop when he heard the thump, he had gone on several miles before pulling up. By some miracle the bag was still full of groceries. This story was guaranteed to have us rolling on the ground.

The laughter baffled the nurses, but not the doctor. He could see it as a release of tension.

But the laughter, though in itself therapeutic, left me feeling hollow, I'd find myself convinced nothing had ever been funnier, then in the next breath I'd feel angry at being so childish. I wasn't meant to be enjoying this, was I? For visitors, the laughter and camaraderie were especially weird. William told me later that he felt like an intruder when he came to visit. We had in-jokes, nicknames, a system of shorthand which had quickly evolved.

Laughter – manic, hysterical, nearly tearful – became our defence against the world. When I'd first been imprisoned in Thailand I'd been puzzled by how much the women laughed. I wasn't puzzled for long. It was a simple choice: laugh, or cry. The middle road was not one which, in either circumstances, I was able to maintain for long.

'One of the things that worries me the most,' I said to the doctor, 'is how on earth is life ever going to be exciting without booze. Booze is associated with excitement, with good times, with bad times, and somehow the thought of a life that is lived on an even keel is very depressing. I can't imagine me ever being even.'

'Don't worry,' he said, 'it's a lot less dull than passing out.'

I laughed, but I still worried about the possible boredom of sobriety. I asked the AA speakers about excitement, but they were little help. AA guides its members back to respectability and stability. Highs and lows, and excesses of any kind, are frowned upon. After the chaos of your drinking life, they said, surely what you want is to return to complete stability? To me, this spelt middle-of-the-road ordinariness, and it filled me with a sense of helplessness. To be sober, was my life going to have to be sober too?

Later on I was surprised that the doctor had not explained the situation more fully. Booze is an anaesthetic that works to inhibit areas of your brain. To start with it lifts, finally it's a sedative only. Any alcoholic who is drinking regularly is experiencing, in the end, only the sedative effects. Sure, booze was providing my excitement, because it was inducing chaos. I'd be swinging into a bender, out of it, through a period of furtive but controlled drinking and then back to chaos again by getting almightily drunk. I'd forgotten, in the interim, that whatever feelings of happiness or sadness I had were just as powerful when left alone. More powerful, because they were real. I was to get to grips with this a lot sooner and faster than I anticipated, and, like most of life's lucky accidents, in a way which was entirely unpredictable.

TEN

From a lilo in the middle of the pool of Bombay's Taj Mahal Hotel, Rosie watched Steve seduce the last girl of his life. She was a blonde Qantas air hostess, with an uneven tan.

Cancer was a winner for seducing women. Steve only had to mutter, 'I'm terminally ill . . .' and the girl would start ripping off her clothes, anxious to give him a last moment of earthly nirvana. The Qantas girl was already sitting astride his buttocks, applying sun-tan oil to his back. I hope she's not another saviour, Rosie thought, recalling the rangy redhead Steve had picked up in London. She called herself Lotus and was into star signs and pyramids. If Steve would sit in a pyramid, Lotus said, for an unspecified length of time, the energy vibes would cure him.

Definitely.

Just before Christmas, Steve's cancer had suddenly spread. Hopes of going to Vietnam to make the film faded. The doctors advised hospital, but an acupuncturist suggested India. 'There isn't anything else I can do. You need a miracle,' he said.

'Sai Baba,' Steve announced later in the day.

Rosie had never heard of him. John had, however. 'It's the only idea left,' he said. 'Apparently the guy's really performed miracles.'

'Well,' Steve asked, 'are you up for going?'

'It's on the way,' said Rosie, watching his face. He looked relieved; despite his public cynicism he'd been frightened at the thought of undertaking the trip alone.

Rosie hauled herself out of the pool and went to sit beside Steve. 'How do you feel?'

'Terrific,' he grinned, 'the sun does wonders and you haven't yet met . . .' He introduced the Qantas girl. Rosie laughed, amazed once again by his attitude. She had never even seen a dead person, let alone seriously contemplated her own death. Yet here was this thirty-two-year-old who, barring a miracle, was going to die in a few weeks, cracking jokes and wondering if he was going to get laid that night. Perhaps Vietnam had encouraged such indifference to death. Or was it just a refusal to accept that he was going to die?

News of the dying man flashed round the hotel staff. They were encouraging about the chances of a miracle. Sashin, the bellboy, spent all his spare time with them. 'I have been to see Sai Baba,' he smilingly proclaimed. 'He is a wonderful, wonderful man.'

'Yah,' said Steve, 'get me another gin and tonic.'

'Yes, yes, I fetch waiter,' Sashin said as he headed for the shadowy interior of the hotel. 'Then I come back and tell you about Baba. Perhaps you like to meet my father, he once saw Sai Baba . . .' It was lunchtime of their third day in Bombay. They were preparing to fly south the following day. The Qantas blonde was now a permanent fixture. In the two days they had spent together, her attachment to Steve had become slavish.

On the way back from the airlines office later that afternoon, John and Rosie wandered into a café called East West, Both are Best. At the next table sat an American couple, the woman heavily pregnant. She wore a cheap sari, frayed and muddy, and her eyes were gaunt and hollow.

'What are you doing here?' drawled the man. John explained. 'Hey, that's far out,' he said, and then proceeded to paraphrase the story to his lady, whose glassy look said that she wasn't taking anything in today. 'Me and my old lady, we're in a bit of a fix,' he said, 'you couldn't lend us a few bucks, you see she's having a kid and we're waiting for a cheque.' His arms were thin and bitten by bedbugs. He scratched them furiously from time to time. His tee-shirt was dirty and a piece of string held up his trousers. Greasy hair fell to his shoulders, but his sunken cheeks and eyes gave him the look of a saint.

'We came here three years ago,' he said, 'and kind of dug the place. Started out up north with the Maharishi, but then he split to Europe and we decided to stay. Then she got pregnant,' he added, 'fuck knows what it's going to be like having a kid here. All the money I've got goes on trying to feed her.'

'Why don't you go home?' asked Rosie.

'I guess things wouldn't be much better there,' he replied, with finality.

John gave him five dollars. 'Good luck with your friend,' the American called after them. The woman never opened her mouth.

The Hare Krishna mantra thundered from Oxford Street to Bombay. The begging Western 'sadus' – holy men – seemed a further corruption of a system that was already corrupt. Rosie hated seeing Westerners mimic Indians. They shaved their heads, wore orange, draped their necks in beads and bells, and then had the nerve to beg from people who were starving themselves. But she also felt jealous; whatever it was they were doing they were doing wholeheartedly and with faith.

She was on the surface of life skating around like a manic waterboatman, always busy, always in the right place, but never committed to any one place or any one philosophy. This country, supposedly so much nearer to God than solid old England was, didn't seem to be giving her any faith either.

She was terrified of doing and saying the wrong thing; she was terrified of Indian food, in case she got ill. She was afraid of so many things, in fact, that it amazed her when people thought she was bold, though she never knew whether to take it as a compliment or not. Sometimes, she knew, there was an advantage in being considered a she-wolf rather than a mewing kitten.

John, Steve and Rosie left the next day, six hundred miles by air to Bangalore and the miracle man.

The taxi-driver recommended the Hotel Stay Longer.

'Nice hotel, nice pool, not expensive,' he said. John thought that was funny. Steve, who was already exhausted and was now suffering from the far hotter temperature, grinned weakly. 'Well, we'll have to prove it.'

They reserved adjoining rooms. Rosie checked the bathroom for cockroaches and found several crawling in and out of the waste pipe, but they were quite small by New York standards. The sheets were clean and the beds were hard and comfortable. John pronounced the hotel OK for a prolonged stay after discovering the efficiency of the room service.

The hotel was on the edge of the bazaar, at the cheaper end of town. Bangalore had been a large army station and despite the blistering heat, trees and flowers grew in profusion. The British had left long straight roads and neat colonial houses. It must have been a civilised posting, with the fashionable hill station of Ootacamund only a few hours away by train.

Pima, the receptionist, commiserated. Her father had just died of cancer. Rosie asked her about Sai Baba. Yes, she knew of him, but her father had not been a believer so the family had not sought a miracle. 'It was his time to go,' Pima said with a fatalistic shrug, 'who are we to argue or to interfere?

'The miracle man is still up in the hills,' she told them, after making a phone call. 'He will be here in Bangalore in about a week.'

It was too long to wait. On Pima's advice John and Rosie plunged into the bazaar to acquire the necessary items for a stay in a hill village. 'You need mosquito net, cooking things, mattresses, sheets, mugs, food . . .' The list was endless. 'And Rosie will need a sari. Sai Baba likes all women to wear saris.'

John packed and repacked the equipment, finally cramming it into seven bags. Pima organised a taxi for the following morning.

During the winter months Sai Baba inhabits a hill station called Puttaparti, about two hundred miles east of Bangalore. In the summer he comes to Whitefields, a centre outside Bangalore, where he runs courses for Indians and Europeans. In southern India he is revered as a god, the incarnation of Shridi Sai Baba, and his powers are reputedly limitless. The point most strongly in his favour, Rosie thought, was that he had never bothered to go to the West, as so many of his fellow gurus did.

Although sceptical about the Hindu Sai Baba, the Sikh taxi driver certainly did well in taxi fees.

As they climbed towards the hills, the heat grew more intense. Rosie looked anxiously at Steve. What little hair the chemotherapy had left lay in damp sweaty tendrils and the ominous lumps that she thought she had seen on his head a few days earlier were now clearly visible. He fidgeted in his seat, groping in his pocket for more morphine.

'I seem to have hurt my shoulder,' he mumbled a little while later. Pulling back his shirt, he revealed a huge contusion on his collar bone. It was the size of a tangerine. 'I fell out of bed last night, can't think what I did to myself.' He dozed off into his fretful morphine stupor. John also slept. Rosie watched the countryside, conscious of disappointment. It was just dirty, dusty and dull. Her new sari itched her armpits. It was red and orange and had taken a long time to arrange. Peeing was a hassle. There was obviously some trick to holding all those yards of material together with one hand.

It was nearly seven o'clock by the time they paid off the driver. The village of Puttaparti sprawled around the walls of the ashram. Inside the gate people wandered aimlessly. John approached a man with long blond hair, who wore the traditional white pyjamas, dhotis. His name was Mark.

'That's just wonderful, really wonderful,' he kept repeating, as John told him the reason for the journey. 'I'll take your friend to sleep inside the ashram: you'll have to sleep outside.'

Steve didn't like the separation but Mark was adamant. 'You must be near Sai Baba at all times, his powers will find you, he'll know you're here and he'll help.'

Mark told other Westerners the news of Steve's arrival. The two or three hundred white faces in the crowds were greatly outnumbered by the Indians. Good, thought Rosie, they come too.

John and Rosie slept in a field that night. The ground was rocky and parched; other disciples huddled in groups around the field. One by one the lights of their torches and lanterns went out, and by about ten o'clock the field was dark and silent. The sky, thick with stars, seemed only inches away.

'Why do you say that miracles are in bad taste?' Rosie asked.

'No one should try to interfere with karma.'

'But medicine interferes with karma.'

'That's different. That's a creation of man and that's OK to use. It's another matter when you start kicking about with spiritual powers. Life is in constant rotation and you can't stop that cycle.'

They were silent. 'Do you think it's going to work?' she asked into the darkness.

'No, I don't. But even if he can't work a miracle he is a holy man, and Steve could do with a dose of that before he dies. Now shut up and go to sleep.'

Looking up at the stars, Rosie wondered what she was doing. The role of nurse/spiritual follower seemed to fit as badly as the sari. She had always relied on life to turn up trumps at crucial moments, to nudge her into new patterns, new places. But was that just another way of abdicating from responsibility? She looked at John's sleeping back, and listened to his regular breathing, and wondered if he ever felt like that. Shouldn't the fact that she was spending the first of God only knew how many nights lying in a dusty Indian field be the product of some sort of careful reasoning?

The field came to life at dawn. They found Steve sitting beside a raised dais, on which Sai Baba was shortly to appear for morning darshan (prayers), surrounded by an eager group. 'Hey, John, listen to all these stories. This guy must be amazing.'

The refrain was to become familiar. Stories, stories, stories, each one capping the last: 'I saw him produce his holy ash'; 'I saw him produce a watch'; 'I saw him cure a crippled boy.'

Sai Baba appeared at six-thirty. The murmur of the crowd

died away, as everyone prostrated themselves before him. He wore a long orange robe, which did not conceal his fat belly. His hair was black and sprouted Afro fashion from his head. Round his neck were numerous gold chains and his chubby face seemed creased into a permanent smile.

Rosie sat with the rest of the women. She could not follow the singing, which droned on for half an hour. Baba then rose from his purple velvet seat and began his walk through the crowd, starting with the sick people who sat to one side.

His policy, she learnt later, was to walk through the rows of devotees, nodding to them, blessing them, sometimes materialising his magic ash – vibutti – over their heads. Vibutti was Sai Baba's chief trick; this grey powder, which resembled the charred remains of bones, fell from the ends of his fingers. Rosie never actually saw it happen, neither did John or Steve. Sai Baba always wore loose sleeves, but in spite of her suspicions she was positive that there were no tubes running up to ash bags hidden in his armpits.

They had been there for two days when Mark came to tell them that the master was leaving for Whitefields the following day. There didn't seem to be any reason for this early departure and Steve was particularly irked by the thought of having to move again so fast. But Mark was used to the guru's unpredictability. To cheer Steve's flagging spirits he recounted a tale of a cancer cure that Baba had performed on an American woman. Steve shrugged indifferently, but the pain and fear that now always danced together in his eyes seemed to lift momentarily.

All that day the Indians teemed out of the village. Sai Baba's teaching could never be described as profound or intellectual; but his contribution to his devotees' happiness was indubitable. Many believe him to be a direct descendant of Jesus Christ and point to the lost years in Christ's life, claiming that he spent these in India, where some karmic connection had been forged between him and Sai Baba.

Jesus said, 'I am in the father, and you are in me just as I am in you.' Sai Baba preaches a similar gospel. Love, purification and meditation, he says, will enable believers to realise the God inside. Throwing in a few miracles en route makes him fun to be around, but dazzling though miracles may be, they only serve as a reminder that, in this game at least, he is the lightfooted God presiding over disciples whose sneakers are glued to terra firma. He encourages people to think of him as their mother, or father, a role he amply fulfils in an uncertain Western mind, disenchanted with the rat-race and content to pursue inner goals on remarkably little cash. Unlike some other Indian Ashrams, Sai Baba's is free, though donations – and they come in plenty – are encouraged. Many of the disciples Rosie encountered seemed to spend a remarkable amount of time assuring themselves that material poverty would ultimately lead to spiritual wealth.

Back in the Hotel Stay Longer, they waited for the guru to arrive in Bangalore. It was so odd to only know someone in the context of their dying, Rosie thought. In the weeks in London before leaving for India she often felt guilty when she had told someone about Steve's illness, making a good story out of someone else's life, or rather, the end of it. Rather cheap, she thought. Yet she had always kept her distance, aware of the charm in his twinkly brown eyes, aware of the romantic lure of death and sadness. She did not want to end up missing him too much. For John it was different; he could compare this wrecked human being with the friend of happier days, and his efforts to shut out Steve's presence – by withdrawing into himself, or downing a couple of morphine pills – became more frequent as the days passed.

There were moments when she felt her own reserve slip. One day while they waited in the Stay Longer, he had asked her to write some letters to friends back in the States. Jokily, he said his handwriting had got rather shaky and would she mind . . .? In truth, he couldn't even sit up in bed. 'Dear John and Lonnie,' began one of the letters, 'how are you. When I get home, John, don't forget your promise of that drink together. Be seeing you . . .' Steve dictated five such letters and fell asleep half way through the sixth. Rosie, not knowing whether to post them or not, carried them around in her bag for ages. When she had been writing these hopeful notes, she had wanted to say, 'Stop, what are you doing?' Or burst into tears. In the event she did nothing. Just wrote. When she finally posted them, the envelopes were dirty and creased.

After a week in the hotel, the Sikh taxi driver was summoned for duty again and they drove out to Whitefields. They soon encountered Mark. 'I've found a place for Steve to live,' he said, 'with this wonderful woman who rents a bungalow nearby.'

Cynthia was about fifty, a large, hearty woman who resembled a gym mistress going to a fancy-dress ball. A faded Cambridge-blue sari exposed sturdy ankles and feet thrust into heavy black leather sandals. Her tone was brisk.

'Come in, come in,' she hailed, when she saw the little party making its way across the stubbly field. 'I've made a bed up for Steve on the sun balcony. No room for you two, though.' She was jocular, but firm. 'Lucky you're here,' she said to Steve, 'only place to be. Doctors really don't know what they are on about. We'll have you fixed up in no time.' Rosie watched her unpacking Steve's bags, tutting over the morphine, the silk shirts, the Nikons. Especially the morphine. 'Have to get you off this.' Steve looked alarmed. 'Even if you do die, you don't want to be addicted when the time comes. Miss all the fun.'

'What the hell is this bloody woman on about?' muttered John. 'Listen Cynthia, it's very kind of you to offer Steve this place to sleep, but he's got to have his painkillers. He's in agony, can't you see?'

Cynthia raised her head a fraction. She was rifling through a camera bag. 'Well, well, for the time being, maybe. We'll have to see. Now, Steve, you just get into bed and I'll arrange the Altar next to you. You two, run along now.'

Cynthia's story was bizarre. She had been born in South Africa shortly after the First World War. Her parents were 'into gold and diamonds' and Cynthia had joined the jet-set; when she was twenty she had married a racing driver, and had had a son and daughter. She had, she said, 'lived a shallow, meaningless existence, in which money was flung about like confetti and the only interests were the race track and the next party.' She had a number of affairs before her husband's death in a racing accident. Two years later her son was killed too, blowing himself to pieces while trying to beat a speed record.

'I just felt so guilty, so out of harmony with myself,' she said. The turn of phrase sounded strange from this matronly figure. 'I came to India for a holiday and while I was in Bangalore I came out here to see the Sai Baba. He seemed,' she added, with a rare touch of humour, 'to be one of the main tourist attractions.' She had stayed, convinced she had found her spiritual home. She was generous with her cash, and Rosie often observed her discreetly passing bundles of rupees to poverty-stricken Indians or Westerners.

Her attitude to Steve, though, was a mystery. On the second night of his stay she moved her bed on to the sun lounge too. Efficiently she organised the construction of a litter, so that he could be carried each morning to the darshan, where Sai Baba continued to ignore him. During the day, she plaited him elaborate garlands of frangipani. He was fading fast, but Cynthia refused to see it. She and John argued endlessly about the morphine but even in this Cynthia was winning. The dosage was being reduced, but Steve was semiconscious most of the time and past caring. Whether he was asleep or awake, she would talk to him constantly. Sometimes she read passages out of the Baghavad Gita, sometimes she urged him to believe he was getting well, sometimes she told him to accept his fate and to believe in the afterlife.

The paradox, which was never answered – perhaps the reason why miracles are in bad taste – was this: if you believe in karma, in some sort of divine fate, and in the theory that your actions, whether in this life or another, will reap their own rewards or punishments, as Sai Baba's teaching dictates, then how can any man, or God, step in and interfere?

Cynthia's answer was simple. 'Sometimes, for reasons of his own, Sai Baba realises that it is not time for someone to die; or to suffer; so he will alter their destiny.'

As the days passed and Baba continued to ignore Steve, whose doses of holy ash were supplied by Cynthia, the fact that he considered Steve to have deserved his fate became increasingly apparent.

One late afternoon, Cynthia suddenly turned to Rosie and asked her to come for a walk. Rosie was surprised. Cynthia had seemed jealous of Steve's affection for her and she was always abrupt when she arrived at the bungalow, happy to see her leave.

'My son,' Cynthia began, as they walked down the dusty lane leading from the ashram, 'would have been the same age as Steve is now. They're the same sign – they even look alike. I felt so guilty when he was killed. Maybe my husband knew what he was doing, but my son was so young and I didn't have any time for him, didn't try to keep him off the track. I just went to parties and had lovers, and –' she turned to Rosie, her eyes streaming tears '– I think Sai Baba has sent Steve to me, so that I can somehow make up for having abandoned my son like I did.'

A mess; but it did explain her manic behaviour, thought Rosie with a rush of anger against Sai Baba who, if he was capable of performing miracles, had not performed one; against fate for giving Steve cancer; against herself for having naively believed that he would be cured; and against her expectations of finding some kind of answers for herself in India.

Exhausted by her outburst, Cynthia sat down on a bank beside the road. Overhead chattered two parakeets, and the smell of cow droppings, mixed with the strong scent of the flowers, was sickening.

Rosie could not think of a suitable response, but Cynthia did not seem to expect one. After a time her sniffles subsided. 'I'm glad I told you. You don't think I'm crazy do you?'

This was the first time Rosie had ever heard Cynthia – or any Sai Baba devotee – express doubt. 'No,' she muttered, too aghast at the arrogance of Cynthia's assumptions to argue. 'We'd better go back. It must be nearly time for the evening darshan.' Picking up the edges of her sari, she stood up and held out her hand to the older woman. Cynthia rose and hugged her. 'I wish my daughter was like you,' she said.

As Steve's life ebbed away, so too did the flow of visitors to the bungalow. John, especially, was relieved about this, as he knew the time he had left to spend with his friend was short. But it was still irksome. At first everyone had crowded round to see the sick man, hoping that they might witness a miracle to be added to their list of stories. Everyone was bored with tales about watches appearing out of thin air. Another miraculous recall from the jaws of death would have fed the camp-fire tales for years. But as they saw that Sai Baba was not intending to work any magic, they stopped coming. Before, they had said that all Steve needed was faith. Now, they said he had too little. No one wanted to know this failure of a human being who was going to die on the master's doorstep. They needed to be convinced that it was Steve's fault and not a sign of Sai Baba's own fallibility.

Steve's breath was coming in shorter and shorter gasps. Since her confession, Cynthia had stopped watching over him quite so protectively and it was John who spent all his time sitting beside him. He read to Steve and when he was conscious they reminisced about days in Vietnam and about mutual friends. Rosie had little place in the closing scene.

He died late one Wednesday afternoon. There were no final struggles, no last attempts to hang on to life in a body that had long since seen the end. One minute he was breathing and the next he was not. It happened so quietly and quickly that it was minutes before Rosie could acknowledge that she was sitting next to a corpse.

There must be a spirit, she thought. It was just as though something real but intangible had suddenly disappeared, like shutting out the smell of summer by closing the windows. She bent to kiss his cheek.

Nobody knew what to do. Cynthia for unknown reasons was adamant that she did not want the body on her verandah overnight. The only solution was to take it to town in a taxi and then try to put it in the morgue.

Darkness had fallen by the time the cab arrived. 'Very bad to travel with dead man,' the driver protested, turning to leave. For three hundred rupees he changed his mind. John wrapped the stiffening body in a sheet, and placed it across the back seat.

'Well, goodbye then.' John held out his hand to Cynthia. She took it and then held it firmly in her own.

'I am sorry,' she said. 'But he did die under Baba's protection.'

They left her mourning the passing of another son.

The driver was scared and drove dangerously. The normal journey took twenty minutes. That night they made it in twelve and drew up, with shrieking brakes, in front of a large hospital. John climbed out, returning in a few minutes to say that there was no morgue. 'We have to go here,' and he passed the driver a scrap of paper.

The next hospital was closed for the night.

'You must get out, here,' said the driver, his hands trembling violently. 'One hundred more rupees.' John held out the money. 'There must be somewhere. And stop by the bazaar, you could do with a drink.' In the bazaar, John bought three bottles of raxi, a cheap, rotgut Indian whisky; one for each of them.

The driver swallowed hard. His spirits revived. 'Maybe I know a place,' he said turning the car round.

'Thank God for that. I was beginning to think that we would have to buy a hat and an overcoat and smuggle Steve into the hotel,' said John. They both started to laugh manically. The driver joined in, though he could not have heard the remark. Racing and lurching through the narrow streets, they must have looked like three drunks out on a spree.

At the third hospital the doctor laid the body on a table in a huge, empty room. 'I'm sorry, but our morgue is shut for the night. This is the only room we have; it does have air conditioning. ' He pointed to a feeble fan on the ceiling, slowly rotating. 'I shouldn't really let you leave him here, we use this room for lectures during the day. You must come and collect him early in the morning to take him for cremation. It would have been better to have burnt the body out in the country.'

The driver dropped them off at the Stay Longer. But we won't, thought Rosie, as they went to their room. Half a bottle of raxi later, she fell into a stuporous sleep, to be awakened by the bedside phone a few hours later.

The hospital was awake and bustling when she arrived. John was still sleeping. Several Indians were standing around Steve's body, lifting back the edges of the sheet and peering. They might all have been commenting on a freshly slaughtered pheasant. A hospital official, waving forms and documents, came across the room while Rosie was standing there, looking at the shrouded form and wondering what the hell to do next.

'You have to take him for autopsy,' the clerk said.

'But why?' she responded in dismay. 'Everyone knows how he died.'

'Because he is American,' explained the clerk patiently. 'We do not want the American Ambassador ringing up next year saying that we murdered him.'

A hospital taxi was summoned and the driver slung the rigid body into the back seat. It felt as crazy as the night before, except this time she was alone and the sun was shining. A young Indian girl leant through the window and dropped some hibiscus blooms on Steve's face. Rosie turned to thank her, but she'd run off, tittering and embarrassed.

The municipal autopsy department was on the far side of the fresh meat market. The Indians seemed unaware of the irony. When they drove back through the market, two hours later, the back of the car contained, along with the mutilated cadaver, four jars in which various pieces of Steve's innards floated in formaldehyde. The smell of the putrefying meat and the sight of bloodstained men plunging huge knives into the carcases of sheep made Rosie's stomach turn. They dropped the jars off at the hospital and turned, finally, towards the crematorium. It was only eleven o'clock but she was exhausted.

Rosie had phoned John to tell him to wake up and buy some flowers. When she arrived, he was standing alone in the empty hall, looking ill and depressed. The chairs arranged around the walls gave the room the air of a deserted dance-hall. The workers at the crematorium knocked together a flimsy cane stretcher and dumped Steve's body on it. John covered him with flowers. After taking the money in advance, the attendant pressed a button and the iron gates opened to reveal the raging fire. The electric floor moved slowly. As the doors closed they could see the flowers curling in the heat.

'I will send the ashes to your hotel,' said the man, 'it takes several hours.'

Later there was a knock on their door and Pima announced with a grin, 'Steve is back.' She handed John a heavy package.

Peeling off several sheets of an old copy of the *Bangalore Times*, John found a bulk-size Ovaltine can. Even for such a seasoned traveller it was a strange final convergance.

ELEVEN

The first world conference on alcoholism was scheduled to take place in a West London hotel during my third week in the clinic. Both Anne and Shelagh had checked out of the clinic. Anne, though, had signed up for the conference and paid her money. It made sense to her: attending an alcohol conference was similar to staying in the clinic and, at £172 for three days, much cheaper.

Two new patients arrived but were spending most of their time in their rooms recovering from their last bouts. There was Cherry, a middle-aged, puffy housewife who seemed to be permanently in tears. The other new face belonged to a Greek shipping magnate called Alex.

As the conference drew near, I grew increasingly jumpy. Two things were bothering me in particular. The first was meeting someone I knew there. Medical correspondents are not part of my coterie of friends, but the prospect of a couple of thousand words about the evils of drink might lure God knows who from their Fleet Street lairs. The second was how to explain my presence.

Could I say I had been flown over from Cyprus by an Arab magazine? I wanted to be honest, yet I was haunted by my predicament when considered from the point of view of the impartial outsider: thirty-year-old lush in an alcoholic home.

I was due to meet Anne at three o'clock on the first afternoon of the conference. I arrived at the hotel by taxi looking, I hoped, competent and efficient. My hair was sleek, I was wearing a smart Harrods' herring-bone tweed skirt and a black silk shirt. My mother's pearls hung neatly at my neck.

I rang Anne's room from the lobby phone. No answer. The girl at the conference registration desk was unhelpful and harassed by the scores of Americans asking questions and looking for meal tickets. There was no sign of Anne. I called her home number, called her room again; still no answer. I waited half an hour, and tried all the numbers again. No answer. It wasn't possible. She can't be drunk again already, I thought. Only three days after leaving the clinic?

I decided to have tea. I missed my friend's support. I dreaded confronting the room full of people, some standing in line for scones and sandwiches, others already settled down at tables. I'd planned all this with Anne, and now I had to deal with it alone. I wondered if anyone would notice, if the fact that I was alcoholic was stamped across my forehead like a brand.

I sat down at an empty table. 'Do you mind if I join you?' I looked up to see a tall American, wearing naval uniform. His face was boyish and clean-shaven. Out of uniform, he would be only one step away from a surfboard. I nodded. He said his name was Phil.

My worries about Anne were growing. I discovered that my companion had been running the US Navy's detoxification and drug rehabilitation centre for the last ten years, but I had no wish to ask his advice. 'Have you had a problem with drink?' he asked suddenly.

I was horrified. So it did show.

'How did you know?'

He laughed at my distress.

'I'm not exactly a stranger to this game. I've been around alcoholics for years, my father was one, there was a good chance that alcoholics would be here, and anyway, you've been asking questions that are too acute for a journalist with just a casual interest in the subject.'

I told him about Anne and the clinic. I felt better. My first confession to another human being. Although it was all probably old hat to him, he treated it with dexterity and a level of seriousness which left me feeling OK. I came to the conclusion that he must be a fine therapist. I was, I knew, going through the initial stage of alcoholic recovery, when you feel startlingly different from your former self. I felt deeply at sea with Phil. I didn't seem to know the rules any more. He was flirting with me and I was being drawn out of my burrow. Uncertain, and afraid.

We were the last people to leave the dining room. We parted at the door. I went back to the main desk and asked again if they were certain that Anne had not checked in. The shifts had changed in the intervening hour and the new face behind the counter was marginally more efficient and less harassed. 'No,' he replied, 'the key to room 605 is still here.'

She hadn't made it. I took the train back to Sloane Square, delaying my arrival at the clinic. I hadn't been in a subway for a long time and I kept searching the faces of my fellow travellers on the five-thirty rush-hour train for signs that they were looking at me. Nothing. I was just like any other girl going home from work on a sunny afternoon in mid September. I walked back down the King's Road, hoping that I'd find Anne at the clinic, full of apologies.

'How did it go?' asked Carol.

'Anne didn't come.'

Carol tried the phone; still no answer.

'When the hell did she get drunk?' I asked angrily. 'I can't believe it, she was looking forward to this, it's only been three days.'

Carol looked sympathetic. I felt bitterly betrayed.

I set off to the conference early the following morning. My press pass entitled me to sit at the back of the conference room, behind a long trestle table covered in dark green felt. I scanned the other faces; one dimly recognisable, though a very distant acquaintance. Next to me sat a fat, overbearing American woman, unmistakably lesbian. She took notes feverishly, commenting aloud to herself when she didn't agree. I gathered from eavesdropping, involuntarily, that she was a strong supporter of AA.

During a pause between speakers she rounded on me:

'You're Rosie Boycott, I'm so glad to meet you!' Her voice said 'glad' in the way others say 'desperate'. Her pudgy hand flew out and she pumped mine with vigour. Because of my involvement with *Spare Rib*, politically-minded lesbians often assume I'm one of them.

'Andrew told me about you. He said I ought to meet you.'

Fuck Andrew, I thought, trying to extricate my hand. Andrew was one of the regular AA crowd who visited the clinic to talk to the patients. He worked for a clothing manufacturer who sold suits to Marks and Spencer, and he was always snazzily, if off-the peggishly, attired. Another speaker took the platform, but she was not to be deterred. Leaning over me, her breast touching my shoulder, she scrawled across my notebook, 'Which meeting do you go to?'

I wrote back, 'My nearest to home is St Mary Abbotts', but I don't go there yet.' I added in a whisper, 'I'm still in the clinic.'

She obviously knew all about me. I wrote in the book, 'Do you always publicise the fact that you're an alcoholic?' She snatched the book out of my hand and wrote, 'No, but if anyone asks, I stopped drinking in January 1971, joined AA and have been sober up to today. My boss is one of ours.'

Ours. I looked at the word miserably. I didn't want to be drawn into an alcoholic net like this. She assumed that since I'd been a drunk and a feminist, I was a natural for societies.

When the lecture ended, I left my seat quickly and went into the lobby, looking for Andrew so that I could throttle him. Instead, a quiet hand on my arm and a low chuckle in my ear.

'That fat bitch giving you a hard time?' I turned round to see Phil, resplendent in his uniform. The room had been dark and I hadn't noticed him, though I had looked. 'I knew where you'd be sitting. What was she up to? She looked as though she wanted to eat you.' My irritation turned to laughter.

'Are you going to show me London?' he asked as we made our way to the coffee shop. 'Whatever you think I should see,' he added, his words loaded with sexual innuendo, the flirt in him taking over the naval demeanour, making him years younger, less intimidating and terribly desirable.

We spent the afternoon in the Victoria and Albert Museum.

'What are you doing tonight?' he asked as we walked out of the museum.

I giggled. 'You know what I'm doing.'

'Dinner? Where shall we go? I'm the stranger in town.'

'I'll figure it out and call you. Eight o'clock.'

I leapt into a taxi and returned to the King's Road, where I bought a black dress, resplendent with a tiger leaping across the right shoulder, its sequined claws coming to rest over my left breast. Gold belt, new gold earrings. Just time to wash my hair, organise a table reservation.

I went back to the clinic feeling buoyant. The irony was not escaping me, the fact that I was living in a loony bin, while planning the seduction of a stranger. I didn't even know if he was married, and suspected that he probably was. At that moment the fact that he was so attracted to me boosted my confidence, particularly as he had only seen me sober. It had a healing effect. Later on I would have to pay for it.

I sat in the bath and tried to remember the last time I had been to bed with someone stone cold sober. A few days earlier I'd written a list of all the times I could remember getting drunk, and losing control. I'd stopped writing when I reached page thirteen, battered with depression about how long the list was. Being a binge drinker meant that the excesses stuck out like pyramids in flat desert land. If I looked at them as transgressions, then a great many were sexual. If I looked at them as defences against a world I didn't like, then the attempts to reconcile the outer and the inner 'me' were lamentable. Either way the list was salutary.

Carol knocked on the door while I was standing in the bathroom, making up my face.

'Where are you going?' she asked.

A NICE GIRL LIKE ME

'Having dinner with some people from the conference,' I said vaguely.

She grinned. 'You look terrific. Are they nice?'

'Very,' I said, pulling the new dress over my shoulders, feeling its thin texture settle softly against my skin. 'Don't be too late,' she said as I left.

My status as a patient apparently on the right road meant that I was free to come and go as I wished. I met Phil in an Italian restaurant in the Fulham Road, long a favourite.

'You're beautiful,' he said, squeezing my hand as I sat down beside him in the bar. 'I thought you were pretty, but you're more than that.'

He was drinking gin and tonic. I ordered tomato juice. He watched my reactions closely, knowing that I was feeling as if I'd never been out with a man before. I knew that he knew, but his knowledge was one of understanding. He didn't patronise me.

'If you want,' he said, casually, 'you can take it as a compliment that I'm drinking.'

'Why?'

'Several reasons. One is that I drink very little, my father saw to that, scared me enough to make me teetotal till I was in my mid-twenties. Even now I regard the stuff with mixed terror and love.' He held up his glass and looked at it thoughtfully. 'Second, I wouldn't be drinking around you if I didn't think that you felt OK enough to handle it. Thirdly,' he paused, 'thirdly, I'm nervous too, so you could say I'm taking an unfair advantage.' I grinned: pleased by all those reasons. Later on, well away from the clinic, I was to treat remarks like, 'I didn't even notice that you don't drink,' as the biggest compliment I could receive. But right now, his were much more than sufficient.

147

During dinner we watched the sexual tension build up between us and revelled in it. We were holding on to that moment in any affair when the idea of sex is so exhilarating that everything appears possible.

I knew that the decisions were mine. For once I was in control. An unfamiliar, wonderful feeling. After dinner we hailed a taxi. He dropped me off at the clinic, before turning back to Kensington. Did I want him to protest, to kick up a fuss? A little part of me did, but my footsteps were light on the steps up to the front door.

The following morning I was back at the conference by seven a.m.

'I want to go to the Tate this afternoon. Nothing interesting happening here. Take my word for it. Love P.'

The note was dropped in front of me later on in the morning, during a particularly dull talk about the effects of alcohol on the natives of Trinidad and Tobago.

We met at the Tate at three o'clock. He was late and I was a bundle of nerves as I waited on the steps, overlooking the Thames. I paced around contemplating the stone lions, wondering what I would do if he didn't show up. I'd told the clinic that I was going to the conference for the rest of the day, and planning to spend the night at home, which was next to the hotel. I was covering every eventuality except one; If he didn't show up then I would have to spend the night at home, on my own. I groped around in my bag and found an abstem pill, which guarantees vomiting if you drink. As I swallowed the first I'd ever taken, Phil's taxi drew up at the bottom of the steps.

Standing behind me in the darkened, humidified William Blake room, Phil's breath touched the back of my neck and the sexual charge of the night before bounced between us.

We emerged into thin September drizzle and walked up the embankment to Parliament Square. The rain intensified. 'The hotel?' he said, raising my chin with his hand.

Both men and women suffer guilt when they drink but women's guilt is far worse. A drunk woman is a far less wholesome object than a drunk man. Wantonness and abandon can be appealing in a man; in a woman they are signs of complete moral collapse. Despite the women's movement, we still have an ambivalent attitude towards women's sexuality. There's no male equivalent of the slut. A sexually inexperienced man is a pathetic baby, or possibly a closet gay, whereas a sexually inexperienced woman, though rare, still holds fascination and charm. A drunk man can be awe-inspiring; his willingness to lose control daunting and impressive to someone who runs tight circles round their lives. A drunk woman has no such charms; she's pathetic, scary because people don't know how to deal with her, the object of pity mixed with scorn and loathing. She's the type of woman of whom men say, 'I'd fuck her, and she'd let me because she's so pissed all the time, but marry her? Have children? Never.'

When I began to drink it was part of the outward proof that I was a liberated woman. Good enough to drink with the boys and good enough to drink a lot of them under the table. When the hurdle in my drinking was crossed and I started to find myself drunk without meaning to be drunk, drunk despite my attempts at controlling it, in bed with people I didn't like, let alone love, my sense of identity – especially my sexual identity – took a hammering.

I remembered a scene earlier in the summer when I'd seduced a friend of William's whom I'd fancied at a discreet distance. William was away, it was the day after my thirtieth birthday and I'd been on a ghastly bender. The man left in the middle of the night, a sign of the sudden plummet that I'd taken in his eyes. He'd never seen me drunk before and when I crawled out of bed the following morning, my sense of disgust was so overwhelming that another slug of Scotch was the only solace. I'd had some weird idea that he would like me, maybe would even grow to love me, fantasies blown out of all proportion as daydreams slowly took over my life. Wanting, always wanting, someone or something to break the vicious circle, unable to admit that the only person who can save the drowning woman is herself.

As the taxi slid into the forecourt of the hotel, I was remembering all this. Remembering, too, slithering with drunkenness on a hilltop in Cyprus. The sun setting over Aphrodite's Rock, the flowers in the inn garden folding up against the gathering shadows, I sat under a huge fig tree lapping glasses of wine, until finally I surrendered my single, narrow and enchanting bed in a white Mediterranean room, with shutters at the windows and a view down rugged hills to the water below, and went instead to someone else's room. Lying there fully awake and wondering: just what is this man doing to me, as I watched a head move between my legs, feeling irritation rather than pleasure. Thinking, Oh well, what the hell, it doesn't matter, it's only one more, it's only a quick screw. But, I'd long ago proved I was a liberated woman, capable of walking away the morning after with manly *joie de vivre*, adding to my score rather than subtracting from my self-esteem.

I'd proved all that long ago.

So was I using or being used, I wondered, as Phil made love to me with gentle hands, and for moments I wasn't faking anything. He was pulling out of me gestures of love and compassion which had been so greedily conserved because I needed them all to keep my drunken, warring self alive.

I was utterly vulnerable to him, as we lay there afterwards, sweat mingled, hands entwined.

'I suppose it's possible to fall in love for a day,' he said quietly. A day, that was not what I wanted. I sensed him withdraw and gather in the emotions which had been spilled with his seed. My own armour crept back to cover up sentiment with brittle humour.

'Hey, don't get sad,' he said, as I patched up my make-up in the huge bathroom mirror. 'Don't look for more in situations than there is. I know what you're in the middle of and I also know enough about you to tell that you're strong. Your strength is not all fake, though I know it probably feels like that.'

I returned to the clinic the following day, after seeing Phil off on a sightseeing tour of England. I'd drawn up his itinerary and he went off jauntily in his hired car to sample the sights of Stonehenge and Glastonbury. The night had been strange and uncomfortable, both of us uneasy with the other, and unsure of the ground.

By ten o'clock that night I was exhausted, my nerves stretched like violin strings.

I was stumbling towards an inner confrontation beyond problems of how to handle dinner parties without drink, problems that came before the first blackout. I couldn't sleep, despite the sleeping pill. Finally, I got up, made some coffee and went into the lounge to talk to the night nurse. Alice was my favourite nurse. By day she trained as a psychologist and at night she baby-sat the drunks. The pay was good and I suppose we were a good source for her research.

She was in her late thirties, though she looked older. Her gentle face always seemed tired and she had the look of a person who has suddenly got thin too fast, leaving her skin slightly sagging, without life and tension. Her eyes were of the palest blue, deeply sunk into her face, which could look beautiful from some angles. She always had time to talk, and her advice was stubborn, pointed, often ruthless but never without compassion. 'What's the matter?' she said, when I came into the lounge, coffee and cigarettes in hand.

'Can't sleep, I'm worried.'

'Did that man upset you?' she asked gently. I wasn't surprised at her question. Although I hadn't told anyone in the clinic about Phil, somehow they all seemed to have found out and were treating my little fling with varying degrees of interest and amusement.

'No,' I answered, 'it's not that he upset me. I seem to have upset myself.'

She waited.

'Being with him has brought up all sorts of things. Everything is all wrong with William. If it was all right then I wouldn't respond so strongly to a total stranger. I feel so trapped in so many lies. I'm frightened. Oh, shit, Alice, what's the matter with me? What's wrong? Why do I feel like this? Does everyone?'

'What do you feel? Go on, cry if you want to, get it off your chest . . .'

'I just feel I'm no good. I've always felt like that, right from a little girl. Not good enough for anyone, not good enough for myself, always being second best, below my own expectation, letting people down. Do you know I failed my Latin O-level twice? I go into a room and I'm terrified, terrified people are better than me, braver than me, that they're looking at me, thinking that I'm hopeless. I spend all my time pretending; pretending in bed, pretending to be brave, doing things to make me feel brave, and they don't, they only make me feel worse. No one has ever found me good enough. He didn't, I mean Phil didn't, he left. Obviously, Alice, I'm not good enough. What would I be doing here if I was?'

I was rambling. Between tears, I was trying to explain to Alice things that I'd never talked about to anyone else. 'I've just failed, failed everything. Told lies, cheated, been dishonest.'

I was almost yelling at her by then, past caring whether anyone heard.

'Who says so?'

'I do. Other people have too.'

'No, I don't think they have. Tell me who told you you were no good.'

'People don't have to tell you those things, do they? You just know.'

She smiled. 'You're wrong, you're really wrong. All of us are nervous, all of us go through times when we feel no good, when we don't want to face the day.'

'But Alice, that's not the point, I don't think I've ever felt good enough. I never believe that people love me, I think they're lying when they say they do. My work is never good enough, I'm just a mishmash of silly stories and adventures, and there's nothing in the middle. I feel like I'm held together with bits of string and I can't find the ends. And anyway there's nothing in the middle that's worth tying up.'

'You've got a very warped vision of yourself,' she said slowly, 'don't you see that you're a leader, that people follow you because they know that you're brave, know without actually being able to say it that you're fighting harder than they are, fighting all the devils, all the fear. You're not covering up, you're living. You are special, you know, very special. You take risks others wouldn't dream of, you look at dark sides of feelings which most people run away from. People aren't saying you're no good, it's more that they can't take you. You push things too hard, maybe, you demand perfection.'

'I wish I believed in God,' I said. 'In something which never let me down, even when I fuck up. I feel so split; there's "me" and another "me", and then a mad "me". The mad me who drinks, who seems to destroy. I'm frightened I'll never be any good with all that rattling around.'

'They're all you,' she answered, 'they're all the bits that make you what you are. They've all your energy. You can't feel guilty about drink forever. And you idiot, you keep telling me you're a liar, but you're one of the most honest alcoholics I know.'

TWELVE

The Ovaltine can twisted through the air, curving out over the river then falling towards the white-flecked water. Steve's ashes found their resting-place in India's holy river, the Ganges.

From Bangalore they'd flown north to Delhi. John hunted out Prem, the second-hand motorbike salesman from whom he had bought a venerable Royal Enfield in 1969.

'You buy new this time, Mr John.' Prem was excited, flattered to be remembered. 'One thousand dollars.'

The powerful 350cc Enfield, the work mule of the Indian Army and the Police, who'd jointly acquired the patent after partition from a British firm, hauled them effortlessly up the steep hills. Their kit was considerable; two mattresses, pillows, sheets with pink roses, primus stove, hurricane lamps, mosquito net, books, clothes, fishing rod and water container. In Rishikesh they stayed at the Maharishi's ashram, which had been turned into a chic hotel, affording splendid Ganges views. The Indian tax department had started nipping at the guru's ankles. To resolve the matter he had left India altogether in 1970.

John had studied transcendental meditation there for three months in 1969 and was aghast to see the huge white monkeys, lurking behind the chalets which had once housed the Beatles, hurling empty tins of baked beans at unsuspecting visitors. 'They're mean now,' he said, coming in one evening from a walk along the river, 'only like this since discovering Western garbage.'

They zig-zagged across the north of India, heading towards the Nepal border. Most nights they camped in the jungle, snuggled between pink sheets watching the moon shimmer in misty relief behind the gauze of the mosquito net.

One night they stopped at a hill station called Missouri. Years earlier the little town, which clung to the Himalayan foothills like a limpet, had been a fashionable resort of the British Raj. The shops sold old pieces of porcelain and charged high prices for the china which the last generation of pukka memsahibs had left behind.

There was one grand hotel in the town, the Savoy. In the dining room they were placed next to the hotel's only other guests, an English couple. Over thin chicken soup, served by a dusky waiter wearing immaculate spats, Rosie discovered that the man, Fred Grunfeld, had once been Jonathon's employer. For a short period after leaving Oxford, while working for *Rolling Stone*, Jonathon had written a column on the underground press for *Queen* magazine. Fred had been his editor. If they'd met in New York or a Paris restaurant, the encounter would have been hardly worth remarking. Here, in rarefied Missouri, it was positively exotic. They might have all been on an American Express Packaged Spirituality Tour, members of the low-life jet-set who replaced chalets and ski-runs in Gstaad with ashrams and hippy trails.

Rosie was by now used to being stared at, to never using loo paper and to remembering always to eat with her right hand. She'd given up worrying about contracting hepatitis from the water. They drank copious quantities of the Indian curd drink, lassi, which evidently discouraged the germs.

John drove the bike. Rosie couldn't hold it upright at stop-signs. John was the war veteran: she the rawest recruit in charge of supplies. One night when she'd forgotten to buy a new box of matches, and they had to make do with only four, he complained at her complacency. She was immediately guilty about letting down the mobile home and rubbed his back with coconut oil for longer than usual.

They crossed into Nepal late one night and the contrast between the two countries was glaring. Indian villages – shambly and lazy, relaxed, just getting by; Nepalese equivalents – tidy and ordered, roofs intact and streets clean.

'How the fuck did we ever think we'd change India, let alone own it?' Rosie said as they sat outside an inn, eating rice and dahl, looking down on the giant slothful continent below. 'I don't feel sorry for the poverty any more . . . not after seeing this village.'

'The British were always piss-awful missionaries,' John laughed.

They left the bike in the care of an innkeeper in the lake-side town of Pokhara in western Nepal and walked into the mountains, following the route to the tiny Himalayan king-dom of Mustang. For two days, their legs ached and their ankles screamed resistance to the unaccustomed climbing, up and down, walking five miles to achieve one on the map. The Nepalese passed them like cars in the fast lane of a motorway, laden down with boxes of Coca-Cola destined for the King of Mustang. They carried their burdens on their foreheads and their breathing never altered regardless of the gradient. In one village where they stayed the night, they had supper with a Gurkha sergeant, who was in the mountains looking for recruits for his British regiment. The following morning the village square was full of young men, stripped to the waist and flexing their muscles like competitors in a Mr Universe competition. After prodding and poking the merchandise, the sergeant selected five and sent the other fifty home.

He had gold teeth and floral tattoos on his arms. He spoke good English. 'It is the only chance for them,' he said, 'I returned with much money. I will open an inn like my friend Tegi.' He referred to the innkeeper of the little hotel where they were staying, whose Gurkha heritage was displayed across his mantelpiece. Coronation mugs, pictures of the British Royal Family, postcards of Buckingham Palace and Windsor Castle. Tegi had a tattoo of a mermaid on the back of his hand.

Before they had left England, Joanna Leary had stayed with them for a week, trying, in vain, to raise money for Tim's defence against drug charges. Her rent contribution had been a hundred tabs of window pane acid, direct from California. In the mountains, they took it nearly every day. They were centuries away from the world. After Pokhara, distances were measured in day's walks; no phone, no radio, no communication except on foot. Within days they were fit and lean, muscles hardened on steep gradients.

The mountains were a constant physical assault. Snakes rustled through the grass. Most were harmless, but once they saw a cobra, sneaking up a cliff, its black body glistening with strange beauty. John caught a five-foot grass snake which shot across the path in front of him. He held it behind its neck, letting the shiny green body twist round his arm.

'You take it.' He passed the head to Rosie, She shuddered,

but picked up the challenge, flinching as the cool smoothness bound her wrist and forearm. She wasn't as frightened of snakes as she was of worms. When she'd been little her father used to play a game which involved throwing earthworms at her. Worms made her shudder, and she was aghast one day to walk beneath the arched support of a swinging rope bridge and find the inside of the arch solidly lined with slimy little brownish-red worms.

To reach the waterfall, a favourite place, it was necessary to cross the bridge, which spanned a deep river gorge. Blown out on Leary's acid, John made her stand under the arch for about fifteen minutes, while worms and drops of water fell on to her shoulders and hair. She then ran off up the mountain track to the waterfall and, throwing off her clothes, swam out into the cavern behind the cascade. John swam in after her and they fucked behind the green curtain, amidst the unearthly sound of tons of water falling from great heights. Returning down the path, she stood under the arch, calmly inspecting the worms. From then on, she called the place The Kingdom of Worms.

Later on, while they were caught in a tropical forest during a monsoon outburst, leeches fell from the trees, digging into their flesh, swelling with blood. They were with two friends who ran around in screaming terror, beating at the fat black bodies with their hands. Rosie plucked them off with clinical lack of interest. So did John.

'Tell us about England,' said an innkeeper's son. 'I want to go to England.'

'You're much better off here,' said Rosie. He looked at her in despair. In Kathmandu she met a novelist, a Nepalese whose books advocating sexual freedom were banned in her own country. 'You're all the same,' she said to Rosie, sitting hunched and crippled with arthritis in a mean room. 'You don't want this country ever to be rich. You just want it for yourselves – primitive and rural.

'Hippies like you are the worst of the lot; at least the capitalists understand why we have to bring industry to the Kathmandu valley. Half of us are starving, others are trying to make livings from people like you. Selling drugs and fake antiques. You know that line from your colonialist poet, Kipling, "and the wildest dreams of Kew, are but the facts of Kathmandu"? I bet you don't find dope dealers in Kew, whatever that is.'

Nepal had banned the free sale of drugs in 1970. By 1974 the only difference the law made to the Nepalese dealers was that they couldn't display their wares in a shop window. Prospective buyers had to mount the creaky steps to first-floor rooms in Freak Street.

Rosie was amazed at her first sight of the contents of the teenager's tapestry holdall. Five varieties of hash, from the different provinces, cocaine, speed, mandrax, bombers, opium and yellow liquid morphine, in vials stamped with the rubric 'Welcome Drug Company, Bombay'.

'This is on your bloody head,' John said, 'here, hold that tight and let it go when I say so.' She clenched her fist three times, watching the blood back up in her veins against the pressure of the makeshift tourniquet. Puncturing the skin inside her arm, he drew back the plunger and watched for the blood to flower crimson inside the syringe. The sensation hit with tremendous speed and she felt her body dissolve into weightlessness. A soft rush at the back of her throat sent her senses dancing, very lightly.

'Listen, I'm going to say this once more and I want you to hear it.' John's voice hissed through his teeth which were clamped down on the scarf wound round his biceps. 'I know why you want to try this stuff, because you reckon that it's one thing that I've done which you haven't. That's fine, I understand, but we're only going to do it for a couple of days and then finish. It's no bloody fun being strung out.

'God, but it feels good.' His eyes cancelled inwards, as he succumbed to packaged peace of mind.

The countryside was relentlessly beautiful. With morphine in their veins, they tore round the hairpin bends, ravines opening beneath them like yawning caverns. The stakes had been upped, but she was no longer frightened of falling. Heroin cocooned her against the recklessness of taking bends at eighty miles an hour. And, once again, they were no longer travelling alone. The first companion died, the second was easily bought in Freak Street. He was feckless, cheap and plentiful.

The sight of the hippies standing outside the post office in Durbar Square, strung out, emaciated and waiting for cheques to keep their habits happy, made her feel superior. Like any addict, she was unable to see her own progress towards dependency, figuring, always, that she was in control. Nursing the habit was like pacifying a snake, always hungry, always dangerous, but appeased when food appeared.

The monsoons were beginning. By three every day the thunder that rumbled across the valley would have given way to sheets of warm rain. The streets flooded with water which the makeshift gutters could not disperse. The Nepalese traders would retire indoors, packing up their array of goods: bags and beads, malas, thighbone trumpets, Indian print skirts and clothes, monk-style shirts which buttoned across the left shoulder and bore a strong resemblance to straitjackets. In the evening they'd appear again, to start peddling their eastern dreams to the western starvelings.

'We gotta move,' John said.

That night in their favourite bar – the Yak and Yeti – they sipped double Scotches and listened to Don Maclean's 'American Pie' on the kitsch jukebox in the corner. Rosie's feet were tapping to the insistent rhythm: 'No angel born in hell, could break that Satan's spell. I saw Satan laughing with delight the day the music died.'

By the time they reached Delhi, tired and quarrelsome, the morphine vials were finished. Prem was offhand about the bike. 'Well, it will take at least two weeks to sell, Mr John,' he said, pursing his lips and patting back his greying hair. Dreadful old queen, Rosie thought angrily, suddenly loathing the town, the prospect of the wait, and the knowledge that Delhi did not have a Freak Street.

'It's shit-faced insanity,' said John later on that evening. They had moved back into the same hotel, and its middle-of-the-road plastic luxury grated after the cosy safety of the wooden Nepalese room. 'If you want it so much you can do it.'

He threw the lump of black opium across the room at Rosie. She rolled it in her hand, unsure what she was supposed to do. 'Stop fucking around,' he shouted. 'Just heat up a bit in a spoon with some water and then –' He broke off and got up from the bed. 'You're hopeless . . . I'll have to do it, like I do everything. This is all your bloody fault.'

She watched him draw off the thick, dark liquid, sucking it into the syringe through cotton wool. She shivered at the sight, but tied the scarf round her arm.

They travelled east into the heart of Asia's golden triangle, where heroin overflowed. The habit went too, like an unwanted but tenacious piece of luggage. Over the crackly radio in the bar of the Constellation Hotel in Vientiane they heard the news of Nixon's resignation. It was August 1974. By nightfall the bar was crammed with revellers. Though the American bombing of Indochina had ceased a year earlier, the US still retained airbases in Thailand. The situation made the democratic Thai government uneasy, as they feared retaliation from the communists if they succeeded in overrunning Cambodia. It was not a good summer to be a non-law abiding US tourist in south-east Asia.

Rosie's weight dropped to seven stone, but, like the anorexic, she was oblivious to her skeletal shape. They never made love. Their relationship danced to Morpheus's tune. There was only one reason to touch – to look for unbutchered veins. It was a wildly unpretty sight.

Smack ran their lives like an hourglass, dominating the times when they went sightseeing, the hours they slept. But she was never bored; the drug removed the restlessness which normally made inactivity intolerable. The only hiatus was finding more dope, and in Bangkok's Malaysia hotel that meant a short trip in an elevator and then a walk along the worn carpets of the dusty corridors. Once up on the gentle plateau, removed from the doubts and fears about just what the fuck she was doing anyway, she'd forget the screaming tensions which the shortage of dope in Delhi had meant; forget the nerve-splitting moments when John's smallest move would make her want to scream with frustration.

They tried to cut down but there was always a reason for the next shot. But if reason made the doses fewer, the habit, greedy like an insect in dry places, made them larger. Life had inverted itself; she felt normal only when stoned, displaced and confused as the effects started to wear off.

'The backache's the worst fucker when you come off this stuff.' John was lying on his back on the hotel bed, consulting a tatty train timetable. 'Bali, four or five days in the surf. Pound out the monkey. Four or five days of feeling like hell and it will be over.'

They boarded the train out of Bangkok, travelling south towards Singapore where they planned to catch the boat to the Indonesian island. In the first-class compartment, lined with teak panels and inset with a small cocktail bar and fold-away marble washbasin, they shot up the last of the dope, hanging on to the rail under the window to steady their hands. John slid back the glass panel and threw the syringes out into the night.

They smoked a joint and packed the rest of the Thai sticks away in a suitcase. Rosie had bought thirty dollars' worth of grass in the market in Vientiane, encouraged by two trading travellers who regularly made the journey. The profits were enormous. Risk? 'Shit man, it's cool, cool.'

The customs officials at the Thai border town of Pedang Bezar found the grass within five minutes. They were not interested in a simple fine. 'It can't be for long,' John muttered on the way to the local lock-up. 'Thank Christ they don't know about the smack.'

He was terrified at the prospect of withdrawal on a prison floor. Rosie was too scared for such thoughts. No one knew where they were. She might be lost for ever, buried in the jungle, growing old, toothless and haglike, her hair falling out due to the diet. She wanted to scream, to turn back the clock, to promise anything to anyone who would get her out.

The door slammed behind her. She slumped on the floor, alternately hot and cold, unable to get comfortable on the concrete floor. She rolled herself into a ball, face curled under her arms, and fought, in vain, to stop the enveloping fears.

The cell measured eight feet by ten. She paced it out accurately and afterwards remeasured her feet to check whether her estimate had been correct. In one corner a low wall surrounded a hole-in-the-ground lavatory. A cold tap provided plentiful water. Standing on tiptoe she could just see out of the narrow barred window. Puffs of smoke appeared over the treetops, evidence of other trains going north and south on that ill-fated line.

Their requests to phone embassies were met with either flat refusals or laughter. She exhausted herself turning over the possibilities; trying to beat the fear with a fantasy of walking away, climbing on to a plane, getting out and then crunching back to reality, to the concrete floor and the iron bars.

'How are you feeling?' John yelled down the corridor. 'Are you starting to feel ill?'

'No,' she shouted back, 'at least I can't separate which part of me is shaking, whether it's H or whether it's just plain fear.' And she couldn't.

Opiates are poisons, and their absorption demands an adaptation of cells and systems. Chemical balances alter until a tolerance is achieved and the drug, in ever-increasing quantities, becomes a necessity. Stop and, like a moving car suddenly thrown into reverse, everything jars, scrapes and protests against the sudden cut-off. Too sudden a cut-off can result, like sudden withdrawals from alcohol, in total seizure, coma, possible death.

She wanted dope, at that moment, in the same way as she

would have welcomed a bottle of Scotch; as an escape into temporary amnesia. But her body wasn't screaming for it. Just get me out of this and I'll never take drugs again, let alone smuggle them, she prayed silently.

On the third day the sergeant announced that they were to stay there for a week and then go to the town of Songkhla on the west coast of Thailand for trial. He gave them their luggage and said they could share a cell. They hardly talked, hardly touched, uncovering huge areas of inadequacy in their ability to mask fear. Better to be alone and afraid, she thought, than to face the fact that we seem unable to comfort each other. It was as if the third traveller had caught the last train to the coast. They were alone, without the music.

The trial, conducted in Thai and lasting under five minutes, resembled an inquisition. The judge, tall, thin and dressed in black, with a beaked nose and piercing black eyes, hardly looked in their direction. Their translator instructed them not to cross their legs because pointing the soles of your feet at someone was a mark of highest disrespect to the Thais. The judge banged his gavel. The translator ushered them out of the courthouse.

'You have to go to prison. Another trial in twelve days when they have completed the case against you.'

The courthouse looked on to the sea. Bathers cavorted in the water and their distant cries filtered through the air. She imagined making a dash for the beach. The sergeant would shoot her in the back long before she made it.

The women's prison looked like a fortress, standing alone in several acres of cleared jungle, with a narrow dirt track leading off the main road to the gates. She climbed out of the bus and walked towards the open door. An old man, grey-haired, with an impressive array of shiny gold teeth and a face so lined it resembled a crumpled paper bag, held out his gnarled hand. She shook it, feeling dumb and awkward and bizarrely reminded of arriving at a county pony-club dance. The old man held a new book in his other hand. Peering at it he pronounced, with difficulty, 'I hope you will be happy here. I trust that you are well.'

The scene had the feeling of a grotesque horror film, ready to dissolve into a nightmare of gnashing teeth and crazed hounds. She smiled, warily, and said she was fine. He boomed with laughter and slapped her back with the side of the book, guiding her in through the doors with the gesture.

Once inside, he stood back while a young woman, wearing a militaristic beige uniform, searched her belongings, removing her money, passport and red Swiss army knife. The benign stand-in for Count Dracula continued to smile and read his phrase book.

'I would much like to learn to speak the English.'

'Yes,' she replied, faking jocularity.

'Good, good.'

He took her arm and led her through a second doorway on to a long path that ran the length of the prison. On each side high walls surrounded the compounds. They turned left at the central axis, walked on a few more yards and stopped outside a small black metal doorway set into the concrete wall. Alice, here we come, Rosie thought as they stepped over the stoop and into the sector reserved for minor offenders. The area was fifty yards square, with a low rectangular hut in the centre; showers and lavatories to one side, a small guard hut to the other. Faces pressed against the barred windows.

'We pleased see you.' A fat woman took Rosie's bedroll and led her down the centre of the hut. Sleeping platforms ran along each side, leaving a narrow passage between. Women prisoners of the Japanese during the Second World War had been held in similar huts: they nicknamed their dormitories the Macfisheries, because the slabs were reminiscent of the display counters for fish back in Britain.

'You want to wash?' The soft voice belonged to a pretty girl, no older than Rosie.

'You speak English?' she asked, unable to believe her luck.

'Little, little,' the girl replied. 'My name is Ravena. I hope you and I be friends. You teach us English?'

'I'm Rosie,' she answered, 'I'd be very happy to teach you English.'

Ravena introduced the other members of the cell; thirteen in all. She and Ravena were the youngest, the fat woman, whose name was Tia, the eldest. A woman called Heya rocked a young baby in her arms.

She walked down the corridor to the washing area at the far end. A low wall shielded a lavatory and taps. What to do, she wondered. She was dusty and dishevelled but uncertain about stripping off. She looked round, wondering if some indication might be gleaned from her inmates. They all grinned encouragingly. She pulled off her shirt and skirt and started energetically to throw water over her shoulders; a slight cough of embarrassment greeted her action and she turned to see the women busying themselves with crochet and books, looking everywhere but at her nakedness. Shit, she thought angrily and struggled into her white Vietnamese pyjamas, the water still streaming off her body.

'Take this,' Ravena said as she walked back to her mat, and handed her a brightly coloured sarong. 'Less hot.'

Ravena was the second wife of a Bangkok policeman, a Moslem. She told Rosie this slowly, perched cross-legged at the end of the mat, offering her small bananas and even smaller tangerines. 'He say I steal. He send me here. He has my baby. Now he has new wife. My mother and father in Bangkok. Long way to Bangkok.'

'How long will you be here?'

'Three years.'

Tia was the madam of a brothel, picked up in a token border raid on the houses of ill-repute, established to service the soldiers stationed in the area, to suppress communist activities in the jungle regions of southern Thailand and northern Malaya. Heya's husband had dealt heroin. He'd escaped arrest through a tip-off, leaving Heya and her six-month-old son to take the rap. They're all victims, she thought.

'Not worry, not worry.' Tia put her arm round Rosie's shoulder. She spoke in Thai to Ravena, who translated. 'She say, grass not matter much in Thailand. You not be here long.'

Her 'crime' seemed hedonistic and trivial in comparison. No one wanted to drag her down with their own misery; a humbling thought, while she fought with her own fears.

Ravena moved her sleeping mat next to Rosie's. 'Maybe I come to London in three years,' she said. Three years, it was an inconceivable time; where did the Thai girl find her calm acceptance of her predicament? She wasn't even bitter.

'You not be sad,' Ravena said, as she curled up on the mat. 'You go soon.' Rosie at least had somewhere to go. Home was always there; there was money, people who loved her; she let her imagination leap forward to when jail would become another story, another laugh-a-line dinner-party episode, and shuddered. It would never be that for Ravena, who had nowhere to go, only a lost child and a lost family.

There was no enforced work for the prison inmates, but there was a routine, roughly adhered to. The door of the cellblock was opened at five-thirty, just after dawn. In the chill morning air, they'd line up for the showers, wash the clothes they had worn the previous day, and have breakfast. Prisoners' own money supplemented the diet of rice and fish, so there was usually plentiful fruit, shared between everyone, regardless of who had paid. After breakfast, Tia would hold energetic dance classes, stomped out in time to whatever tune was playing on the tinny portable radio. The popular song in Thailand that year was the Beatles' 'Let it Be'. One day it came on the radio twenty-three times.

After dancing, another shower, then the lengthy business of make-up and hairdos, which could last for up to two hours. All Thai women, like other Orientals, have little body hair, but any stray hairs were always removed with tweezers. They set to work with relish to tweak the hairs out of Rosie's legs; a process which was as painful as it was long.

By ten-thirty the sun would be high in the sky and the courtyard insufferably hot. Under the shade of the terrace roof, which connected the sleeping hut to the guard hut, Rosie tried to hold English classes. The guard, a young woman with a pleasant, smiling face, joined in. After the first lesson she went to town and bought pencils and paper, and two English/Thai guide books. In the afternoons they would sleep or read. Rosie had brought one book with her from the suitcases which they had left at Pedang Bezar: Simone de Beauvoir's *The Mandarins*. It was the longest book she had.

Rosie received no visits from the police, nor from any officials. Every time the gate of the compound opened she'd look up, hoping to see a panama hat and cream safari suit which might herald the arrival of a Grahame Greene-style British consul. She fretted, alternating between despair and an odd type of exhilaration, and scribbled notes in her diary:

There is some truth in the notion that freedom is in the mind. None of these women fight their circumstances, and in that way they survive. They don't resent the past, hanging on grimly to what happened to them, I'm sure they don't think, endlessly, as I do, If only I hadn't done that, and if I never do it again just get me out of here. They really do take each day as it comes, which makes sense, since they would go mad if they thought of years here. For moments I can do the same, shut out the terror and the fear that it may last for God knows how long. But wherever I am I'm always thinking about the outcome of what I do, how it will look, what its effect will be ... there are moments here when I actually stop doing that and for brief seconds it suddenly doesn't matter where I am. Is this what the Buddhists mean living in the moment?

A later entry read:

Tia in particular is concerned about my skinniness. She's been feeding me endless scrambled eggs after discovering that I like them. I try to stop her giving me eggs, but that upsets her. Does she think I'm too proud? Horrors. Arranged with the guard to buy eggs from the market. The English classes progress slowly. I'm a hopeless teacher and everyone ends up laughing. Last night Ravena was sitting by the barred window, looking at the full moon, which was so close it seemed to balance on the outer prison wall. She said to me, 'Rosie are you sick home?' Yes, I'm very sick home.

A letter from John arrived the next day. All mail had to be read out loud in front of all the prisoners, and Dracula, who was known as the prison father, did the honours.

> The conditions here are awful. We're locked up from four in the afternoon to six in the morning. There are twenty-five people in my cell, which is about fifteen feet by eight. The only place for me to sleep is with my feet across the piss bucket. I get no sleep because people use it all night. Someone, very drunk on the liquor they brew here, knocked it over the other night. But spirits are high. I've been adopted by the prison's King Rat – he's just like the guy in James Clavell's book. Robert (who's a Malay Indian), is an ex-policeman who went – wait for it – to Oxford. He likes to talk about literature, and it's very bizarre to have such conversations here. He's a great cook and runs the prison woodshop. Also because of being in the police, he knows the legal system and says we won't be here for long.

The days, though, were frighteningly long. The few novelties that life had to offer were soon assimilated.

> I've now been here for ten days and yesterday was such a strange day. Tia was trying to pull out hairs from under my arms when she suddenly saw an old needle mark. Thought that they had all gone. She got Ravena to ask me what it meant. I wanted to lie, to say it was an inoculation, but, finally, couldn't do that. They've been honest with me, so I told the truth. I expected at the least disapproval. Instead they looked rather awestruck, which makes me guilty and confused. Tia hugged me and asked if I was now OK. Said I was and returned to puzzling over how this monkey has disappeared. I now can look at myself in the mirror and see how thin and dreadful I

A NICE GIRL LIKE ME

look, so no wonder they picked us up at the border. How could
I have thought that we looked smart and straight? And I must
look better now: after eating like a horse all this time. Can
mental fear really overcome the withdrawals? Apparently, yes.

In the afternoon something else happened which was very
moving. A guard who I'd never seen before came into the cell at
about three o'clock. Singled me out and started playing with
my hair. He was very ugly, swarthy, rough, with a thick broken
nose. Like a fighter.

A squirrel was sitting on his shoulder, attached by a piece of
string tied round its tail. I stroked it, trying to divert attention.
I moved backwards and he grabbed my shoulder. I was really
frightened, catching the feeling from the others. Suddenly he
jerked the string and the squirrel's tail fell off. It was unbelievable, I can't understand how it happened. But there was the tail
and there was the squirrel. No blood. The squirrel was on the
ground, whimpering. I bent down to it and he grabbed me. I
didn't dare shout, it was prisoner and master, that sort of thing.
Then the others got up and stood between us, in a line, like sen-
tries. The warden took the guard's arm, he stumbled, nearly fell
but picked up the squirrel, and lurched away. Very drunk.
Found out later that he comes very rarely, that no one likes
him. But they protected me, they said I was one of them.

Dracula told her that her trial was due to be held in two
days. The women prisoners set to work to smarten Rosie up.
Ravena offered a straight cotton skirt and a pair of high-
heeled shoes. Another woman proffered a cream silk shirt.
Tia plucked her eyebrows, checked over her now hairless
legs, and experimented with eye make-up. A rattle of keys in
the gate after lock-up that night attracted the prisoners' attention. Rosie, deep into *The Mandarins*, didn't bother to get up.

'Rosie . . .' Ravena's voice was loud. 'It's for you, you free.' Everyone helped pack her bag, hurrying with an urgency that seemed to imply that if they weren't quick then the offer would be withdrawn. Within two minutes, she was outside the cell, turning back to hug Tia and Ravena who pushed her away, exhorting her to hurry and go.

Dracula handed back her penknife, passport and money. He shook her hand warmly. He pointed to a young police-man, standing beside a red 175cc Honda. 'You go with him.'

She climbed on the back, balancing the bedroll on her knees. 'What's happened? Why am I suddenly being let out?' she yelled at him through the wind rush. He lifted his hands off the bike to express non-comprehension. They lurched towards a ditch. She shut up and gazed at the trees, curling over the road like arms. Parrots skittered through the sunset, their incessant shrieks and cries suddenly wonderful. In prison she'd hated the sound. The wind flicked away her tears before they had time to fall.

The policeman dropped her outside a square wooden hotel. He pointed across the street: 'Mr John.' The hotel and the men's prison were adjacent. She booked a room and immediately went to it, closing the door behind her, locking it securely, delighting in being mistress of her own keys for the first time in three weeks.

In the morning the guards smiled cheerily. 'You come to see Mr John?' They showed her to the visitors' area. Beyond bars lay the central compound. Male prisoners were not sep-arated according to the severity of their crimes, so murderers jostled with rice smugglers, gun runners and petty thieves. She realised with dismay that she hadn't brought any pre-sents. All the other women lining the bars waiting to catch sight of their men were laden down with carrier bags stuffed with fruit and tinned food – condensed milk, Heinz baked beans, Campbell's soup.

They crouched on the ground, holding hands through the bars. The nightmares fell away. 'God you look well,' they both exclaimed. Robert stood to one side and John stood up to introduce him. 'I'll come to court tomorrow, because I know I'll be saying goodbye to Mr John,' he said. Robert was tall and well-built, and except for his dark skin, his physique and features were wholly European. 'I made you this,' he said to Rosie and handed her a wooden vase carved out of a single thick section of cane, delicately painted with flowers.

John looked cocky and optimistic while they waited outside the courtroom the following day. His trial was scheduled for the afternoon and they waited in the little café by the building. Robert drank gin and lime which Rosie had brought along in a thermos. His King Rat status in the prison had gained him a day pass. The night before she'd met a stringer from AP, an Australian on his way home from Cambodia who'd stopped for the night in the border town. He claimed to have met John in Vietnam years earlier and he trailed along behind Rosie to the courtroom, intent on renewing the friendship.

'Who is he?' John asked. Rosie explained. 'Never seen him before,' he said, but his spirits were buoyant and Mike sat and drank Robert's gin and lime, ignoring protests from Robert that it was his and his alone. 'Singapore tomorrow night,' John said gleefully.

'Don't come in with me,' he said, standing up when the policeman came to fetch him. 'Stay here with Robert. I'll be back in five minutes.' He was, his face crestfallen. 'I've got to stay inside for a full month. They charged me with the rap. You're officially innocent. No fine . . . just the time.'

'Listen, when I get out . . .' He stroked the inside of Rosie's wrist. 'Shit, I really thought it would all end today. Well, I want to go home. Too many risks, too much danger. I want to be in America.'

The AP stringer mumbled his sympathy. 'You're not to bloody file this,' John said.

'No, no,' he replied.

The story was in the papers two days later. 'Steinbeck's son arrested for drugs on Thailand-Malaya border.' The US consul in Songkhla was contacted by his ambassador in Bangkok who'd received panicky enquiries from John's relatives in America.

Rosie went back and forth from the consul's house to the jail, conveying messages which found their way from New York. Immediately on her release from prison she'd written to her parents to say that she was sorry not to have been in touch for so long, but she'd had hepatitis. It was a thin excuse, but the best she could think of at the time. She planned to tell them the truth when she was back in England. The AP wire story, though not certain to have been picked up in England, just might have been. She sat down to compose another letter home:

Dearest Mum and Dad,

I don't know what, if anything, has appeared in the English papers. My last letter was untrue. John and I were arrested for attempting to smuggle some marijuana into Malaya. I was released after eighteen days. John was sentenced to a month. This happened on 22 August. John will be released on 21 September.

Now please try to take this: it's time our relationship was more open, even if you do disapprove of my activities. It has

happened now, nothing can be done to change it. The
marijuana was in fact mine. John urged me not to do it. We'd
met so many people who had done this successfully. I
decided to take the risk. I got caught. John has been amazing
and I feel guilty about it.

Please don't be angry or worried. It's been an enlightening
experience and one day I'll be able to tell you all about it. I'm
sorry and I know you will be hurt, but I'm still the same
person, your daughter, whom you know; I won't take risks
again and I love you both very much.

Please write or cable care of John, CBS, Hong Kong.

Later on she was to think it was one of the most inadequate
letters she'd written in her life.

On the morning of John's release from prison, the
American consul went to collect him from jail. His sentence
included deportation from Thailand, which necessitated,
according to the police department, that he be watched from
the moment he left the prison till the moment he was safely
outside the country. Since neither of them wanted to stay
anyway, they viewed these formalities with grim annoyance.

In the departure lounge of Bangkok's Don Muang airport,
they sat next to a thin, wispy diplomat who had reluctantly
sacrificed his Saturday afternoon at the beach. He was wearing a grey pin-striped suit and a pink shirt. Odd clothes for
the warm weather. In his hand he held their air tickets and a
sheaf of papers relating to John's case.

'What do they say?' John nodded his head at the documents.

'No idea,' the young man said wearily, 'I can't speak a
word of this damn language.'

The airport wait seemed interminable. The diplomat caught

their nerves and rapidly got drunk on dry martinis. 'Lucky for you that you weren't caught with heroin.' He burped, and spat his olive stone on to the stone floor of the bar.

'I met a member of the border patrol while I was waiting for John to get out,' Rosie said to him. 'You know how they smuggle heroin out here? Cut the stomachs out of babies, girls always, they're cheaper, and then send the fake mother through the customs, pretending the baby is ill. This man, God, he was awful, terribly rich too, he said that he knew of more than twenty cases this year alone.'

The diplomat said he felt sick. Rosie realised she was drunk.

'Shut up,' said John, 'that's an awful story. It's not true, is it?'

'Yes,' she replied. 'I met him with a strange English man, an Etonian who was travelling with this Chinese boy. Anyway, the border patrol man was the Chinese guy's uncle. I went to a night club with them and all this man did was tell these awful stories. Christ, I want to get out of here,' she mumbled, downing the rest of her martini and ordering another.

An hour later they were airborne, curving north out of Thailand towards Hong Kong. John ordered champagne and Rosie curled up in his arms.

'Listen, I don't know what to say about the fact that you stood all that . . . that it should have been me, since it was my grass. My stupidity and all that . . .'

But John was already ahead of the trauma, packing it away like winter clothes when summer comes.

'You can never again say that I'm not a gentleman.'

The music picked up again, as the South China Sea slipped away beneath them.

'I feel . . . like a virgin, like we're going on our honey-moon.'

For a brief moment John and Rosie were equal.

At the CBS office in Hong Kong, her father's replies to her letter waited in triplicate. She called home, bursting into the early morning calm of her parents' country house. 'I'm fine,' she shouted, 'fine . . . can you hear me?' The line crackled and hissed.

'You can't imagine how worried we've been . . . what are you going to do?'

'I'll write something about it, honestly, it was all right.'

'No,' her father's voice crackled back. 'Don't write about this, how do you think we'll feel?'

'OK,' she shouted back, 'I won't,' but she'd already begun a first draft of the story.

Her mother came on the line, heard her voice and started saying goodbye. Rosie wished they'd stop thinking about the phone bill for once, but hastily added her goodbyes and hung up.

Two days after leaving Bangkok she had lunch with a reporter for the Hong Kong *Star* in the Press Club. The girl, an Australian in her late twenties with curling titian hair and a loud mouth, quizzed her for two hours on the subject of feminism in England, and the lives of the women in the Thai jail.

'Well, you must know a lot about Asian women now,' she concluded. 'Tell me, what do you think of the Chinese women in Hong Kong?'

Rosie looked out of the window which faced towards Kowloon. The ferries criss-crossed the harbour like bullets, miraculously avoiding collisions on their electronically con-trolled dodgem track. 'I don't know,' she replied, her attention drawn back to the table and the white cloth, with a single hibiscus bloom in a thin vase set dead centre. 'I haven't met any of them yet. This city feels strange.'

The reporter sucked her ballpoint pen. 'Are you going to write about being in prison?'

'I don't know about that either. I feel very close to it all.' The girl cocked an eyebrow; she was obviously puzzled why anyone would pass up such a good story.

The piece about Rosie appeared in the paper the following day, turning her overnight into a mini-celebrity in that star-starved colony. She was asked to come and speak to the Hong Kong Women's Liberation Group.

There were twenty-eight women at the meeting. The opulent apartment, on the fifteenth floor of a block three-quarters of the way up the peak, opened on to a huge verandah. They were sitting outside, on rattan chairs and colourful cushions. Hong Kong twinkled below, busy even at night, pouring dollars into the world money markets.

'Why are there no Chinese women here?' she asked.

Sybil, who had invited her to the meeting, looked uncomfortable. 'We do try to talk to them. Go out to the ghettos and try to get to know them. But they're suspicious of us, suspicious of the foreign wives.

'They resent us; that we're interfering, trying to patronise them.' The woman was drunk, her body swaying slightly in her seat; she fixed her eyes firmly on Rosie.

'Yes,' said Sybil, 'you become a do-gooder when you try to tell people something. What you're saying is that your life is intrinsically better than theirs. Our lives are richer, but . . . We never talk to the really rich Chinese at all,' she added. She was big-boned with shoulder-length mousy hair, pulled back into a ponytail; archetypal American earth mother.

'We're like the memsahibs from India days,' an English woman commented. 'Wives of important men. I find it distasteful.'

Rosie remembered going out to Heathrow airport two years earlier to write a story about Asian women employed to clean the lavatories. Unprotected by any union, they worked for sums which no one but those on the very, very bottom of the heap would consider. Standing in the loo in terminal three, interrupting a cleaning woman in her work, she'd felt the hopelessness of the gap. The movement may have had ideas of being for all women, in all places, and in all states, but at times like that the idea seemed like a monumental impertinence. Arrogance at its worst.

'Because we can't do anything – in the way that Sybil says,' said the wife of an American banker, 'we just talk about ourselves. Our men, our sex lives, equality in the kitchen.'

'But we can't go much further than ourselves. At least we've got to have ourselves in shape in order to be any use. The personal is always very political,' Rosie replied.

'Some good shape, some equality,' said the woman who was drunk. 'I've spent fifteen years following my husband's career. I don't have a choice, bugger it.'

'Neither did the women in the Thai jail,' Rosie said. The most overwhelming emotion to emerge from prison was the sense of solid sisterhood. She had never before known that level of acceptance and caring. She remembered Tia's sarongs, always brightest red though a little worn round the edge, and wondered what the hell she'd think about a Western woman's preoccupation with orgasms. We're all pawns, to a greater or lesser degree – us, the prisoners, the Chinese women living down by the ferry, she thought. The sophisticated orgasm hound could claim a link with the poor and deprived, but could it ever be the other way round?

But her remark missed its target by several miles. She wasn't sure whether John understood either when she tried to explain to him why she saw the links between the prisoners' and bankers' wives. He was thinking of America, of home, of returning to his spiritual teacher, the Tibetan guru, Chogyam Trungpa Rinpoche. Rosie was thinking of New York, of working again. Feminists there, she was sure, would understand the story.

At night, the junk they had borrowed swayed peacefully on the sheltered waters of the Yacht Club harbour. For a few days they relished its peace, a lull in the frenzy of the last eight months. But she knew they were only resting, that solitude was not their game. When she saw John going off to check out airline charters to the US, she wondered what extra dimension they would find to keep their relationship on the boil.

THIRTEEN

'Every symptom of alcoholism – barring acute physical deterioration – will be experienced by the spouse of the drinker.' These words had kicked off a series of early-morning talks on alcoholism and the family by an American couple, Ted and Gail Clark.

She was a therapist, he a recovered alcoholic who now worked with other alcoholics.

'I'm the daughter of two drinkers and the wife of one, so I'm more qualified than most to talk about the contagious effects of alcoholism,' Gail continued.

Shelagh groaned beside me. She was never much of an early riser, but I'd urged her to attend these talks with me, partly because I wanted the company, partly because she was having acute family problems herself. Shelagh's drinking had begun in reaction to her husband Andrew's affair with a younger woman. Drunk, she was helpless; helpless, how could he leave? But she was as aware as anyone of the lunacy of such behaviour; not only had his love turned to muffled hate, but her children were learning how to cover up for mum.

'Close relatives will feel guilty, angry, ashamed, isolated. They'll start to lie to cover up. Everything that happens to the drinker, though not necessarily in the same order.

'In my case,' Gail went on, 'anxiety was the first thing to hit. Terrible anxiety. I'm very social, but I was nervous around my friends because all the time I was worried that Ted was going to get drunk. At parties, I always had one eye on him, one on my watch to see when we could reasonably leave. Before he got too pissed, I'd hope, though that didn't always happen.

'Second was my sense of isolation. Parties were no fun. We were no fun. Our friends knew that Ted was liable to be soused by the end of the evening, so they stopped inviting us. We were more or less alone.

'Then I started to feel guilty. What was wrong with *me*? Why did Ted prefer the bottle to me? Didn't I love him enough? Didn't he love me enough? I didn't understand alcoholism as a disease, as something which the drinker cannot stop on his own. I was taking the blame for his drinking. I wasn't good enough, sexy enough, loving enough. It was terrible. My sense of uselessness spilled into my work. I was like Ted, dying to get home from the office, to hide from people, convinced of my own personal failure. I'd cry, threaten to leave him, hide the drink, give him drink, anything. Nothing made any difference. I got more and more lonely. Ted would be out of it in the evenings, so I'd be there all alone, much too proud to go and talk to a friend about what was going on.

'My value system was going haywire. I was having to call his office and tell them he was sick when he was drunk, cancel arrangements for the same reasons. I wanted to believe Ted when he said he would stop, but time and again he didn't, so I began to distrust him too, distrust both of us. I thought I was responsible. Should I go, I kept thinking, would that make it OK? Was I so awful, so horrid, that I was actually forcing him to drink?'

'Andrew said just that to me the other day,' hissed Shelagh. She seemed paler and smaller than when we had entered the room. The substance of Gail's speech was not entirely lost on me either. I remembered William cancelling dinner dates because I was too pissed to go.

'I ended up nearly losing my job because of having to stay at home and look after Ted. That was almost the end. My anger was flying around in all directions, against him, against me, against the world for being such a mess. I also started to get ill, physically ill, through lack of sleep and a rotten diet; after all, there wasn't any point in cooking good meals in the evening, when Ted was too drunk to eat them. So I'd go without food too.

'Ted finally went into treatment when he was sacked. That was his bottom line. I'll talk about that tomorrow and how the family deals with it.'

Shelagh and I left the room together. 'God, I'm frightened,' she said, holding on to my arm as we went up the staircase towards the dining room. 'Frightened for me, but more for them.'

'Isn't that enough to stop you?'

'I wish it was, but nothing seems to work. I mind about the children most. You know they won't bring their friends home? They go to their rooms a lot. David's nine, but he still carries his teddy bear around with him as though it's the only thing he trusts.'

The following day Gail picked up where she'd left off.

'When the drunk goes into treatment, people forget about the spouse. The drunk is understood at last, he finds a whole lot of new friends, he's the centre of attention. Unless the spouse gets some help too, she's going to feel bitter and resentful, like I did.

'An alcoholic partnership produces a weird intimacy. It's inconsistent, and after a binge, very desperate and insecure.'

That shot home; memories of mornings when I'd wake to see William standing there with a cup of tea in his hand, and an angry look on his face. 'What the fuck are you going to do? It can't go on.' I'd cry, make endless rash promises about never getting drunk again, about how I was unhappy, how I did love him, and how I'd be lost without him. And at the time, wasted and paranoid, aware that my world was out of control, I'd believe it.

'So the drunk has all these new-found friends, and he's terribly pleased with himself for having sobered up and undergone his conversion to sanity. Ted,' Gail turned at last to her husband, 'you take over from here.'

'Hi, I'm Ted, I'm an alcoholic. You know my story now and as you can see, Gail and I are still together, but it took a lot of work. There was so much mistrust. How was she to know that I wasn't going to start drinking again after having therapy? I'd made a whole lot of promises in the past and I'd always failed to keep them, so why should this be any different? She wasn't to know.

'I started going to AA every night, so I was still seeing as little of her as when I was drunk.'

'That felt like a reinforcement of my earlier paranoia,' Gail interjected. 'Drink had been most important, now this organisation seemed to be more important. I still felt a failure. I got jealous.'

Ted continued: 'I met people who said that their wives had been to Al-Anon. I told Gail and she went. From then on we both started to work together. Believe me, it wasn't easy, but at least we were together.'

I couldn't see William going to Al-Anon meetings. More to

the point, I thought gloomily, did I want William at Al-Anon meetings? I wasn't in love with him so what was the point? Wouldn't it make it all much more of a mess?

Gail was talking again: 'Women of low self-esteem tend to marry alcoholic men. It's all part of a really complicated power game. A drunk husband, however much havoc he's creating, puts you in control, paying the bills, getting the kids to school, making all the decisions about the house, calling the shots. It puts enormous power in your hands.' She paused. 'I have a theory (maybe I'm just bolstering myself) that the loss of self-esteem occurs when the husband starts to drink, not before. That women don't go searching around for a potential drunk with the idea that he will give them confidence.'

'Any questions?'

'Yes,' I said, 'does a man with low self-esteem marry an alcoholic woman?'

Ted answered. 'I don't think so, I don't think many men would take on a practising lush. It's a hard truth, but women drinkers have it worse. They're not exciting challenges like men who drink.' He grinned at his wife. 'But, both sexes can hide their problems behind the drinker's problems, which are more upfront, more immediate.'

It all made a lot of sense. I'd get drunk, crawl into a state of dependency and insecurity, and for a period the ball would be in William's court. When I was going through a period of not getting drunk, my confidence would come back a little, and I'd feel like moving out somewhere, because I could see the holes in the set-up. Then the power would swing round. He would be the one saying, 'Do you love me?' and, 'Why aren't you more affectionate? Why don't you like to make love any more?' Then, bang, I'd get drunk and we'd be back again at the beginning. Totally exhausting for everyone.

In this cycle, William's problems never got a look-in.

'The recovering drinker has to balance his own needs and the needs of his family,' said Ted. 'I've known many marriages break up when the boozer stops, because they have been founded on the wrong reasons, things like paranoia and need, rather than love and mutual support, but I've also known them break up because the booze was, so to speak, keeping a lid on what was going on. But, and there's no way out of this, the boozer's treatment has to come first, if it's going to work.'

'Everyone has to change,' Gail said. 'I had to let go control of the house, control of Ted, which I realised that I had, and work to heal myself. If you reckon that many drinkers have been drinking for up to fifteen years before they finally get treatment, then it's a long haul back. I'd say sometimes it takes six years to bring a couple back together. But I could, I realise now, have done different things while Ted was actually drinking.

'The first thing, if you're living with an alcoholic, is to recognise the fact,' Gail continued. 'You have to realise that you're not going to sober him up on your own. Divorce threats might keep him off the booze for a while, but he needs help. But you can help yourself; keep going out; don't become a victim of the drinker's reclusiveness. Tell people, so you have people to talk to. Don't believe his promises, and don't let him cover up for the mess you're both in by endless platitudes. Keep on rubbing his nose in the mess he is causing.'

'Covering up for the drinker's crimes is bad for both of you,' said Ted. 'I know that when I drank, I was always desperate for forgiveness and concealment. I made Gail an accomplice.'

I understood that only too well. I had always tried to gain forgiveness from the people nearest to me. Their complicity in my game gave me a longer rope with which to hang myself. In transactional analysis terms, I had a series of patsies; my shrink, my father, my boyfriend. I made them feel guilty for my state.

I can remember times when I'd meet William's eyes, challenging him while I poured a drink. Knowing that he was thinking, Oh God, is she going to get drunk again? Knowing too that I could make him feel guilty about his suspicions, which may or may not, depending on the occasion, have turned out right.

'The main thing,' Ted said in conclusion, 'is that you cannot do it alone.'

William was by this time in the Middle East. Before he left we had had one short meeting with the doctor. William had deflected the conversation from himself and us to me and my drinking habits. But like other people he had thought that I could be changed. With security, love and a happy home. He didn't say this to the doctor, who commented on it to me later. 'Yes,' I said, 'I think that's true. But perhaps that's what I was after too.'

Anne checked back into the clinic the day after the conference finished. She was shaky and miserable and spent the next twenty-four hours shut in her room. In the evening I went in to see her.

'Cheer up,' I said, dumbly, holding her hand, stroking the back of it with my thumb, looking at the blotches and enlarged veins rising on the skin's surface.

'Oh God, what am I going to do?'

'What happened?'

'I feel so useless to everyone. My children don't need me, my business doesn't need me, no one needs me. You know, my son rang up and said, "God, Mum, you're drunk again!" and then hung up.

'His father used to drink, you know. Then all he'd say was, "Oh Dad's gone on the piss again," and shrug it off. But not Mum. They've never once been to see me in here. It's as though I'm completely evil. They think I'll contaminate the children. And all they do is to take, take, take. You know my daughter, she's been using my house down in Lyme Regis all summer long. I pay all the bills, but when I'm in trouble, then they just turn their backs.'

I didn't know what to say. Anne's family were acting like the families of female alcoholics always do. I had noticed the way that women speak about their alcoholism: I'm evil, said Anne; I'm wicked, said Shelagh; I've committed sins, I thought. The rules of womanhood, particularly of motherhood, mean that once you crumble into alcoholism you've fallen from grace. Women's drinking may be covered up for longer: by husbands who don't want to admit that there's a lush in their bed; by the secret patterns of drinking alone; by doctors who send a woman home with a bottle of valium to cure the shakes; but once it's out in the open, then forgiveness is harder to come by, self-esteem harder to restore.

Statistically, women are far harder to cure than men. The state of 'learned helplessness', which begins in childhood, stays with women all their lives. They cannot believe in their own worth. When things go well, fortune is smiling; when disasters come, they are deserved. With so little sense of their own worth, is it surprising that women sometimes find it impossible to scramble back from the bottom? If you continually find yourself in situations where you have no control, your life structured by a husband, father, boss, or the bottle itself, you give up even trying.

Anne, it seemed, was trying; but she had no knowledge, no resources inside her. She started to cry quietly.

'What do you want out of life?' I asked.

'I want my home. I want someone to love. I want someone to make me feel worthwhile again. Someone to care for, someone to care for me.'

To care was her reason for being alive. Since infancy she had been taught that women care and men are cared for. Deprive her of that, replace it with a weakness for drink, and you've got a vicious circle which is almost impossible to break. Anne couldn't see that she was the only person who could do it, because she had never been taught responsibility for herself; responsibility for whether she was sober tomorrow or not. She was taking her own failure to heart, seeing it as her weakness and so reducing all the time her little reserve of the strength which she would need to fight back.

'God, I wish they would ring up. Just ring up and ask if I'm alive, if I'm OK.' She hugged her pillow, and pulled her nightdress up around her shoulders. 'You know, when I was in hospital once, with a liver gone wrong because of the booze, they came every day. Flowers, sweets, magazines, and they brought the kids and they'd sit there for hours. You see, that was OK. Mum was in an ordinary hospital where Mums and Grannies are supposed to be. But they won't come here. They never even try to understand, and I've given them everything.' Through her sobs she choked out, 'And do you know what Adrian said before he hung up the phone? He said, "God, Mum, you're spending all our money in these clinics." It's as though they don't want me to get better.'

I sat there stroking her hair. 'Anne,' I finally asked. 'Why did you get drunk instead of coming to the conference? I mean, you would have enjoyed it.'

'I don't know, I don't know. I never know. I thought I'd have one, I suppose, thought it would be OK. Then I felt guilty. I didn't know how to face all those people either.'

'But I was there.'

'Yes, but you're young, you're pretty, you have lots of friends, you've got a father who loves you, a boyfriend. What have I got?'

'You've got friends though, there's me and Brian and all of us.'

'It's not the same. You know it's not the same,' she said sadly. 'Oh, I'll be OK tomorrow, and I'll fit into this place again, and I'll feel quite happy for a while, and confident, but don't you see, I've been through all this before, over and over. The same things are always waiting for me, nothing. No one really cares.

'God, I wanted to die this week. I even got as far as shoving old sheets around the garage doors.'

Cherry, a new patient, was sitting in the lounge. She had taken over Brian's room. Cherry was fat and blowsy, with puffy ankles and wrists; her face was blotchy and little capillary lines ran like wireworms away from the bridge of her nose. She was wearing a pair of black nylon stretch slacks and a floral blouse; unflattering garments for her figure.

'We haven't seen too much of you lately,' she said.

I stared. I hadn't seen much of her either.

'You look better,' I hazarded, cautiously, because she didn't in fact look any better than three days earlier when I had first run into her in the kitchen. 'Thanks,' she smiled. A sweet smile. She must have been pretty once upon a time, and I offered up a silent prayer of thanks that my looks, at least, were still reasonably intact. Most women alcoholics start drinking heavily around forty; so, although the disease ravages them more quickly, society's reluctance to deal with them means that by the time they finally get into treatment their looks have gone.

Statistically, though, women alcoholics are getting younger and younger. All victims of the same revolution, which though it may have brought sweet freedom in many respects also brought unwelcome demands which we hadn't been brought up to meet.

I was torn between wanting to be a career woman and wanting to be a stay-at-home mother who didn't have to cope with the big world. Anne had her family, she had her job, but these alone were not enough.

'Has your husband been in to visit?' I asked Cherry, who was gasping on a cigarette.

'Yes,' she said, 'he's been and my sons have been in too.'

Poor Anne, I thought. Alone in that godforsaken room. Flowers at least would have been a visible souvenir.

Cherry and I went down to dinner. Brian was sitting in the dining room holding Angie's hand.

'Come on, Angie, you must eat something,' he said patiently, 'you haven't eaten since yesterday.'

'What should I eat?' Voice small and hollow, eyes staring into the middle distance.

'Fetch her some yoghurt,' Brian said to me. She picked at it desultorily, scooping up a glob and then letting it run back over the spoon, some of it into the carton, some on to the table cloth. Cherry twitched in discomfort beside me.

'Anyway, Brian, how are you getting on?' I asked, to break the awkwardness. The question was redundant, since Brian had been popping in and out of the clinic since leaving, mostly to see Angie but also, I suspected, because he was finding it hard to break the umbilical cords that joined him to the place. London, after all, was not his home.

'Fine,' he replied, grinning. He looked unbelievably fit and well; face lean and finely drawn, arms tanned. 'I just can't think of a reason to ever get drunk again. When you think about it, there isn't any reason.'

'Do you feel that emotionally, too?' asked Cherry suddenly. 'I mean, do you really accept it deep down?' She asked the question casually, unaware of how close to the mark her query was.

'Oh sure,' he replied easily, 'I mean, there's no sense in drinking.'

'I'm not talking about sense, I'm talking about feeling,' said Cherry obstinately.

'Well, yes I do. I know I'm an alcoholic, I know I have to stop drinking, I know I can't start again.'

Cherry didn't pursue the point. Later on, when Brian was drinking again and I found myself in the role of 'relative of an alcoholic' I was to remember the exchange. She was right: sense and reason did not necessarily imply commitment.

FOURTEEN

The flight from Hong Kong to Los Angeles took eighteen hours, long enough to draft a letter to *MS* magazine outlining the jail story. Rosie was excited; the article she was proposing seemed to grasp the essentials of sisterhood, a word feminists had used so often it had become a cliché. The prisoners had found sisterhood naturally. Probably none of them understood the word consciousness, let alone attended classes to have theirs raised.

In California she mailed the letter to *MS* in New York. The magazine had started in the same month as *Spare Rib*, and there had been occasional contact between the two. By the end of 1974 *MS* was the largest-selling feminist magazine in the world.

John's elder brother, Thom, was living in Los Angeles. The three of them drove to New York to spend Christmas with the boys' stepmother, Elaine Steinbeck. En route, they stopped to visit their natural mother, Gwynn, who was living in Tucson, Arizona. Neither son had seen Gwynn for an embarrassingly long time. The reunion in her small condo apartment was emotional, and they all ended up drunk.

The reply from *MS* was waiting for her in New York – a rejection. Rosie was surprised and depressed. The editor wrote: 'The story is too much of a hippy saga, too unreal for American women to appreciate.' What exactly did they mean? Was the story too sleazy for them? Was it that they lacked confidence in her ability to tell it?

Here was an example of women genuinely oppressed, and genuinely holding together – sisterhood in action. A change at least from that trivial crap about oppression depending on who washed the socks. And they said it was not interesting or relevant.

In the meantime there was no shortage of commissions. She accepted two from *New York* magazine. One on the new-style graffiti in women's lavatories, the other on the latest diet fad – staples in your ear which connected to the hunger centres – a crude form of acupuncture.

'Tony gives good head,' she read on the wall of the Ladies in Maxwell Plum's, the renowned Second Avenue singles bar. Was this a new sign of liberation? Though she was secretly relieved not to have to defy her her father's wish for radio silence on the Thai story, she was irked and unhappy. She owed the women prisoners a debt: and at the moment there was no way to repay it.

The physical practicalities of writing were the first problem. It was cold, they had little money and nowhere permanent to live. Her anxiety was all-pervading. The articles were not going well. The commissions, she knew, had come on the strength of her reputation as an English feminist magazine editor. How could she now admit to herself that she was wholly dependent on John? The inevitable kill fees just covered the bar bills.

John was 'organising' their life, which was about as nomadic as it had been in Asia. But there, it had made sense. Travelling was a valid way of life. At no time in Asia had

Rosie considered that she was on holiday. But now, living between the Village and the Upper West Side, with her knickers in Waverly Place and her overcoat on 92nd and the borrowed typewriter hovering uncertainly in between, she just felt homeless and hopeless.

She missed the diversion of danger. City centre paranoia was no substitute for leeches, snakes and diseases. But New York was a combat zone, nonetheless, with plenty of do-it-yourself emotional danger.

John hung out with friends who'd been in Vietnam, in particular with Louise, the wife of the photographer Dana Stone, who had disappeared in Cambodia with Sean Flynn. Rosie was jealous of Louise, because she'd been to the war. Admittedly second-hand, admittedly courtesy of her husband, but John picked up on the sentiment quickly: 'It's penis envy in action,' he said. 'You're a war groupie.' Rosie shrugged the comment off with a laugh. But wars were the ultimate in female macho and Vietnam the first war in which a few women had shone as news reporters and photographers.

John seemed to enjoy the inactivity. He'd sleep through till one o'clock and then go out to a bar. Rosie'd wake at eight and sit bolt upright, immediately worrying about how to con her way through the day. For John, the waiting had a purpose. Chogyam Trungpa was due in New York in February. The reunion with his Tibetan Buddhist teacher was evidently going to fix their location in some way. Possibly in Boulder, where the Tibetan's headquarters were.

John's search for his personal Holy Grail took them to a loft in Soho. At eight one evening she took off her yellow boots and added them to the large pile of slush-covered footwear at the entrance. Most were stout, expensive boots, a contrast to the cheap open sandals she'd seen in similar heaps outside eastern Buddhist temples. John moved into the crowd, greeting his old friends. For him, it was school-reunion day. Rosie sat down, crossing her legs, annoyed that there was a large ladder in her tights.

She waited in anticipation. The meeting had all the fraught connotations of a first encounter with prospective in-laws. It was important that she like Trungpa but important that the liking be spontaneous. She looked round the loft – smart suits, smart people. All eager and elated. She felt a stab of jealousy, as she had felt for the Hare Krishna followers in Bombay. An envy of any faith with no room for scepticism.

Twenty minutes after the lecture was due to start, Chogyam Trungpa Rinpoche limped on to the platform. 'Early,' commented the man on Rosie's left. The guru wore well-cut English tweeds, perhaps meant to disguise how short he was, and how plump. His face was flat as a plate, his complexion sallow, almost jaundice-yellow. But he had a mischievous, winning grin which he offered the company while checking that his water-bottle (containing sake, she later discovered) was in its place on the table.

Physically he wasn't inspiring – more like a sales rep for Sony than a spiritual teacher whose birth had excited as much interest in Tibet as Christ's had in Galilee. Trungpa was born in a cattle byre in a tiny village in north-east Tibet. Flowers bloomed on the day of his birth, despite it being winter in the world's most rugged landscape. A pail full of water was found to contain milk. A rainbow appeared in the sky.

Indications given by his lineage led monks to the village, and finally to identification of the baby. They set him certain tests picking his predecessors' personal possessions out of a group of similar objects – which he completed unerringly. He seemed to know, too, that he was a reincarnation and even as a tiny baby made gestures of blessing towards the monks, who, like the Three Wise Men, had followed signs towards the child. The baby was a reincarnation of an abbot, the ruler of one of Tibet's most important monasteries.

After the talk she lined up to greet Trungpa personally. Without thinking, she twisted a ring off her finger, a round band of gold set with semi-precious stones which had belonged to her mother. She dropped the ring into his out-stretched hand, proffered for her to shake. 'Thank you,' she said. He cocked an eyebrow at her, looking her up and down with an expression which was almost, but not quite, lecher-ous; sizing up her tits as well as her soul. The sensation was weird. Normal onceovers check the packaging, but this one seemed to be asking if she was wearing her spiritual Guccis as well.

Rinpoche had left Tibet in 1959 when the Chinese invaded. He'd fled to India, and from there to England. In 1970 he arrived in America. For someone reared to be celibate, he was evidently at ease with women.

She was surprised afterwards at her gesture. The ring had been sentimentally precious. What exactly had he touched in her? She hadn't intended to impress. Ever since John had first mentioned Trungpa she had had mixed feelings. His books, *Meditation in Action* and *Mudra*, struck her as sane. But you don't go for a guru because your boyfriend does. She'd followed John into enough bizarre situations to be wary of following him into his spiritual life, particularly since John was by now – two months after arriving in New York – having an affair with a woman who rated high in Rinpoche's court circle.

One weekend towards the end of January they had stayed with some friends of John's who owned a farm in upstate New York. On the Saturday night they were joined for dinner by a singer called Carol. John zeroed in on her like a homing pigeon.

The effect was to diminish Rosie's already shaky self-confidence still further. Carol was slick, sharp and witty. So was Rosie, but she didn't have a hit record. What made it worse was Carol's position as a long-time student of Rinpoche's.

Carol had been in at the beginning. Like one of Christ's original disciples, or a Beatle fan who'd been at the Cavern, her early start bestowed distinction. Whatever she did, Rosie could never catch up.

Carol herself was not too subtle to underline the point: 'Haven't you met Rinpoche yet?' she said to Rosie, flicking her dark hair to one side. 'No,' Rosie replied, thinking, you bitch, you know the answer already . . .

Later, in bed, Rosie curled herself away from him, wanting to touch him, wanting to restore their closeness, but knowing that the person he actually wanted to fuck was asleep in the next room.

Two days later in New York John spoke to Carol on the phone. Rosie was hovering in the kitchen, glad that at least he had the balls not to lower his voice, but angry. 'So you're going to see her tonight? You're going to see her at the club?' she said, hoping her voice sounded steely and cutting, controlling its nervous tremor.

'Yes.' He was dialling another number. 'You can come if you want.'

She said no and sat through the afternoon like a martyr, hating herself for her crippling pose, but knowing no other way to deal with her jealousy. John sang in the bath, then clipped his fingernails. 'See you later.' He was gone, banging the door of the apartment. They were on 92nd Street at the time, in a small second-floor apartment, just one large room, with a kitchen and bathroom.

She poured a drink. She was half-crazed with a new kind of fear. The jealousy felt like a surgeon's knife, eating into her self, her esteem. She watched TV. All the rules of being laid back were useless. The Scotch bottle stood there like an ally. She drank till she passed out.

Through a thick haze she looked at her watch. It read nine o'clock. Morning? The bed was empty. She was on the sofa, her clothes suffocating her, twisted and turned into knots and wrinkles. She threw them off and staggered into the bathroom. Shivering under the cold shower, she tried to imagine her life without John. She couldn't, any more than she could imagine an old age spent alone. Would it be different if we were married? she wondered. Maybe then he'd stay.

I've just walked myself into one more liberated trap, Rosie thought, huddling under the covers. Courage was such weird stuff, indefinable really. She supposed she was what people describe as good in crises, at least she didn't crack up when Steve died, or in jail. But she couldn't handle this.

Carol was promoting her new album. She arrived in New York at least once a week. The phone would ring in whatever apartment they were in. It was the signal for John to get out his smartest nylon shirt and go to meet her.

Thinking of them in bed together struck like physical pain. She loathed herself for minding so much, for being so possessive of someone's body and someone's mind. It was fucking ironical too. Just the other night, in an attempt to prove that she'd conquered her jealousies, she and a girlfriend had seduced John, rolled him into bed and then played with his body like two expert geishas. In the morning he'd woken up like a bear with a sore head, and growled off to the kitchen for coffee. He hadn't remembered a single moment.

'I'm going back to England for the spring,' she said to him finally. John had decided that they were going to Boulder, Trungpa's headquarters, in May for the start of his summer university called Naropa Institute. Rosie was uneasy, she was jealous of Carol and her in-status with the guru, jealous of Rinpoche himself. She felt left out because she didn't know the jargon and the Buddhist in-jokes.

'Rinpoche's going to England in April,' John answered, 'I'll come over then.'

'I suppose Carol is coming too?' Rosie asked, petulantly.

'I don't know. Stop being so fucking jealous.'

He spent the night with Carol while Rosie started to pack. She was leaving in two days' time.

She moved back into the house in Shepherd's Bush where she used to live. John followed in ten days. Rinpoche, his English wife Diana and Carol, three days after that. The party moved into the Ritz.

'What's a spiritual teacher doing staying in the Ritz?' her mother asked over the phone. Rosie had told her about Rinpoche and Betty had started reading his books, interested but wary.

'Why are the best things of life necessarily non-spiritual?' Rosie countered.

'I don't agree with that kind of hedonism,' Betty replied. She was obviously nonplussed by this crazy oriental who liked sake and women and safari suits.

Rinpoche held court accompanied by the tinkling sounds

of the fountain in the Palm Court of the Ritz. Previously the English had treated him warily and while in the country he had wondered how he could adapt Buddhism to Western tastes. A car accident resulted in partial paralysis and he abandoned his monastic way of life. 'No longer,' he says in his autobiography, 'could I hide behind the robes of a monk.' He married an eighteen-year-old English girl and together they travelled to the US. His English students hadn't approved of his new materialistic life.

Watching him delicately eating the Ritz's cucumber sandwiches and drinking pale China tea, at home in the Western world's most bourgeois surroundings, Rosie was impressed. Not only had he overcome his celibate upbringing, but his non-materialist notions were obviously stuff of the past as well.

There were several such tea-parties and each one was an ordeal. Carol's intimacy with Rinpoche was easy and familiar, while Rosie still floundered like a schoolkid. Carol's suite overlooked Green Park. John commuted between them – between spiritual wisdom and Bollinger and the often hysterical outbursts that awaited him when he came back to Rosie.

In Shepherd's Bush the household watched the pantomime sceptically. Rosie drank and sniffed heroin which had, in the intervening two years, become alarmingly common among some of her friends. A girl she knew sold Rosie a needle, and she slid through John's Ritzy nights gentled on opiate clouds. Sitting at the stripped-pine kitchen table one night, too out of it to notice what she was doing, she loaded the syringe and injected the contents. Someone seemed to be throwing a soft ball at her heart as she slid away. Physically, she was conscious of falling towards the floor, uncaring of possible pain, just going, going, onwards, downwards, out.

'Stop it,' she muttered. Someone was shaking her shoulders, banging her down on to the floor. It was annoying, disturbing; she didn't want to be dragged back out of this calm sea, this gentle and rounded black womb.

'Christ. Thank heavens.' Her old friend David Jenkins sat back on his heels and looked down at her. 'You were almost dead, you maniac. I've been giving you the kiss of life. You were blue.' His face swam into focus, full of concern, a rough edge to his voice masking the fear.

Dead, the word echoed from afar. It would have been an accident, she thought sleepily, and dragged herself upstairs to bed. 'Thank you,' she said politely, standing at the foot of the spiral staircase. 'I'm perfectly all right now.'

The following day she woke properly. God, what am I doing? Nearly dying, dying, dying. She shivered with fright.

Two days later, the musical chairs started again. Rinpoche and Diana moved on. Carol went to Europe, John and Rosie packed to return to America. They arrived in Boulder in the middle of May, laden with baggage. John was travelling with all his worldly goods.

'Going home,' he said, though he'd never set foot in the town before. They checked into the Hotel Boulderado. Their room faced east, outwards towards the plains. Behind the town rose the Flat Iron mountains, the last gasp of the old America, thrown up when the continents cracked and divided, sending Africa wandering east and South America drifting south.

Boulder was into youth and Trungpa Rinpoche's summer university blended into the curious mixture that already inhabited the Rocky Mountain town. There was no central campus; the main lectures, given by Rinpoche himself, took place in a Catholic school which had been hired for the two-month duration. Naropa students slept in the university dormitories, hiked in the hills and studied such subjects as creative writing, Tai Chi, Buddhism, mathematics and Japanese calligraphy.

Most of the people who gathered around Trungpa had found their way there via another spiritual teacher. In 1975 he wasn't as well known as the Maharishi or the Kid, whose spiritual disciplines offered safer ground. Rinpoche's teachings were vaguer, the opposite of ashram life. The shrine room in Boulder looked regal and ornate, with red and yellow meditation mats arranged in rows on the parquet flooring, but the community was no joss-stick-tainted playschool.

In many ways more happened at parties than at workshops or seminars. They certainly fostered the frantic games of one-upmanship. Have you been to seminary? How long have you been involved with the scene? Are you in the know? Does Rinpoche sleep with you? Does he sleep with your wife? (Even this lent cachet.)

The poets, who all lived in a condominium near the mountains, gave the smartest parties. One night Ginsberg, Burroughs, Corso and Anne Waldman hosted one to welcome some poets from California, Ted Berrigan, Diane de Prima and Joanne Kyger.

Corso sidled up and clamped her hand in his. It felt sticky and damp. She pulled her hand away and confronted his wizened smile, broken teeth and alcohol-ridden face. 'I just came in your hand, baby,' he lisped through the gap between his front teeth. She looked at her palm. Difficult to tell in the half-light what was clinging to the centre of her hand. 'Snot,' someone said later, 'one of Gregory's favourite jokes.' Should she be flattered?

Burroughs loomed in one corner, his thin face satanic. The noise was deafening. She poured another drink and walked towards the next room. John was deep in conversation with a girl she didn't recognise.

In the doorway she collided with someone heading in the opposite direction. Rosie's drink splashed down the front of her blouse. 'I'm sorry.' Gentle voice, polite manners. Different. Everything around her felt competitive, as though people were only there because they wanted to be the people who went to the poets' parties, unlike the junior students who were probably hanging out at the Hungry Horse saloon, drinking 35-cent beer and playing that odd game called shove on the sawdust floor. But maybe it was only her. Another manifestation of her spiritual failing, of her fear of being left out.

Buddhist doctrine said you should experience everything without fear. And she was so often afraid.

'No sweat,' she answered, shaking off the droplets of wine.

He took her glass and turned to fetch another drink. She followed, fascinated by his looks. He was deeply tanned with huge black eyes, long black hair caught back in a ponytail.

'Have you just arrived?'

'This morning, from Bolinas. It took all night in the car. I came with Joanne.' He indicated the other side of the room where Joanne was deep in conversation with Ginsberg. She was short-haired and intense, not pretty but energetic; hands waving, words spitting.

'I'm teaching a course for the two weeks as well. On movement, on the spatial relationships between man and nature.'

His words flowed. Apart from being unofficial mayor of Bolinas, he turned out to be an ornithologist, an anthropologist and a writer. She told him she was attending the university. He invited her to have lunch the following day. She agreed. 'One o'clock in the Boulderado bar?'

The affair blossomed. On the night before Peter was due to leave, they sat in the garden, watching a party in full swing inside. As they turned back up the lawn, emerging out of shadows into sprinkled light, they saw John and Joanne standing together on the balcony hurling glasses down on to the terrace.

In the autumn Rosie started work as assistant editor on the Naropa journal, called *Loka* – the Tibetan word for space. Never before had she welcomed office hours – ten to six – so thankfully. At last she could honestly say she was doing something again, in her own right, without John. And the work, editing and re-writing, was familiar to her, and she revelled in feeling competent.

The journal was to be published the following year by Doubleday. Some contributions were original, some were taken directly from lectures which had been held during the summer. All centred around the growth, development and influence of Buddhism on American culture.

Rinpoche joined the Boulder Chamber of Commerce. John had an old friend from Vietnam days who was then Treasurer of the State of Colorado. Sam Brown, once a member of the Peace Corps, now lived in Denver and expressed a tempered interest in the goings-on in Boulder. He could see that Rinpoche's presence brought cash into the state, and a meeting was fixed between Rinpoche and Sam along with the Governor. John made the introductions. He was unashamedly delighted to play a part in Trungpa's elevation into public office.

One weekend Sam took John and Rosie to the State Rodeo. Rosie was thrilled to see the real-life cowboys ride broncos and bulls. Sam nudged her arm. 'For a monk from the Himalayas,' he whispered, 'that guru of yours isn't doing too badly.'

But though Rinpoche indulged in most aspects of Western materialism – chauffeur-driven cars, hand-tailored suits, beautiful mistresses and first-class travel – the message he continually hammered home was that the teaching (the dharma) is doing the dishes, washing the nappies. The dharma is meditating. Sitting on your bum for hours. Experiencing life as it is with no magic potions, no mystical relief.

A friend of hers called Anne, who had married a member of the east-coast aristocracy and lived with her two children (the eldest, born in 1967, was called Mandala) in a large house at the edge of the mountains, employed a girl called Sue to water her garden. 'I have to have someone working for me so that I have time for meditating. Sue also looks after the kids.'

'But what about the dharma being the dishes and the nappies?' Rosie asked.

'Well, I do do some of that. But Sue needs the money.' Sue found the situation irksome. She was from California and had hitched to Boulder.

'I realised that the only place on this planet that I wanted to be was Boulder,' she said to Rosie one day while they waited for one of Rinpoche's lectures to start. 'So I bought a tent and I camp in Anne's garden. She lets me stay for free in return for the watering and childminding. But she's so in control of her life, there's no space for anything to happen.'

'Like what?'

'Well, she takes birth pills, so she's stopping her natural cycle. Dividing herself at the neck . . . head controlling body.'

'But you haven't got a baby.'

'I've just thrown away my birth pills. Now I'm into surrender. It's fantastically exciting to live in a united body.'

In 1968 Anne had been involved in running the Woodstock Festival. Now she was into the New Age. Busy with the spiritual hierarchy, seeing people's places as ordained, karmically controlled. A long way from the love generation.

In the hamburger joint, the waiter complained about his boredom with meditation. At the hairdressers, the effeminate owner said he found spiritual peace by gazing at his goldfish tanks. The real-estate agent who showed you round a house recommended a room for meditation rather than a site for a barbecue pit.

William Burroughs once asked Rinpoche if he objected to psychic practices like astral projection and telepathy. His own view was that these things were fun, like gliding and skiing. Rinpoche parried by saying that since these things were a new dimension, not everyone could share in them, and this lessened their usefulness. Dollar bills, he concluded, were far more real, and his only experience of astral travel came courtesy of TWA.

Rinpoche's English wife Diana solved the problem of being married to a philandering guru by spending a lot of time on horseback. Occasionally she and Rosie went off for weekends together when Diana was competing in horse shows. They'd share a bedroom in a plastic motel. One weekend Rosie arrived at the stables, complete with a left-hand shiner that was almost shutting her eye. Diana's right eye was similarly abused. 'Suitcase fell off a cupboard when I was packing,' she said airily, soothing the horse before urging him up the ramp of the box. 'You too?'

Rosie nodded, then decided to tell the truth. 'No, John thumped me. I was pissed.' Falling suitcases, she knew by now, never caused black eyes, and she was fed up with lying. Would Diana reciprocate the confidence? Rosie waited. She had no intention of asking the guru's wife such a direct question. Diana remained silent. Pulling down their dark glasses they climbed into the box.

Two nights earlier she and John had been to dinner with some friends called David and Mary. As it turned out only Mary was there since David was on a spiritual business trip to the east coast. Had she known before that John fancied Mary? A little, but she'd refused to acknowledge it. After dinner, John had whispered in Rosie's ear and how loud it had sounded, surely everyone else must have heard him – that he wanted to screw Mary. Would she, Rosie, somehow get out of there and go home? What to do? She could hardly shout into the smoky room that no, she was bloody well not going to do anything of the sort and how dare he even suggest it. Mary simpered on the carpet, all sleek black hair and green eyes, lithe limbs, slim hips.

Rosie'd gone in the end, without complaint, feeling sick in her stomach and frightened. Back in the Boulderado she'd finished off a bottle of Scotch, then thrown all the bedclothes out into the corridor. Luckily they were on the top floor at the south-east corner. Few people passed that way at night. John finally came back and tripped, swearing, over the bundle of sheets, blankets and pillows.

In the morning she had a black eye. They must have had a fight, but she couldn't remember. She could rarely remember their fights. The only evidence was the morning-after bruises.

Disadvantaged by lack of memory, she usually conceded it was her fault. On the other hand, John never had any bruises.

But was it right to turn Rinpoche's teaching into self-indulgence? Where was compassion in that? Did honesty – like John's desire to screw Mary – justify the repercussions? Was she wrong to feel such hideous insecurity? Did that reveal a shallow spiritual capacity? If she could trust in herself, in the security of the moment, then would such things not matter?

But they did matter, she thought angrily, as she and John bitched and whined at each other. And, what was worse, Rinpoche sanctioned all such behaviour. In London, it would have been the permissive society, here in Boulder it was the path of spiritual growth. The Rocky Mountain spiritual Peyton Place.

They moved out of the Boulderado Hotel shortly before Christmas. John's mother Gwynn arrived from Arizona, and Thom, who had moved to Boulder too, set up house with her. John and Rosie lived downstairs. Over Gwynn's excellent cooking they played uneasy happy families.

At the office she helped edit work by Allen Ginsberg and William Burroughs. John submitted an article to the journal about a Buddhist monk he had studied under in Vietnam. Rosie, as ever intrigued by his war stories, laboriously typed out his handwritten script. When he'd finished he went on a week's meditation retreat. His packing included two half-gallons of Scotch.

When he returned, Rosie signed up for a retreat too. The journal was due at the publishers. She would go the day afterwards. Brief periods of solitude were considered indispensable for all Rinpoche's students.

Just after Christmas Gwynn was taken ill. Overweight,

weakened by asthma, she died three days later of heart failure. Two days after that Rosie went into solitude.

Retreats were conducted up in the mountains, on land owned by the Buddhist community. The region was wonderfully beautiful; high and rugged, with valleys surrounded by wooded hills, cut through by small streams. Students had built wooden huts, each one isolated and equipped with wood-burning stoves. She was immediately terrified to be so alone, full of remorse that she had been drunk the night Gwynn died.

Her cabin was octagonal, with a sleeping platform above the living area. The journey up the ladder was sheer terror. Once up there, things were no better. Would she roll off in the night? The wind howled through the pine forests, the creaking branches sounded like footsteps through the snow.

For the first two days she sat in a heap, sipping the one bottle of Scotch she had brought, but ignoring the cans of baked beans. Too miserable to meditate. Was she, she wondered, in the wrong bloody life for all this? On the third day she ventured out for a walk across sun-sparkled snow and looked into a deserted caravan parked at the bottom of the valley. Under the folding seat she found a cache of novels: Harold Robbins, Len Deighton, Irwin Shaw. She cast a guilty look outside to see if anyone was walking up the valley. But as usual it was deserted. She stuffed the books under her coat and set off briskly back to her cabin.

She felt guilty to be reading the books, but they kept the worst of her worries at bay. Would John be sleeping with someone while she was gone? What work would she do now that the journal was finished? But the books must have belonged to someone else who found it hard to live in peace with themselves. Once she'd discovered them, meditation became far easier. It wasn't so hard to stay with it for an hour or so when she could look forward to getting lost in someone else's imagination.

The question of obedience to the guru was always complicated. Obedience to any living presence is never easy to understand or to rationalise, obedience to a teacher who claimed certain divine rights was even harder, particularly for a woman.

When she'd first come to Boulder, Anne Waldman, the poet, had invited her on to a radio show where the subject of feminism and spirituality had been discussed. The answers of the participants were decidedly fudgy. Anne could see the contradiction in submitting to male authority – to any authority – while working through your own, female, sense of oppression. The other participant, the singer Rachel Faro, saw no contradiction. Rosie saw masses. Most of them stemmed from Trungpa's style rather than from the fundamental question of whether or not feminism and spirituality could mix. She believed that they could.

Both were personal beliefs, and as such need not contradict each other. But the externals clashed – feminism's attention to detail versus Rinpoche's feudal, and sexist, approach to life. And Gods, spiritual or temporal, were nearly always male.

Rosie's retreat did nothing to help her peace of mind. She frequently got drunk. Unconsciously she was turning to helplessness as a means of making John stay, acting on the dubious assumption that no man would dare leave a woman who was patently incapable of coping alone. But drunken helplessness is hardly pretty, hardly endearing and a lousy weapon.

Her visa came up for renewal, and her immigrant status

was in question. Marriage was the answer, but once they had agreed upon it she became even more desperate to hold him, even more paranoid about his small philanderings which nowadays never went further than chatting someone up in a bar. The rows got worse, frequently erupting into fights and ever-increasing amounts of Scotch.

Soon there was no even ground on which to meet. Though she could see the relationship going wrong, could see that her clinging was driving them inexorably apart, she did not stop. After arguments she'd always be able to think of the right thing to say, but of course by then it was too late. In the mornings she'd have to hope that his words would fill in the gaps. The blackouts were terrifying. Black eyes faded, turning from violent purples, through blues and greens till they resembled smudgy eyeshadow. But blackouts were just holes.

Charles and Betty wrote expressing pleasure about the marriage but, between the lines, a wariness. John, who never wrote letters, still hadn't written to Charles, though he frequently agreed to do so. The days passed; letters arrived from Ludlow concerning the church and the canapés, the guest-list and the hymns for the service. Still John didn't write. Sam Brown came over from Denver to take them out to a celebration dinner. The evening went well, and when they got home Rosie tried again. John told her to stop nagging.

The truth began to dawn; he no longer loved her. She wavered between love, hate and need. Apologising for her behaviour all the time was a pathetic way of trying to keep his love; such abjectness made her turn her hatred on herself as well.

'Why don't you go to England ahead of me?' John finally said, weary of fighting. Rosie snivelled and agreed.

'You will come?' she said tearfully. At eight in the morning Stapleton Airport bustled with tourists returning from their Easter holidays in the Rockies. Children in sheriff badges and Indian feathers jostled round the departure gate. John nodded.

The plane curved up the side of the mountains, north towards Chicago. She ordered a large vodka, ignoring the stewardess's offer of coffee and doughnuts. I'm running away, she thought. Running because I can't hack this any more. It's my fault, I'm a failure in love, a failure spiritually. I didn't even say goodbye to Rinpoche.

Betty picked her up at Heathrow. Another eight a.m. tussle with airport crowds. It was only when they got to the parking lot that she asked Rosie where John was. The last time she'd spoken to her daughter, two weeks earlier, the topic had been weddings and churches.

'It's over.' Rosie stood clutching the door handle. The wind whistled through the open sides of the highrise building. 'Oh, Mummy, it hurts . . .' The years slid backwards. Fourteen again, being comforted because a boyfriend hadn't danced with her at the pony-club dance.

The phone calls from John came infrequently. Within six weeks they stopped altogether. Rosie was doubly wounded, losing not only John's love, but his friendship too. She stuffed herself with Betty's cooking and Charles's booze, going to bed at night drunk enough to ensure instant sleep.

After two months she moved back to London, to her old house in Shepherd's Bush. The sameness depressed her; the only new element was shabbiness. As an ex-editor of *Spare Rib* she found freelance work easy to come by. But discipline was elusive; Scotch was solid.

On the day the scales registered eleven stone two, she

could no longer kid herself that she was only a little over-weight. She was fat. Like Georgy, Margaret Forster's heroine, she was hiding behind her flab. She fasted for eighteen days and trimmed her weight down to nine stone nine. But it seemed pointless, any attempt to pull herself together hollow. The rug had been pulled out from under her and she didn't know what to replace it with.

Once trim, though, she began exacting her vengeance, picking up Mr Goodbars and then throwing them out of her bed at four in the morning, screaming that they were smelly and disgusting, and how dare they come near her. There were others, too, who took off on their own accord, never to phone again. Their rejections turned her passing interest into mini-passions, fuelled by that ghastly twist of human nature which dictates that you love most what you cannot have. Later she was to shudder; condemning a stranger's virility in the small hours can be a dangerous business.

She was arrested for drunken driving. The magistrate fined her £263 and suspended her licence for three years. Her mother came to court. 'Why didn't you tell me that you'd had a previous conviction?' she asked. 'Your father would never have bought you the car if he'd known.'

'Last time, well . . . it hardly counted. I was only just over the limit. So little that I wasn't even fined for that, only £7 for speeding on the motorway.'

Betty frowned. 'You ought to do some exercises. You've lost weight too fast. And you smoke too much.'

Rosie grinned brightly. 'I'll cut down, honest. And the booze too,' she added, pre-empting her mother's inevitable query.

John telephoned in November. 'I'm in New York for a couple of weeks. I kinda miss you.'

It was all she needed. She arrived in New York drunk and left, four days later, still drunk. In the middle of their useless reunion an armchair in their hotel suite burnt down, causing fire alarms and pandemonium in the corridors. She flew back in despair and rage. Once home, tired and hung-over, she called him in New York.

'Just to tell you what happened on the way home . . .' Her voice was aggressive. 'I joined the mile high club.'

'You bitch, get off the phone, get out of my life. What the fuck do you mean by calling me up to tell me this. I've kept you in Scotch and champagne for four days . . . Goddamn it, Rosie . . .' His voice trailed out. The phone clicked.

He'd hung up.

FIFTEEN

'Listen, Daddy, I can't check out of here just like that. It's not a hotel, or a health farm. I don't know when I want to go.'

'But darling, we don't know whether or not the insurance will pay. You have to tell me when you're going to leave.'

'I can't.'

'You must. What's the matter with you? You know I'll come and stay or you can come here. What good is it doing you? You've been there for three weeks now.'

'You don't understand. This is life and death to me.'

'Don't you see that this is costing a fortune?'

'I'll bloody well pay.'

'Stop shouting at me. I'm only trying to help.'

I slammed down the phone. It was after nine at night and the doctor came into my room, hearing my raised voice.

'What are you arguing with your father about?'

The doctor was calm and matter-of-fact, defusing the hysteria that often overwhelmed me when I talked to my father.

'He thinks I should leave. I don't. Stalemate.' I was crying, even though I knew how infantile it was.

'When you argue do you become like each other?' he asked.

'Yes. We both say the things that hurt.'

'Which one of you is the most likely to be able to change?'

'Well me, I suppose. I'm younger.'

'Right, ring him back and say you're sorry you shouted and put the phone down. Let him talk. Can't you understand that it's no fun for him to have his youngest daughter in here?'

An understatement. My mother had died fifteen months earlier. Now I was in the drunk tank.

I picked up the phone.

'I'm sorry. I don't want to argue.'

It was the beginning of the slow process of healing the scars left by his hurt and puzzlement at my drinking. I was also trying not to fall back on the role of the darling daughter. I knew he felt responsible for me, both because he loved me and because (being a father of the old school) I was an unmarried daughter.

Meanwhile, the clinic bill had topped the three thousand pound mark, and was rising every night I slept in that room. It wasn't clear how much, if any, of the costs were covered by insurance.

This was a crucial question: how long should the alcoholic remain in a clinic? Should he go into clinics at all?

Alcoholics divide into two categories: primary and secondary. Primary alcoholics are those who show no other sign of being psychopathologically disturbed beyond the problems that addiction to booze has caused. Secondary alcoholics have far deeper levels of disorder, present before the drinking began. The doctor made little attempt, initially, to separate the two categories. He maintained that while you were drinking and while that was causing problems, then it was impossible to work out the real source of a problem. For many alcoholics, stopping is enough.

I'd figured out for myself, and he had concurred, that I fell into the category of primary alcoholic. I wasn't manic-depressive, poly-addicted (addicted to more than one drug at a time – although since the age of seventeen, I'd always been addicted to something), and there was no history of mental illness in my family. There was no history of alcoholism either. Later, when I'd been out of the clinic for some months, I was to go through the family tree with my father, wondering if I would discover some genetic cause for my drinking. He confessed to a couple of maiden aunts who had lived solitary lives and could possibly have been secretly on the bottle, but there was no real evidence of this. I was the freak.

Fifty per cent of all alcoholics have an alcoholic parent. Studies of adopted children have shown this genetic tendency. Alcoholic parents, especially single mothers, are high on the list of parents who give their children up for adoption. American research has shown the same incidence of alcoholism, fifty per cent inheritance, cropping up in offspring who have been raised in stable, non-alcoholic homes.

I was first-generation, primary alcoholic but I hadn't stopped drinking on my own. Asylum was necessary. I have friends who claim to have stopped on their own, aware of the dangers, and able to lay off the booze from one day to the next. Does that make them less alcoholic? I tend to think so.

The debate about whether or not a drinker who drinks alcoholically can ever return to social drinking is never-ending. No hardened drinker is going to want his doctor to tell him to stop. A programme of behaviour modification is far more acceptable. But statistics show that this rarely, if ever, works. AA, the world's most successful organisation for helping alcoholics, says it is impossible. My doctor broadly agreed:

'Show me one, just one, successfully rehabilitated alcoholic who now drinks normally, and I'll change my mind.' There were no certain answers.

'It doesn't make much sense to me,' I said, when the subject was being discussed in the group. 'Controlled drinking isn't normal drinking. If you have to control it, to think about it all the time, then life can't be much better than it was on the booze.'

But there was another point about trying to control drink as against giving it up completely, though it took me a while to realise it. One common trait amongst alcoholics, certainly true of me, is an all-or-nothing approach to life. To the outsider this ability to be instantly enthused and just as instantly bored probably makes the alcoholic seem even more unstable. But it was a pattern of my life that I was sure wouldn't completely change. I was sure I could give up – but could I stay sober? Month after month? I contemplated a lifetime without booze, and found the prospect dreary and miserable. At those moments, I'd fall back on the idea of not drinking today: following the AA line of keeping it simple and not looking too far ahead. But that notion seemed childish and unrealistic.

It helped to think of the Buddhist creed – live in the present. Human misery and suffering are largely caused by failed expectation. I felt better when I figured this out, as though it gave me a basis for staying sober, a firmer basis than thinking simply in terms of not drinking today.

'Of course you only know that you're alcoholic when you really hit the bottom line. I had to hit it twice.' The speaker was an AA member who was giving the group an evening pep-talk. 'Most people have to hit it twice,' he added.

'Why?' I asked. 'Are you saying that I'll have to go through this again before I know I have a problem?'

'Well, a lot of people get very cocky – it takes the second nosedive to make them humble.'

I sighed. Doctors endlessly debate the question of the bottom line. AA maintain that no one will get sober unless they hit rock bottom. They follow the old adage that it is impossible to treat and cure an alcoholic who is dragged protesting into treatment. But Phil had told me that he had the same rate of success with drunks sent to treatment at gunpoint, threatened with the loss of their jobs if they didn't shape up, as with those who came in voluntarily.

Anne's relapses, Taylor's relapses (and we had had news that he had been drinking back home), Shelagh's constant relapses; why did they happen? Would I constantly relapse too?

They all approached the problem in the same way. They were prepared to come into clinics to appease their families, or in Anne's case, literally to keep her alive, but that was the extent of their adjustment.

There are five clear stages of treatment. Conflict, which in my case meant anger, frustration and rage and the unwillingness to admit to my alcoholism. Commitment, which meant acceptance and a giddy sense of euphoria stemming from the physical sense of well-being, the lack of dependence. Mourning, which was a crucial period when you missed the booze like a deceased relative, and it was critical to move forward and make decisions that would ensure sobriety. Following mourning, though, comes denial: 'Oh well, I've got a drink problem, it's incurable and what the fuck can I do about it?' The drinker's life is so protected from reality by booze that the required changes seem like a threat to his survival. At least, while drinking, he's been alive.

If the drinker can work through these psychological barriers then, the therapists tend to agree, he has a good chance of being both sober and happy – stage five.

Anne, Taylor and Shelagh all seemed stuck in the middle, which is about the worst place to be, fully aware of their drink problem, and its only solution, yet unable, or unwilling, to move themselves past that point. The result is a shambles; clinics, followed by brief patches of sobriety, followed by benders, followed by clinics. The twilight world of the well-to-do boozer.

Later on I was talking to Anne.

'I'm just so miserable, I stay off the booze and as nothing gets better. I'd rather be drunk.'

I longed to grab her by the shoulders, literally to shake the life back into her.

Mrs Taylor brought Taylor back into the clinic one Wednesday lunch time. She was in despair and her usually immaculate appearance was ruffled and untidy. Taylor was stubborn. He sat on the edge of the fat orange lounge chair and regarded the doctor through jaundiced eyes.

'I just don't *want* to stop,' he said, his voice firmer than his trembly hands. His eyes strayed towards the window, towards the Potter. He was at that critical moment of withdrawal when only a drink will do the trick and take away, instantly, the shakes and the burning behind your eyes, fusing your vision with reality and making your voice stop echoing round the rooms as if you were in the Grand Canyon. Just one drink, and all these stray ends would be pulled together and your mind diverted from its misery into considering the possible pleasures of the day.

Mrs Taylor flopped into a chair. 'I can't cope, doctor.'

I went down to have lunch. Brian was sitting with Alex, the new Greek inmate, and I joined him.

'You read Rosie's life story, then?' Alex asked Brian, looking at me.

Brian considered this for a moment. 'She's seen more ceilings than Michelangelo.'

I watched the door of the dining room waiting for Taylor to appear, pour his usual glass of apple juice and shuffle over to sit down. He didn't come and I assumed that he had gone to bed.

When the story finally emerged, disordered and fragmented in its telling, it was several hours later and Taylor had gone. Carol pieced it together. 'Taylor finally agreed to come in just for three days, just to dry out. Then he started panicking that he hadn't got pyjamas or slippers, or a toothbrush. You know he can't stand not to have everything just so.' She looked embarrassed. 'Well, Mrs T. went off to Peter Jones to buy the stuff, the doctor went to see a patient and I went to have lunch. Taylor said that he would just sit in the lounge as he was feeling too ill to come down to the dining room. Hell, he seemed OK, resigned to the fact.'

The moment Carol's back was turned, Taylor had got up, walked downstairs into the sunshine, and across the street. Half an hour later, his distraught and angry wife found him seated at a corner table in the Potter, empty glass in hand, a tough and contented look on his face.

'Ann, I simply refuse to go back there. There's absolutely nothing you can do,' he said. 'So you might as well sit down and have a drink as well, since I'm not going home until I've had a few more.'

Ann did sit down, and they spent the remaining hour till closing time drowning their private and separate sorrows, he in vodka and she in gin. She then drove him home, complete with the new pyjamas and washing kit. The whole incident had passed off so quickly and predictably that we were soon laughing. To Brian, Taylor's determination not to listen to his wife was cheering. He felt the old boy would be much happier that way than ending his days playing a sober door-mat.

The ability to find the saddest situation funny was not uncommon. We'd all been in appalling scrapes at some point or another in our drinking careers and the stories, though often macabre and scary, were hilarious. Brian's worst debacle had occurred while he was Christmas shopping in New York. Loaded with parcels he'd tripped on an escalator. His tie caught between two stairs, dragging him upwards while simultaneously throttling him as the material was eaten up by the grind of the machinery. He was two bottles of vodka to the good at the time, effervescent with Christmas bonhomie. It took him several moments to realise that he'd probably be dead if something didn't happen before the escalator reached the top and turned over on itself.

He was saved in the nick of time. Someone pressed the emergency stop button and he landed like a fish on the top of the stairs, with just enough leeway round his neck to breathe. We often used to wonder why on earth we weren't all dead. By the laws of averages we had had more than our fair share of luck.

One night we were sitting up on the terrace when Anne turned to Shelagh and asked her how many clinics she'd been in.

'Three,' said Shelagh.

Anne looked triumphant. She had been in six. Taylor in four.

'You could write an Egon Ronay guide to good alcoholic homes,' I suggested. 'Four stars if it's near a pub, like this one, no stars if it's way out in the country. Food, facilities, gullibility of nursing staff, room service, laundry charges, endless things.' I warmed to the subject. The book never got off the ground, but we'd talk about it often, and the idea entered our jargon when anyone referred to other homes. The Charter was good on food, fair on rooms and cleaning services, low on facilities (the jacuzzi bust again), irritating because of the nutcases from the third floor, but excellent for access to the outside world and the off-licence, and for hiding places for any patient who wanted to bring in booze.

Drinking in a clinic always seemed to me to be the height of insanity. Far better and more comfortable to go to a hotel and hole up there, I'd said to Anne, when Shelagh had confessed that she'd been bribing a third-floor schizophrenic to bring her vodka which she hid behind the bathtub. Even after considerable pressure from the nurses, Shelagh never revealed her source.

But there was little the staff could do, anyway. As Carol said, 'We can't go and search everyone's room every day. We look at their bags when they come in, but that's it. You have to trust people.'

On the whole the system worked; but not with Cherry. After six days she was beginning to look a little better.

No shakes, no tremors, but still rather green despite an extraordinarily fast change of attitude which followed confessions about her home life, her husband's recently deceased father, his lost job, his interest in other women. Rejected, completely dependent on her husband, Cherry'd come into the clinic after a couple of stays in National Health beds, threatened with the end of her marriage if she didn't shape up.

On her fourth day, she announced that she knew she was

an alcoholic, knew she had to stop drinking, and more to the point, knew that she could.

'I'll never touch the stuff again,' she pronounced vigorously, 'I've got one last chance and I'm going to take it.' The doctor looked sceptical. I wondered whether she'd seen some magic light overnight. Her schedule of recovery was out of line with everyone else's. 'That's fine, Cherry,' he said, 'how are you going to cope on your days without booze?' She had it all worked out; she was going to write a book, get a part-time job to give her financial independence, take cookery classes, learn gardening, go to keep-fit classes, and take up dressmaking so that she could improve her wardrobe on a limited budget. It was a fantastic programme.

Three days later, I sat down beside her at breakfast, noticed her eyes red with weeping and asked what was wrong. 'Nothing,' she sniffed, producing a grubby hanky and dabbing ineffectually at her eyes. I shrugged and didn't pursue it.

Cherry was late to the group therapy session, and when she finally came in, she looked even more tearful. The skin round her eyes was so puffed up that they had almost disappeared beneath the fleshy folds. Like a drunken whale, I thought. She sat in silence, twisting her handkerchief backwards and forwards. Finally she coughed and leant forwards. 'I've got something to tell you.' Her voice was little more than a whisper. 'I've been drinking.'

The doctor started. 'When? Last night? This morning?'

'No, all the time.'

'You mean from when you arrived, Cherry?'

'Yes, I brought it in a suitcase.'

'What did you have?'

'Beer.'

'How much?'

'Twenty-four large cans of Special Brew.'

A whole suitcase of beer! Even Shelagh looked impressed.

'I've just run out,' added Cherry miserably, though this fact was by now patently obvious.

The doctor frowned.

'Didn't any of you notice?'

'No one knew what Cherry was like sober,' said Anne. 'How was anyone supposed to tell the difference?'

'Didn't you smell it?' We all looked at each other, feeling like children who just failed an exam. 'Why didn't someone look at her luggage?'

The nurse simpered. 'I don't know. I'm not sure who was on duty at the time.'

Buck-passing was not going to appease him. 'I want a staff meeting after lunch.'

Everyone gazed at Cherry with awe. From being a shambling faded blonde she had suddenly assumed heroic proportions. She burst into a fresh bout of weeping and got to her feet. 'I feel awful,' she said. 'I want to go to my room.'

One of the questions raised as a result of Cherry's drinking in the clinic was whether or not the patients should take abstem or antabuse while in treatment. Disulfram, the anti-booze drug, comes in two forms: antabuse, and abstem, a milder version of the same chemicals. The pills are taken daily and produce no noticeable side effects – though research at King's College, London, has shown that they build up negligible quantities of toxins in the liver. If you drink on top of them then all hell is let loose, and heavy drinking while taking antabuse can result in death if you suffer from a dicky heart. Both Shelagh and Taylor had drunk while taking the pills and had sworn never to attempt such madness again. The pills, taken daily, build up in the body: reactions will occur for up to ten days after taking antabuse, and up to three days after taking abstem.

To sneak such a drug into someone's breakfast cup of tea, as desperate spouses have been known to do, is very dangerous.

At Phil's clinic in the States, patients were put on to one or the other of the drugs the moment they were detoxified. He recommended that they continue for a year. There was no such procedure in the clinic, mostly because there were mixed feelings about the drugs themselves. A cop-out is the verdict of most Alcoholics Anonymous members, who consider that real sobriety cannot be achieved while the ex-drinker resorts to any form of chemical help. We didn't hold such strong views, but we did think that we wanted to do it alone, without help. On the other hand, as Brian said, they were the only pills, the only concrete help in fact, that the medical profession has devised to keep people off booze. But somehow it seemed pathetic to fill yourself up with lethal chemicals when all that was needed was willpower to keep your hand from the bottle.

I changed my mind when I realised that I was using the word willpower again. Using my willpower to control my drinking had not worked.

'You have to remember too,' the doctor had said, 'that if you're taking abstem and you stop taking them for some reason, like "accidentally" forgetting, then you're holding the stable door open for drinking, you're allowing that chance to arise.'

Later on, after I was away from the clinic and editing the ex-patients' magazine, I wrote a piece about taking abstem and had compared it to using anti-nailbiting products. The day I decided to give up biting my nails, at the age of thirty, I went and bought every vile-tasting product available and used them liberally for the next two months. The result is that today I don't bite my nails – but I never felt guilty about using a crutch.

Abstem, when taken regularly, removes the possibility of drinking, and in the first months without booze that's a blessing.

I confided to the doctor that another reason I was reluctant to take them was the fear that I'd want to try out the effects; play Russian Roulette with those innocent-looking white tablets. He'd cocked his eyebrows at me and said, 'Well, I know your style and your habit of trying out everything, but you're not that much of a lunatic, are you?'

His advice was to listen to a few more stories, learn from someone else instead of always having to learn everything the hard way.

When Shelagh drank on antabuse, she felt a similar rebelliousness. 'What the fuck, I thought, I'm desperate for a drink and the doctor might be conning me completely. They might be Smarties for all I knew. I'd been taking antabuse for about three weeks, so the pileup in my system was considerable. I drank half a bottle of vodka, fast. I remember that I couldn't breathe, that I seemed to be dying. Then the next thing, it was twenty-four hours later and I was in an intensive care unit. I'm not even sure what they did to me, because I was so frightened at having almost died that I didn't want to talk about it. I was just lucky that a doctor lives next door. He knew what to do.'

Shelagh's reaction was very extreme. The effect of a drink after taking a single abstem pill is fairly mild, though decidedly

unpleasant: red face, galloping blood pressure and vomiting –
a sufficient deterrent to most people.

Life in the clinic was starting to make me irritable. 'A sure
sign,' said Alice, 'that you ought be leaving.'

The feeling that I had more or less got what I could from
the place was growing. The group therapy was now repetitive, the confinements of institutional life irksome. I'd given
up going to the community meetings for the past few days
and had been taken to task by the head of Occupational
Therapy.

'But they're so bloody stupid,' I said to him crossly as he
waylaid me in the corridor. He looked annoyed, so the following morning I stayed on after breakfast instead of beating
my usual retreat back to my room and my typewriter. The
subject under discussion was where to take the third-floor
lunatics for their weekly outing. The suggestions veered from
the mundane, a trip round the Royal Hospital Gardens, to
the ludicrous, a visit to the massage parlours in Soho. No
one bothered to read the papers to find out what was going
on in the vicinity. The other problem was transport, since in
the past patients had been lost on the tube if the expeditions
entailed travelling anywhere out of walking distance.

'I want to go to the antiques show,' pronounced a middle-
aged woman called Anna. The staff looked sceptical. Anna
was a kleptomaniac who only avoided prison sentences by
going into nuthouses and convincing magistrates that she
was working on the problem. A large antique fair would provide good pickings. However, the rest of the inmates were
moderately enthusiastic and the antiques fair had the advantage of being only a couple of hundred yards away.

Anne, Shelagh and I were sitting to one side, downing

black coffee and adding to the smoke-laden atmosphere. 'Are you going to come?' one of the staff said.

'No,' came the answer. The staff looked despondent. The day was beginning particularly badly for me. The night before I'd had the first of what were to become a series of nightmares about booze. In the dream I'd been driving along a country road. It was very early on a summer's morning and the sky was growing lighter. I think I was coming home from a party, and at one point in the dream there had been someone in the passenger seat of the car. Sudden wailing sirens filled the air. I pulled the car over to the side of the road, expecting the cop car to pass, but it had skidded into the kerb in front of me. A swaggering policeman stepped out, an American policeman, although the road was definitely English. He wore a gun in the holster around his waist.

'Been drinking then?' he said, looking in through the window. My hands were shaking. I was sweating. Even in dreams I'm terrified of the law.

'No, my friend can tell you that.' I turned to the friend who had vanished.

The cop began to laugh, huge bellows emanating from his stomach making his copious flesh shake like jelly.

'Hey Joe, we've got one here,' he shouted back to his companion. 'Says she hasn't been drinking, says to ask her friend, and look, there's no friend. Out,' he shouted, yanking the door handle.

'Breathalyse me,' I begged. 'Honestly, I haven't had anything to drink.'

He started to laugh again, and the laughter kept on coming, interspersed with 'You're drunk,' 'You're drunk,' 'You're drunk.'

'But I'm an alcoholic,' I screamed back, tears pouring

down my cheeks. 'I don't drink, I can't drink, don't you understand.'

I'd woken up with the words still on my lips: 'I'm an alcoholic.' I was shaking, wet with perspiration, and my heart was pounding.

I hadn't felt like this since Cyprus. I lit a cigarette with trembling hands. My dream was only a moment away, just as the bottle, and all that would probably go with it, was only a swallow away. The room felt confining. The ghastly orange picture glared down at me, full of menace. Its pseudo-pastoral qualities seemed to mock my attempts to save my life.

'You're a nut, you're a loony, once a drunk always a drunk, there'll always be people like those cops who will never believe you, you'll be the victim of suspicion for ever.'

'But that's a good sign,' said the doctor later in the day, when I told him about the nightmare. 'It means you're starting to accept your alcoholism subconsciously. It's common. You can expect the dreams to go on for some time.'

The dream was to recur frequently over the next three months. The variations on the theme were slight. I always awoke, my face creased in tears and my body sweating as though in the grip of alcohol withdrawal, grappling with the fact that someone, usually a policeman, did not believe that I was sober.

'You're drunk, you're drunk!' would echo through dream corridors and reverberate into waking like the clanging of a church bell or the sound of the Muslim priests, calling the early-morning prayers from a mosque and clattering into my sleep on countless Arabian dawns.

FOURTEEN

'Wanted: Editor for Arabic woman's weekly. Salary: eleven thousand pounds p.a. tax free, all expenses paid. Minimum age 30.' The advertisement in *The Times* caught Rosie's mother's eye; she cut it out, consulted Charles and pursued the matter with her daughter.

Six weeks later, in mid-January of 1977, Rosie and Betty were in Libertys carefully selecting a suitable suit for the interview.

Rosie was astonished that her application had even been considered, let alone that she had passed the first round. For a start, she was still only twenty-five. Two days before she had attended a preliminary interview at the North London headquarters of Lord Thomson's international newspaper empire.

Lord Thomson's representative looked like a former army officer who had spent three decades destroying his physique over expense account lunches. He was benign, almost paternal. Rosie thought at first that he fancied her, then concluded that the human warmth was generated by neither alcohol nor sexual desire. It was as if he were sorry for her: it should have made her suspicious.

'I'll put you in the picture,' he began. 'To be frank, they're an odd bunch. Not at all what you'd expect.'

Rosie found herself wondering what the kindly inter-
viewer believed her expectations might be. It was clear
already that he would recommend her for the job. He had
said, in effect, that she was 'one of us', by assuming that she
shared his own approach to the Kuwaitis. She had no
approach – she scarcely knew where the place was.

'We were in the process of buying the magazine ourselves
and then the Government suddenly told us to forget it.
They're no longer letting foreigners buy anything, now
they're so bloody rich themselves. I gather they're nervous
because so many Palestinians have moved in and begun running the show. So we're left acting as agents – we said we'd
find them someone, it's good PR for the future.'

'What exactly are they looking for?'

'Who knows what goes on in their heads? But I'll tell you
one thing.' He leant confidingly across the desk. 'Forget all
that stuff about the noble Arab – sheiks, hawks, hospitality,
old-world manners, all that. They're not like that any more.'

'But what *are* they like?'

'Well, just between us, they seem just like the old-fashioned wogs, the kind who tried to sell you dirty postcards in
Suez. Crooked as they come, sly, predatory, dirty-minded,
devious, precisely like your old-time wog. Only difference is
nowadays they've got money coming out of their ears.'

He had seemed surprised that she still wanted the job. As
she left he said, 'And the best of British luck – don't say I
didn't tell you they're, well, an odd bunch.'

In honour of their supposed oddity, Rosie and her mother
chose a blue velvet suit of classical severity. Shoes and match-
ing handbag were lent by Anna Raeburn, a friend serving as
Agony Aunt on *Woman* magazine, and therefore in funds. Thus
attired, Rosie turned up to meet her prospective Arab boss.

Fauzi was chubby but dressed to kill: biscuit suit with blue pin-stripes; darker blue shirt; Gucci shoes; a watch and a ring worn on the little finger of his left hand that both seemed hewn out of fair-sized gold nuggets. As the magazine was in Kuwait, Rosie assumed Fauzi must be a Kuwaiti national. Later she learned that it wasn't so simple. Nothing was. Fauzi in fact hailed from Iraq. 'Why do you want the job?'

Rosie improvised, giving a list of jobs in the past. A Chinese girl (girl-friend? secretary?) sat elegant as a cat in cream silk and diamonds. When Rosie said 'My career structure has been unorthodox', she made a note in a black leather book. On the tube Rosie had examined the latest issue of *Harper's and Queen*, memorising the major display ads. When asked about advertising, she ran through her list and said these were the kind of products they should go for.

Fauzi listened attentively enough. But it was only when he asked, 'You've read *The Oil Sheiks*?' that something in his tone gave Rosie a clue. This was the only question that really mattered.

In fact it was more of a statement than a question. At the time Rosie assumed that he had taken it for granted that anyone applying for such a job would have read the recent bestseller claiming to expose the Arab world. Later she realised his assumption stemmed from a truly stupendous belief in his own, and his race's, self-importance. But she hadn't read the book for the simple reason that she never thought she stood a ghostly of getting the job.

'I've met Linda Blandford,' she said finally, figuring that this might deflect attention from her ignorance. 'She wrote a story about me when I started *Spare Rib*.'

Now Fauzi looked positively enthusiastic.

'She was rather rude about me.' And gambling on her hunch, 'Just as she was about the Arabs,' she said.

Fauzi beamed. 'Terrible, terrible . . . what she did, taking all our hospitality and our generosity. You know, I know people in Kuwait whom she wrote about and she never even met them. Shocking. It's not that we minded her being a Jew . . .'

'I'll have a vodka on the rocks, please,' she smiled at the air hostess.

'Sorry, only Pepsi or Seven-up.'

Christ, the airline was dry too, she thought, regretting that she hadn't packed a small bottle in her handbag. It was two months after that first meeting, she was on her way to Kuwait and she was dead nervous. A drink was definitely in order. She thought back to her friends in England, how amused and pleased they'd been that she was going to a dry country. She was pleased too, and figured that Kuwait's dryness must have figured in Betty's enthusiasm. How else to explain why a mother would encourage a single daughter off into the heart of the Arab world? The boozing had been steadily increasing and Rosie welcomed the chance to see how she did without it. Welcomed, too, the chance to see if she could really hack things alone. Bar Fauzi, she didn't know a soul in the desert country.

He was waiting at the scruffy airport, Gucci and Savile Row replaced by a white dishdasha (traditional male Arab dress), which tastefully concealed his paunch. Inside his brown Cadillac the air-conditioner hummed, cutting through the stifling heat and dust of the atmosphere. She stared out of the window at the first sight of her new home. It wasn't inspiring. Wrecked cars littered the highway. Houses rose like ghosts out of the flat desert. Trees huddled in clumps, growing well in the clement spring weather. By July they would have fried.

They turned off on to a bumpy road which wound between a forest of apartment blocks. Left, right, right, left.

'Do I have an address?' she asked as the elevator chugged upwards. 'No . . . a box number. Far easier,' Fauzi said, and opened the door into a little apartment. Beige lino covered the floor and an ugly brown nylon three-piece suite squatted by the naked window.

'You will make this nice?' Fauzi muttered, a shade anxiously.

'Did you choose this furniture?' Rosie asked. It was a far cry from his smart penthouse overlooking Hyde Park.

'No, Tarek – the advertising man. He did.' But this admission, although attesting to Fauzi's taste, confirmed the fact that he'd never set foot in the place before.

'Do you want a drink?'

She nodded, sitting down on the sofa and easing off her yellow high-heeled sandals. The heat was already making her feet swell. Fauzi disappeared out of the door and reappeared moments later with a half of Gordon's.

'Gin? But I thought . . .'

'Well, it's not always easy to get,' he said pompously, going into the kitchen to fetch some glasses. 'Tonight's something of a celebration, isn't it?'

'Not always easy to get . . .' She was to remember that over the next two years, as she poured sugar, blackberries, yeast and water into dustbins, brewing up her local speciality called Rat.

She sipped the gin. The spirit bit into the panic and she grinned. No one could say it wasn't an adventure.

A driver collected her at eight the following morning in a beaten-up, un-airconditioned Toyota with bust springs. Fauzi's comfy Cadillac was nowhere in sight when they pulled up outside the low office buildings in the heart of the city's industrial zone.

The Thomson man was right, she thought. The place was a shambles. Fauzi rolled in at two and summoned her across the courtyard to his palatial office. 'How have you got on?'

She glared at him. 'How do you think? No one speaks English. You know I don't speak Arabic. The office is a mess and the bathroom's a health hazard.'

'Always in a hurry,' he mumbled, reaching for the phone. 'There – it's all fixed,' he said a few moments later. She bit back the comment that so far, less than twenty-four hours into the job, everything he'd talked about in London had failed to come true. The apartment, the beaten-up car, the language problem – all, he had assured her, would be the tops.

But within a week, the office had been cleared and knocked into an open-plan design, the bathroom replaced. Carpets were fitted in the apartment. Her translator, an obsequious, obese Egyptian woman called Efat, who had previously taught English, turned into an ally.

Fauzi bristled in and out of the country, full of advice about French fashion (when he'd just returned from Paris), American sofa beds and Korean cooking. The staff were frightened of him, of his hot temper, his accusations of slacking. Rosie didn't know what they thought of her, until the day when Efat pointed out that someone had run a caption under a picture of a chimpanzee which said, 'Rosie, Bahrain's famous ape'. She looked at the snap, looked at Efat's worried face and started to laugh. In minutes the whole office was laughing. The reviews editor invited her to an Arabic play, another journalist sought her advice on an article, and Tarek, the advertising manager, suggested lunch at his home. No one ever confessed to the misprint.

'What's the hardest thing you have to handle?' The question was asked by a Rumanian journalist whom Rosie was meeting for the first time over breakfast in the Sheraton Hotel.

'My age,' she replied, unhesitatingly. 'I expected it to be my sex, but since I don't work at something the Arabs consider important like banking – it doesn't matter.

'There's such value placed on the wisdom of years! I have to do everything myself, at least once, just to prove that I'm not so inexperienced.'

Alina was big and old-fashioned. Her hair was grey, neatly parted to the right, and she wore a floral blouse and plain straight skirt. She'd defected from Rumania to America five years earlier and was in Kuwait with her architect husband.

'What do you think of Arab women?' she asked, between mouthfuls of buttered croissant.

'Hard to know. I had lunch with someone called Nawal the other day. She's got a good job in the health ministry, but what she talked about was the disaster of her arranged marriage. She asked her father for permission to meet the intended for tea, hated him on sight and said no. She says the whole family has lost face and that she'll probably never marry now.'

'They have money, freedom to travel, flashy cars, good education and they've always had equal pay. But rights in love . . .?'

'Yes, the reverse of England or America. You could have fifty illegitimate children there but no equal pay. Can you imagine an illegitimate child here?'

'It wouldn't happen. If it did, you'd be locked up in the women's quarters for ever. But what do you plan to do?'

'Sort out the censorship first. We were banned the second week I was here for running photos of the garbage problem in the city. So dumb . . . they trashed the issues and added to the problem.'

'I'll take you to meet Salman, the Minister of Information. He's a good friend of mine. Do you want a series of articles on divorce and children's rights when families split up?'

'Can you get them through the ministry?' Rosie asked.

'Yes . . . Salman's a chicken. He likes pretty girls to come and have tea with him.'

Rosie laughed. 'Will he accept pictures of how to feel your breasts for cancer? Fauzi said we'd never be able to run them.'

'You bet,' Alina answered. 'But it may take seven visits for tea.'

Their first joint assignment was interviewing the Egyptian doctor and writer, Nawal Sadawi. She had long been involved in trying to halt the barbaric custom of clitoridectomy, still carried out in Egypt and extensively practised in the Sudan. Sadawi advocated the complete overthrow of traditional Arab culture. 'A necessity before anything will improve at all for women.'

Fauzi read the interview. 'We cannot use this,' he said to Rosie over the phone. 'It's too strong. It's not true.'

'I'm not going to argue about its truth. The point is, she's important, what she says will make people think.'

'But Rosie, we are a family magazine. Not political.'

'Salman says it's OK. Actually he thinks it's interesting.' Rosie played her trump card, hating Fauzi for making her resort to it. As an Iraqi – a foreigner like her – he couldn't condemn the view of the Minister of Information.

'Oh, well.' He sounded angry. 'I suppose Alina thought of it?'

'No, we did it together.'

He didn't want to blame his protégée; he would blame Alina instead. 'Magda won't like it.' He hung up. Magda, the owner of the magazine, was away in Florida, where she owned two houses. Rosie knew that Fauzi's livelihood depended on her. Kuwait society consisted of sixty per cent foreigners, ruled by the minority. Each level revered the one above, despised the one below. The Kuwaitis looked down on the lot, permitting only a few chosen foreigners into their homes. Fauzi had given her one helpful piece of advice when she first went to Kuwait. 'If you want to get to know the Kuwaitis steer clear of the British community.'

She had no trouble following his advice. The British community, mostly second-rate, homesick and full of petty criticisms of the Arabs, clustered together round their barbecues and home-made brews and swopped wives and mortgage stories to pass the time. They resented the Kuwaitis because they were never asked to their homes, and resented Rosie because she was. In her first summer she had a brief affair with an English banker; like herself, a single oddity in a community of couples, he had introduced her to a crowd of rich, single, playboy Arabs, who accepted her as a friend and took her along on boating trips and desert picnics.

She made friends as well with a Kuwaiti woman called Lulwa who ran the local art gallery and children's bookstore.

Lulwa was beautiful. Thick black hair surrounded a classically perfect face, and fell to her waist. She had studied at London University, returning to Kuwait in 1972. By '76 she had retreated from campaigning, resigned from the Ministry of Education and opened her bookstore and art gallery. The year before she'd arranged for Andy Warhol to exhibit in the main government gallery.

'Once I thought I could change conditions for women here. Not any more.' Lulwa was sitting on the edge of the swimming pool. It was after lunch at her mother's house, a traditional weekly family gathering. The meals were delicious; spiced meats and fish, rice and jappatis, eaten very quickly with fingers. Rosie was invited every Thursday and treasured the invitations.

'Why?' Rosie was lying in the pool, sipping a campari and soda.

'No one will listen. No one takes you seriously. All I can do is what I do – sell non-sexist children's books from Sweden. As an outsider, you have more chance. At least you don't have a position to maintain.' Lulwa's position was a topic she rarely talked about though the rest of Kuwait did.

When she first returned from London full of zeal and a fast line of Western chat, she'd stuck out in her bohemian clothes and flamboyant jewellery. She was already in her thirties in 1972. After her student life in London no Kuwaiti would seriously consider her as a wife, though her pedigree was impeccable. The years took their toll. Lulwa, and Rosie was to notice the process over the next two years, withdrew physically from the world. Spending time with her family, venturing less into the fray, worn down and battered by never being listened to, by toeing a line over which, in another time and country, she had stepped.

But Lulwa was wrong, at least over one crucial element. Rosie did have a position to maintain, and the more she and the Arabs got to know each other, the more complicated it became. Fauzi wanted her as pet and protégée. The Arabs

wanted her as an asset to their drawing rooms. The Brits
wanted her at their parties because she was well known.

At a dinner one night she met a Lebanese businessman of
high standing in the community, witty, urbane, attractively
grey. Jean was in his late fifties, successful, a longtime Kuwait
resident. He invited her to dinner. She arrived to find she
was the only guest.

Oh, well, she thought, as she sat down, accepting Scotch
and soda, I can quiz him for my *Financial Times* article. As an
immigrant and right-hand man to the mayor of the city, Jean
was in a unique position; a foreigner with real access to power
and influence, with the subtlety to understand the complicated social structure which operated in the country. 'The
Kuwaitis aren't such fools as people think,' he would say. 'No
foreigner gets seriously rich here. They don't allow it.'

Rosie gazed round the apartment, at the huge marble
coffee table, surrounded on three sides by Roche Bubois
sofas, the fourth opening on to a spectacular view across the
Gulf.

'But you're not doing too badly,' she hazarded with a grin.

'Nothing – not on their scale at least. You know Mustapha
H? He accepted a bribe of twelve million dinars this year,
and that's a regular occurrence.' Jean downed his drink and
flicked his fingers for the uniformed butler to serve the
dinner: a selection of delicacies, prettily arranged on fine
bone-china plates.

They munched away in silence. Jean was no longer the
easy conversationalist. 'I want to sleep with you,' he suddenly announced. Rosie shook her head, trying to turn the
issue into a joke. He began fidgeting under his white robe.
Suddenly he lifted up the skirt, exposing a swollen penis.
Grasping it in his hand, he masturbated furiously for a few

seconds. She wanted to run but couldn't take her eyes off the spectacle. He came in great flying globs, which spattered, sticky and white, across a plate of fried brains.

She arrived home half an hour later, shaking; glad, not for the first time, that she now had a tenant. William was an Englishman, doing business in the Gulf. His wife had just left him, he'd been temporarily homeless and was renting Rosie's spare room. She told him the story. He laughed and, finally, so did she.

'But don't they pick you up all the time?' he said.

'No, out here they're too concerned with face to be as pushy as we all imagined in London. One refusal is usually enough. None of those horrors you hear about in England.'

'Do they still think you're plotting your own version of *The Oil Sheiks*?'

'Not so much. To start with everyone asked me that. You know, what Blandford really missed in that book was the danger of this country. The feeling of being in their control. Ugh, I hate it.'

She poured another Scotch. Jean had offered two bottles: she hadn't turned down the gift. Booze was hard to come by, and home brews disgusting.

When she first arrived, she hadn't wanted to drink. The newness was exciting, compensatory. But now, as her fears started to rise, booze turned back into a trusty friend. There was a layer of hypocritical craziness in the country with which, because she was barred from reporting it, she felt she was colluding. Like Jean's sexual frustration; like the lot of Lulwa and the double standards applied to women. In the early summer she'd been to a high-society wedding. The main party consisted of two thousand women, dressed to the nines, with diamonds and sapphires sparkling on Dior and Balmain. No men were present. The women danced wildly, the sexual ripples unconcealed beneath the silk, releasing desires for glamour into this giant harem.

Waiters, hovering with trays of orange squash, might have been eunuchs for all the attention they were paid. As a spectacle it was riveting; as a symptom of a segregated, repressed society it was disheartening.

Just before Christmas, Rosie and two staff reporters were invited to compile a Bahrain issue of the magazine. The trip had been under discussion for weeks: the red tape interminable. Fauzi was excited and kept ringing her up with exhortations to 'go in and show them how to do it'. His manic enthusiasm rapidly turned what promised to be an interesting trip into an ordeal of perfection.

Two days before she was due to go she got drunk; rip-roaringly drunk and out of it for two days. The bender began with a wish just to dull her tension and flew out of hand somewhere between the third and fourth glass. Thirty hours later William was shaking her awake, saying she had to be at the airport at noon.

'God, what have I done?'

'Don't you remember? You were crying, yelling . . .'

Rosie shook her head. Waves of fear swept over her. Drunk, in a dry Muslim country.

'Why do you drink like that?' William's face was full of concern. He was thirty-four, slender, the product of an upper-class English home. His face was unlined; indicative of a life which has left no traces. She looked at him miserably, wondering, as she always did when wallowing in hungover self-hatred, where her life had gone wrong.

'Is it your work?'

'Yes and no. Oh, the job is hard, sometimes it seems like I'll never make it work. Fauzi is impossible – expects me to do everything with no money, expects me to be his perfect little editor, never to put a foot wrong. And, I'm the darling of all these boring old Brits. Try as I might, I can't avoid them. Even the ambassador likes me. Called me a useful product for our country, the other day. Product, product . . . fuck that.'

'But you're very popular,' William murmured, lighting her cigarette as she was too shaky to manage it herself. 'You're asked to every party.'

'Yes, and you know why,' she said viciously. 'Because no one knows what to make of me. I'm the only single girl in the country who's not working for an airline. The men can't take it because I earn as much as them, the women are jealous because they think I'm going to pinch their husbands. They all wonder whether I'm fucking the Arabs. But they ask me. I have curiosity value. Christ, the office . . .'

'It's OK, I went there yesterday morning and told them you were sick. I said you'd meet them at the airport.'

'Thanks. Thanks very much. I don't know what I'd do without you. I mean it,' she added, sensing that she'd sounded abrupt, almost sarcastic.

The flight down the Gulf was mercifully short. She hid her eyes behind dark glasses. They interviewed members of the government, members of the royal family, members of the women's groups. Rosie toured the countryside seeing homes for the handicapped, craft centres and model towns. She scribbled notes and dictated into her tape recorder. On the fourth day she got up at five and drove out on the Budaia road towards Budaia village.

She arrived at the remains of the fifteenth-century Portuguese Fort as the sun was starting to climb the sky. She slid down the edge of the pit to greet the heavily clad woman who was digging into the rock face with a trowel, carefully removing shards of earthen pottery. Sheika Hayya, an archaeologist and a member of the Bahrain royal family, was in her late sixties. Her agile, tough face looked as though it had seen as many tears as laughter.

They talked about her work and about the museum she was helping the government establish. Rosie asked her what she thought the problems were for the young women of the country.

'Romance,' Hayya replied. 'Western ideas of romance. Arab marriages, arranged marriages, are the right way for people to live. It's impractical to think that two people will love each other for ever. Hopeless. So we see it as a business. The parents know that their child will be happy with a man from the right family – they will have similar interests. Maybe they will have lovers. That's all right, but the marriage is a deal. Now people have these ideas of being in love with the man they marry. They demand it. And what happens? After a few years, they fall in love with someone else.'

Rosie shrugged. 'Maybe. But it seems wrong that people shouldn't choose whom they marry.'

Hayya wagged her finger. 'Just look at the divorce rate. Think of it in terms of unhappiness, unhappiness for the children, then ask yourself if love is really worth the price?'

'Well, do you agree with her?' Rosie put Sheika Hayya's scenario for the perfect marriage to Faisal. They were lying in her bed at three in the afternoon, both slightly drunk.

'My marriage was arranged, I'm not in love, I'm not getting divorced. But I can't say I'm that happy.' He rolled over on to his side, sliding his brown hand down her stomach.

Their affair had been going on since the spring, when the desert had suddenly come alive with flowers after the rains and the camping expeditions had begun in earnest. Kuwaitis took their camping so seriously, they even moved telexes and telephones out to their tents. Rosie had been invited on a hunting camping party, staying overnight in a private tent, one of a circle of black bedu tents around the central fire. A generator fuelled the fairy lights, the video machine and the fridge. Bollinger came with the roast lamb. Rolls-Royces hovered behind the tents; the seventies version of trusty camels.

Faisal had driven her home, and, soused on Chivas Regal, had pulled over to the side of the earth track, tumbled her out of the car and made love to her amid miles of yellow daisies. 'Are we good in bed?' he'd said, teasingly, his fine face hovering inches from hers. She'd nodded. Embarrassed, because it was true. His skin was palest brown, sleek like a wet otter. She'd fancied him for ages.

In Kuwaiti terms Faisal wasn't a rich man. He'd bought his house with the £50,000 government grant to which every citizen was entitled. He was employed by a downtown bank, handling foreign exchange.

'Why,' she wrote in her diary, 'do you have to go and fall for the poorest Arab you have encountered in this country?' and knew the answers. Faisal's energy matched her own. He drank too much, wept too much and did everything with passion, suddenness and total commitment. He decided he was in love with her and told her so while they drove back that day across the desert. He was restless about his life, his job, and his family; loyal to his friends, sharp with anyone who disagreed with him, and observant enough to see the mess his life was in.

'What do we do all the time?' he said to Rosie rhetorically.

'Go bathing, go water-skiing, get drunk, play cards, go to Beirut for the weekend, pick up girls . . . wallow in money. You, you outsiders, you're jealous of us, you want a piece of our action. You have an idea that we betrayed you, that we replaced all the simplicity you claimed to love – that Lawrence and Thesiger found in the desert – with materialism. Don't you see, it isn't worth shit.'

Faisal could remember growing up in a hut, and his mother walking to fetch the water. Now he drove a BMW and kept a jeep in the garage for visits to the desert. He owned suits as well as dishdashas. He loved Bob Dylan and the Rolling Stones.

They drank and got drunk. Fought and made up. Rosie panicked about the danger, about what would happen to either of them if somehow the affair came to light – prison for him, deportation for her. She went out with other people and Faisal sulked and groused in fits of jealousy. Finally he walked out, angry with her for having dinner with a Lebanese film director in the Hilton one night; angry because in small-town Kuwait the news reached him almost before they'd started on dessert.

Rosie wrote him a letter – short, apologetic, genuinely unhappy not to be seeing him any more, and hand delivered it to his bank.

Faisal arrived at the house at nine. Rosie was at home alone, sorting through a pile of magazines and clippings that had arrived that day from London.

Rao, the Indian servant, opened the door and showed him in, bowing obsequiously to the Kuwaiti.

'Faisal – you came. But you're wearing a suit.'

'I can't come here any more unless I do. I might be recognised. Why did you send that letter?'

'I wanted to talk to you – I didn't want you to just walk out like that.'

'Are you drunk?'

'No.'

'Thank God for that. I hate it when you drink and you drink too much.' He sat down on the sofa. 'Listen, I love you, but I want to be proud of you. I want to live with you, maybe one day even marry you.'

Rosie didn't want this. 'My job, Faisal,' she said slowly, 'Magda would destroy me . . .'

He turned her face round to his. 'You're lying. I know your face by now. Like a chameleon you change colour when you're not telling the truth. God, I must be mad. I spent all day alone on the boat, drinking, talking to myself, wishing you were there, playing games with the boat, like trying to chase bigger boats. I go home, shower, prepare my room. I want you, I want you in my home, and I've never wanted anyone there.

'We're different, I have to protect you. If ever, any time, day or night, you need me, you can't handle it, you are in danger, call me, and I will tear open my guts and put my flesh and body around yours. I don't care what state you're in.'

'Some part of me does love you, you know that, don't you?' she said.

He nodded. 'Come home with me – just tonight. I want you there . . . just once.'

She draped her head and body in yards of thin black silk, covered her face with a net mask, traditional to the Kuwaiti women. They drove through the night in silence.

'Take your shoes off,' Faisal said, 'leave them in the car.'

She padded along the corridors of the women's quarters,

following Faisal's directions. Holding her breath, excited and frightened, she wondered what she would do if they bumped into someone.

Safely in his bedroom, she threw off the veil. They made love with a silent frenzy, biting off cries which might awaken the household.

Rosie stayed till nearly five, then slipped out into the early dawn. Driving back through the still-deserted streets, Faisal was cocky. 'Now you know how all the Kuwaiti ladies have affairs,' he said, looking at her raven-like appearance. 'The more liberated they get, the more important it is to retain the veil.'

William and Rosie moved out of the little apartment and into a large villa. The brief spring brought dust-storms. The skies turned dull yellow and the fine particles of dust seeped through the doors and windows. If she didn't wash her hair every day her head itched. The whole city was tense.

In the office, tempers were short. Some days the dust clouds were so thick she could scarcely see across the court-yard. In Iran, the Ayatollah rallied against the Shah.

Faisal's emotional outburst closed the doors on a casual relationship. By May of 1978, when she was twenty-seven, Rosie was going out with five different people. Two Arabs, one Corsican, and two Englishmen. She was exhausted.

Fauzi had said she could fit her annual holiday in with the rest of the staff, but after she'd worked out the dates when the others planned to leave, she realised that she wouldn't be off till the end of the summer. Fauzi kept up an erratic sched-ule; while he was absent, Rosie consulted Magda.

Magda never came to the office, insisting Rosie came to her house if she wanted to see her. She lived in a large villa, surrounded by wispy trees. In the garden the water hoses worked all day, keeping the small lawn green and lush. Inside was a jumble of bad taste. Fake antique chairs, lavishly covered in gold chintzy fabrics, were arranged round ornate coffee tables. Shiny gold ornaments embedded with multicoloured stones perched on the sideboards.

Magda always covered her head. On the death of her husband, she had embraced the Mouhajabah movement.

Mouhajabah – literally the wearing of a head-cover – was an extreme reaction to the westernisation of the Muslim countries. An American friend of Rosie's called Sally, who was married to a Kuwaiti, explained its philosophy. 'A reaction to a deep sense of alienation. Not entirely spiritual. Women who become Mouhajabah are opting out of the materialist ratrace. Where I teach at the university, ten girls out of the fifteen in my class now wear the veil. They're young, pretty, sexy, and the veil removes them from sexual combat. It says, I'm not interested. And can't you see their confusion – they come from segregated homes and schools, suddenly into a mixed class. In one sense, wearing the veil says treat me as a person, not as a sex object.'

'What about the older women?'

'They've seen what has happened to the men in the country – the boredom, the schizophrenia that results when a whole society starts breaking all its religious mores. They're afraid. I don't think they know quite what they do want, but Mouhajabah gives them breathing space.'

Sally was large, overweight, with long mousy hair. She'd been married for ten years, spoke fluent Arabic and seemed, superficially, to be well integrated into the society.

'What they're really doing,' she continued, 'is taking themselves out of competition with Western women. Look, for the last twenty years, all they've been told is that Western women are the best, the brightest, the most beautiful. Arab men want them for wives . . . they want their women to copy them.'

'I heard a story – probably told by a man – that Mouhajabah women are cheaper to run. You know, now they don't want Dior clothes, and trips to Paris, and Italian repro furniture.'

Sally smiled wanly.

Magda vetoed an article on the Mouhajabah movement. 'Why?' asked Alina. They were all sitting uncomfortably on her upright, dainty little chairs, drinking revolting sweetened lemonade.

'It is not right to talk about these things.'

'But it's happening, it's important, and it's something we should discuss.'

'It's too personal and too political,' she said with finality, echoing Fauzi's words about Nawal Sadawi.

'That woman makes me so angry.' Alina swung her blue Buick out of the driveway and they headed back to the office. Rosie sighed. She knew that Fauzi did not like Alina, and was looking for an excuse to fire her. This run-in with Magda, which would be reported in detail to Fauzi, might be his excuse. And she didn't know what to do, trapped in the middle, with almost a full year of her contract to run. The last time she'd seen Fauzi, he'd mentioned to her that he had heard she'd been drinking too much. Rosie had thrown off his remarks, trying to turn them into a joke, but underneath, worrying, worrying, worrying. Who had he heard it from? Was it becoming a matter of gossip?

Lulwa at least was realistic about the gossip. 'What do you expect? What else is there to do but gossip?'

'Like any colonial outpost,' Rosie replied. 'It reminds me of some women I met in Hong Kong, too much time on their hands, their husbands having affairs. Nothing else to talk about but each other. But I understand it,' she added. 'I had dinner the other night with some journalists from the *Financial Times* and I felt so dumb, my conversation was so limited.'

Lulwa laughed bitterly. 'What do you think I feel like? By the way, what did Fauzi say about that piece you wrote for the *FT*?'

'How did you know?' Rosie stared at her. 'It wasn't under my name – my contract says I can't work for anyone else. Fauzi doesn't know.'

'Oh, doesn't he?' Lulwa replied, with raised eyebrows.

Fauzi did know. He stormed with anger. 'You have enough work to do here, or do you think you can lounge around at my expense and get drunk?'

In July he fired Alina. He left the job of conveying the news to Rosie. She went to Alina's house early the following morning and they drank gin and orange for breakfast.

'I ought to resign in protest,' Rosie said. 'My so-called authority is nothing but a myth.'

Alina shrugged. 'What to do? They have us over a barrel. We want their money, they hate us for that, we hate them for knowing. Everyone plays little games to pretend this isn't so, but it is. It's bloody ironic that you are one of the only people out here who came for the job not the cash.'

In the fifteen months that Rosie had been with the magazine the circulation had doubled. Unfortunately, Fauzi had been lying about the figure for so long that under 'improved management' they were still lying. As a consequence, where once he'd said it was 50,000 when it was 25,000, he now said it was 100,000 when it was, in reality, only 50,000.

Fauzi's exaggerations resulted in problems. The London office, through which a large number of the adverts were sold, persuaded a shampoo company to offer a free sample. Following Fauzi's boasting they asked for a hundred thousand sachets of shampoo to be shipped out to Kuwait. These duly arrived. Fifty thousand were sent out with the magazine and the rest were left to swelter in the sunshine. But not for long. Three things happened: the excess shampoo disappeared, samples started appearing in the souk and the Egyptian in charge of the print works bought a new Toyota.

In England at the end of August she spent two thousand pounds on clothes, finding solace in such extravagant consumption. Walking into St Laurent and dropping six hundred pounds in fifteen minutes felt like some kind of affirmation. She told her friends that life out in Kuwait was intriguing, trying to imply by her giddy stories that she was well on top of both her job and her life. She wanted to show, somehow, that she had changed in the last eighteen months, that she no longer drank excessively, that she was making tons of money, that she was glad to be away from London and the economic collapse.

Before she left she gave a party for sixty people where the champagne flowed and the smoked salmon was served up by neatly attired waitresses. She wore a gaudy St Laurent suit, and electric green shoes. She pulled her hair back from her face, painted her lips dark scarlet, and made up her eyes heavily. She was upset when an old boyfriend said she looked hard and businesslike and then realised that that was exactly what she did look like. Someone, renowned for his inability to handle booze and his unfailing ability to drink too much, was sick in the dustbin outside.

Rosie watched from the upstairs window, and passed fa-
cetious remarks about his drunkenness. But she couldn't
forget the last party she'd been at in Kuwait, when she'd
passed out on the sofa of a plush house, in full sight of thirty
people. Since she couldn't distort the picture to make the
truth any more palatable, she would try to erase it, criticising
the behaviour of others in the hope of salvaging her own.
Fauzi suggested an article about alcoholism in Kuwait and
the office in London sent a large bundle of press clippings.
Rosie read them feverishly, holding them down on her lap so
that the rest of the office could not see what subject had so
caught their editor's interest.

'Do you find yourself getting drunk for no reason, or
when you didn't mean to?' The question on the drink problem checklist jumped out and held her attention. Somehow,
its phrasing seemed to imply a leavening of responsibility, a
passing of the buck on to some mysterious force which was
out of her control.

'Do you make excuses for getting drunk, both before and
afterwards?' She ticked that question too, realising, as she
did so, that if the checklist was accurate, then she was certainly an alcoholic. But she pushed the term aside. It was too
gross to deal with, too frightening. More frightening than
the excessive drinking, more frightening even than the blackouts. Anxiety lived inside her like a caged animal. It was like
a spasm, a sudden twitch of the mind, a corresponding
twitch of the fingers, and then the presence of total fear.

William forgave and forgot. He never mentioned the times
when he drove her home from a party when she was too
smashed to drive herself. He covered up for her, inserting
himself into the worn fabric of her self-image like glue, holding the edges together while the inside continued to crumble

into confusion. She sensed that somehow she would never be whole in the way that William was. She wept at her deficiencies of character. She was twenty-seven and she felt old. She seemed to have travelled huge distances, both physically and emotionally, which had left her with scars and stories which no one really believed. Her reference points about emotional stress were way beyond others' ken.

William was out of Kuwait for nearly three months that summer, organising the English end of his business. On his first night back they drank a bottle of champagne. It seemed natural to go to bed.

'You know I love you, don't you?' William said. 'I really knew it during the summer, being away for so long. Missing you so much.'

'I love you too,' Rosie replied, knowing that she meant something entirely different. She loved William like the brother she had never had; a mate, a friend and a conspirator. She needed his friendship, his respectability. She loved him for those reasons, loved him because of and despite his overwhelming Englishness, which was suffocating yet reassuring in that foreign desert. She loved William's routines and neatness. His whisky and soda, punctually, at seven o'clock. His tidy clothes and crisply ironed shirts. His carefully cycled four pairs of Gucci shoes, worn one after the other to prevent undue wear and tear. The picture of his old Cambridge college on his desk. His unhappiness at missing the shooting season as winter drew in. It was very solid in the whirlwind.

Rosie used to watch William drink Rat; he could handle large quantities, but he also knew when to stop. She didn't. Some time into the third drink, or the fourth, she'd get carried away on a notion of her own power, a wish to maintain the high, and then there'd be loads more drinks and she'd be waking up the following morning, wondering how she got to bed.

On 16 January 1979, the Shah of Iran was finally deposed from the Peacock Throne. The British Embassy in Kuwait was beseiged with exiles, leaving the country via Iraq or arriving from Abadan, the oil town across the Gulf. They were full of tales of riots and rumour. The Shah's power had been non-existent for some weeks, but during his reign he'd survived *coups d'états* and rebellions. What had happened this time? Was he ill? Was he dying? No one knew. No one knew either how Khomeini, with his president, Bakhtiar, would manage. The returning Brits were scathing about the wild-haired, hysterical religious leader. 'He can't last,' they said. 'He hasn't a hope of uniting that vast country, all those tribes.'

Two days later Rosie smashed up her car. She was drunk. Rounding a bend near the house she went straight on to a larger road, ignoring the white line. She crashed into a Chevvy driven by a uniformed army sergeant, who was accompanied by a minor police official. No one was going fast and the damage to the sergeant's car was minor. Rosie's Toyota received the full weight of the impact on its nearside front wing, and the car was bent and buckled, the front axle hopelessly twisted.

By a million-to-one coincidence, William was driving towards the house at the moment of the crash, arriving within seconds of the collision.

They went to the police station. After half an hour, William had persuaded the police that she wasn't going to skip the country. He drove her home, then set off to rescue the Toyota. Rosie drank four glasses of Rat and passed out, welcoming unconsciousness.

She woke up the following morning, her head alarmingly

clear in the pale dawn light. The memory flooded back. She looked at her alarm clock: six-fifteen. Dare she wake William? She was in her own bed, he was in his. She got up and went to the kitchen and choked down a glass of Rat. What happened now? Her stomach lurched at the idea of prison. She made William a cup of tea, then went to his room to wake him. Her own company was intolerable.

He sat up in bed, rubbing the sleep from his eyes and drawing his fingers through his tousled hair.

'What will happen?'

William sipped his tea. She envied his steady hands and clear eyes. 'Ring up . . .' William said, naming a member of the royal family whom they knew. 'Tell him exactly what happened and get him to fix it. He can. But you must do it today, don't let your papers get to the central office. It's got to be stopped at a local level.'

Rosie nodded. 'You've got to do something about the booze . . .' He stroked her hair, brushing it behind her ear. 'It's not making you happy.'

He's mad to love me, Rosie thought, standing under the shower, hoping the cold water would make her feel better, hoping it would smash the glass wall which surrounded her, making the world feel distant and unreal. She stepped out of the shower and checked the time. Almost eight. She drank another small glass of Rat to steady her nerves and picked up the phone.

'It'll be OK, don't worry.' The rich Arab tones were reassuring. She dressed and collected her briefcase. The office need not even know, she thought. She had not been due in the previous afternoon, and she'd only be half an hour late this morning. The reason for the crash had to be kept from Fauzi, who was currently in England.

Fauzi arrived back the following week and knew the full story within a day.

'Rosie, why did you say you just forgot about the white line, that you just weren't concentrating?' His voice was stern. She sat twisting her fingers, reminded of schoolmistresses. 'Why didn't you tell him you were drunk?' She said nothing. 'Didn't you know I'd find out? You're my responsibility in this country, you're here on my invitation, my visa, and you do this and then not tell me?'

Fauzi ranted on, like an aggrieved lover. She was so dependent on people – on Fauzi, on William, on Kuwaitis for getting her off drunk-driving raps, on others for organising the installation of her phone, the renewal of her Kuwaiti driving licence. She didn't know any more which part of her she owned. 'Do you want to fire me, Fauzi?' she said, looking him straight in the eye.

'No,' he answered. 'I'm not going to renew your contract, though. I don't suppose you want me to?'

She nodded and wished that she'd managed to resign first.

William and Rosie retreated into domesticity. They went out less, and Rosie repeatedly turned down invitations from former boyfriends. Soon the phone stopped ringing. Life with William was secure, at least.

But his continuing devotion was a mystery. He always forgave her drunken excesses; he even forgave the Sheikh Ahmed debacle.

Sheikh Ahmed was a member of the royal family whose Negro features betrayed an ancestor's penchant for black slaves. Ahmed himself loved pretty Western women, especially blonde Californians.

Ahmed volunteered his assistance – in the form of customs clout – to odd Westerners wishing to smuggle suitcases of drink into the country. The first time William and Rosie worked the scheme it went off without a hitch. Barring two smashed bottles of gin, the liquor which they had bought in Bahrain was safely delivered to their house. Intending to supply their leaving party generously, they decided to operate the plan again. In Bahrain they packed the cases; one dozen gin, one dozen whisky, four boxes of Australian wine, and assorted bottles of rum, vodka and, for the Sheikh, three bottles of tequila.

The cases travelled freight; Rosie and William economy. Later in the day they rang the Sheikh who said that his henchman would make the pickup in the morning. Two days went by. They heard nothing. They rang again. Ahmed was vague and off-hand.

'Drunk,' said William. 'Damn him. I suppose he just can't resist a windfall like this.' The days passed. Ahmed's excuses wore thinner.

A junior diplomat at the British Embassy was hosting a farewell thrash. Both Rosie and William got drunk and, buoyed up on Dutch courage, decided to tackle Ahmed personally. During the previous week, he'd stopped even taking their calls.

Rosie remembered arriving at Ahmed's apartment block, riding up the escalator, and walking through the door. Ahmed was slumped in an overstuffed armchair, watching his video. The apartment was fussily furnished. The next thing she remembered was waking up in his bed. It was dawn. Sunlight fell across his mink bedspread, necessary in the chilly air-conditioning.

Ahmed snored beside her, black and shiny like a leather hunting boot. She slid out of bed, dressed and left the apartment. A bedu rattling past in a Japanese truck gave her a lift home.

William was awake and in a rage. 'Fuck you, fuck you . . . what the hell were you doing?'

She collapsed in tears. 'I don't know . . . I don't remember what happened.' Her head was splitting.

'I'm leaving. What do you think I feel like? I go and have a pee, come back and you've disappeared with him into his bedroom. When I try to get you out, his bloody henchmen throw me out, kick and punch me. My head hurts like hell, I think I've burst an eardrum, I'm bruised all over my ribs, my jacket's torn. I could have been killed – and so could you. And there's nothing we can do. Don't you understand?' He was shaking her shoulders. 'Nothing . . . he rules this country, we can't even murmur. But you're not my problem any more.'

'You can't go, you can't go . . . I can't live without you,' Rosie cried. In that awful moment, it seemed like the truth.

'Goddamn it. You don't love me. You never have.'

'I do. Honestly. It's just the booze.'

'Only the fucking booze. Fucking Ahmed has drunk it all. And there's not a thing we can do about it.' He paused. 'If I stay, will you cut down?'

A chink in the armour. Rosie worked on it with promises, as she was to do so many times over the next two years. William softened into forgiveness.

Two weeks later they were packing the Range Rover, preparing for the drive back to England.

By silent agreement, the incident entered the realm of things which were not spoken of, like Rosie's life in America, the Far East, or *Spare Rib*. William had been to the hospital, where the doctor had diagnosed a burst eardrum and a broken rib. At each jolt of the car over the bumpy desert roads, he winced. Neither of them had forgotten at all.

They didn't know as they drove along the Trans-Arabian pipeline, across northern Saudi Arabia towards Jordan, that an English nurse called Helen Smith had recently 'fallen' to her death from a Jeddah balcony. But when the news of that May 1979 drinks party hit the papers later in the year, along with the charges of a cover up which were being made by Helen's father, Ron Smith, Rosie started wondering.

The confusion and contradictions were such as to leave no doubt that people were lying. And there could, she thought, be only one reason. For a cover up of this magnitude, a Saudi royal, ranking equivalent of Sheikh Ahmed, must have been present at the party. The Dutchman, as Helen's boyfriend, must have tried to prevent the Sheikh's advances towards Helen. The Sheikh's bodyguards, probably drunk as well, would have dealt with him. Maybe they meant to kill him, maybe not. Nonetheless, Johannes Otten died that night. Silencing Helen, after sexually abusing her, would have been the next step.

Unless you've lived in a feudal Gulf state, Rosie well knew, it is almost impossible to comprehend the power wielded by the ruling families. A word in the ambassador's ear, and the cover-up would be on the road. She herself could have been Helen; William, Johannes. He too tried to protect her from a Sheikh, and who's to say what would have happened if his beating up had resulted in his body 'falling' from the fifth-floor balcony? Would the British Embassy in Kuwait have opened up the case, demanding justice? It seemed unlikely.

SEVENTEEN

I picked up the phone and dialled the number.

'Hi, you're back,' came the familiar tones of a close friend. 'How was Cyprus? Did you get my letters? Why didn't you send any postcards?'

I fluffed my answers.

'Lunch tomorrow?'

'Yes, fine, Joe Allen's at one o'clock.'

I put the phone down, still undecided about what I would say to this particular friend, who asked direct and blunt questions and who was not easily fooled. She worked as a gossip columnist; I was worried at the thought of becoming a useful piece of news to fill in dead airtime during dinner parties. I made some more calls. Half an hour later I had one lunch date, one party invite and two meetings for drinks. I was paralysed with fear.

While a part of me was longing to return to normality, the other part was scared – of confronting people, of picking up the strands of my work, of fending off the questions. Undecided too. I couldn't conceive of ever willingly telling someone why I didn't drink. I wanted to stick my head under the pillow and postpone it all. I could make the mental leap to life in a few months' time, and I could look backwards, but trying to project how returning to life would actually work out was almost impossible.

My worry though, I noted curiously, was not that I would drink. At least not in the immediate future. In group therapy that morning we'd discussed the question of confidence; how much was necessary, how much was dangerous.

'How much do you think you need?' the doctor asked me.

'Well, enough to know that you can cope, but not so much that you think you can handle drink again. Wary, but prepared to try anything.'

'What do you mean?' asked Cherry.

'Well, I know my life has got to change, and change for the better, but I don't intend to stay at home. I don't intend never to go to a party because I'm frightened I might drink.'

'Are you still worried about being bored without booze?'

'No, not so much being bored, I'm worried that I won't find excitement without it. I'm worried that I'll be duller.'

'Come on,' said Anne, 'you're not dull now, so why should you be dull outside?'

'I won't be on the right wavelength . . . left behind in sober respectability.'

I'd made a list in the second week of my stay in the clinic of all the practical problems I thought I would encounter. As I hadn't had a chance to try any out realistically, the list remained the same. Fear of looking weak headed the list. Second was fear of someone thinking that I was an alcoholic when I asked for soft drinks. Fear also of looking conspicuous at a dinner table, of being duller, of not being able to get pleasantly pissed on occasions, of never tasting good wine again. Two weeks on from writing that list, the second point was the one that worried me the most; and it connected up with the rest. How to say I'd been in the bin (if I ever admitted it, I thought at that point), how to say that I had been forced to lock myself up, gone temporarily stark raving loony. The other overriding fear was that my life, with or without booze, was a mess.

I knew that if I didn't do something constructive, I'd end up back on the booze. The dry drunk syndrome was one we had been hearing about. According to AA, many people who stop drinking are sustained only by the fact that they do not drink. No inner development takes place at all; the lying is still there, so is the irritability, so is the tenseness and disharmony. Working on the premise that life without booze must be better, people stop drinking and then wait for their world to improve, as though they are owed a favour for having made the supreme sacrifice of cutting out the sauce. To a small degree life does get better, because you are not actively making it worse all the time. But the dry drunk posture is impossible to maintain. Sooner or later, the dry alcoholic is going to say, 'Well, nothing has really improved, I'm more miserable without booze.'

AA changes people's lives by bringing them into a large circle, reckoning correctly that many alcoholics have lost their friends while drinking, and that the havoc of drink created a spiritual vacuum which needs to be filled. This was the special insight of AA's founder, Bill Wilson.

Wilson was born in New England on 26 November 1895. His father drank. Bill started to drink when he was in his late teens, immediately finding that alcohol gave him something he had been looking for; confidence, an inner glow and a quiet calm which verged on spiritual contentment. But his drinking went haywire and with it his life.

After a prolonged binge Bill found himself, for the third time, in Towns Mental Hospital, New York. He was terrified, and aware of needs which were beyond his powers of articulation. He saw three possible paths ahead of him: to go on drinking, which meant he would go insane; to stop drinking; or to die.

Alcohol, which he described as a cancer eating into him, had already killed his mind, his will and his spirit. He knew that it would not be long before it finished him off physically as well.

What happened next changed the life of Bill Wilson and subsequently the lives of thousands of others. Bill described a great light flooding his little room, a joy and ecstasy sweeping him up and giving him back a strength that was greater than his own and investing him with a power that was outside of him, unknown, but utterly trustworthy. 'Was it real? Am I sane?' he asked his doctor later, when he felt panic once again start to rise.

Yes, he was sane, replied the doctor. More to the point, although the phenomenon could not be explained away in any scientific terms, Bill had better hang on to it. It was so much better than what he had a couple of hours before. The experience brought Bill into his present. While others looked at him to see what other signs might appear, Bill was content to live for the moment. Life, which had been so nearly snatched away, was his again; for the moment, that was enough.

The treatment of drunks, until the founding of AA, was in the hands of doctors and psychiatrists. It was unrewarding work, unclassy, a dead-end street of medicine. Wilson stumbled across the major strength of AA; the person who can most help an alcoholic is another alcoholic. No one else can ever have the understanding of what drinking alcoholically actually means. The racking sadness and madness that the drunk endures are all clinical terms to the non-boozing doctor, who is baffled and confused by his patient, irritated by his attitudes and forced to fall back on two lines of thought; that the patient is indeed mad, or that the patient is terminally sick and in the grip of a disease from which he will never really recover.

Wilson came into contact with an ex-patient of Jung's, a man named Roland H who had drunk away most of a fortune and spent the rest at Jung's clinic in Zurich. He was drunk within weeks of leaving. Jung said there was nothing he could do; in his experience the only thing that ever worked for drunks was some kind of religious experience. Bill hammered his message home to the drunks he knew, determined to pass it on. If he could do it, then couldn't they? But they weren't receptive. Bill's vision of a network of drunks across the country – even the world – who would help each other slowly faded.

He returned to his doctor, who told him bluntly that he was putting the cart before the horse. 'Tell them about the disease aspect first. Tell them that it is certain madness to go on, tell them they'll die. Get them to listen, to see that you're a drunk who's made it, and then hit them with religion. Too much religion makes anyone feel guilty, or rebellious.'

Wilson's mistake was to do all the giving himself. But shortly after his meeting with the doctor, he found himself needing help. His business was going badly, he was broke, the only source of income for the family came from Lois, his wife, who worked in a department store. Bill entered into a deal which backfired and he found himself stranded in Ohio on a hot Saturday afternoon with little money. He wanted to drink; the desire was irresistible and he panicked. He needed another alcoholic to talk to. A call to the local vicar provided some numbers and soon Bill was sitting in the house of Dr Bob Smith.

He didn't try to convert; he simply asked for help. He talked about the mess of his own life, and his understanding of the nature of alcoholism.

Despite his medical background, Bob Smith had paid little attention to the physical nature of his illness. Moral collapse, only to be helped by spiritual strength, had been his concept of alcoholism, but hearing Bill talk about the twin spectres of madness and death opened his mind.

Bill Wilson evolved AA's famous line: One day at a time. He knew that there was no point in telling any drunk that he had to stop for ever. I'm not the only ex-drunk who can't cope with that idea. But I can see it as a contrast to my drinking days, when I lived in a vacuum, suspended between the guilt of what I'd done and the fear of what I might do. I was far too busy to appreciate the present. Ceasing to worry about tomorrow, by concentrating on today, starts to make life rich again.

Bill Wilson, through his group of drunks, was able to pick up the threads of recovery where Jung said that psychiatry had failed. By tapping the spiritual needs of the alcoholic he gave him a reason to live which was beyond himself, encompassing both the notion of a higher power and the knowledge that he, himself, could help others. Anyone who's been a bloody nuisance to everyone for years, and who suddenly finds that he is needed, will find that healing in itself.

When Bill was in his early sixties he wrote to Jung, outlining the principles of AA and telling the old man of the progress of Roland H, who had recovered through AA. Jung's letter of reply was Wilson's most treasured possession:

His [Roland's] craving for alcohol was equivalent, on a low
level, of the spiritual thirst of our being for wholeness,
expressed in medieval language, the union with God. How
can one formulate such an insight in a language that is not
misunderstood in our days?

   You see 'alcohol' in Latin is 'spiritus' and you use the word
for the highest religious experience as well as for the most
depraving poison. The helpful formula therefore is 'spiritus
contra spiritum'.

To Bill, Jung's letter meant a master's confirmation of what
he, as a layman, had struggled to prove: that the alcoholic can
only be rescued through experiences which must be
accounted spiritual. But the whole question of God in AA is
also a stumbling block. Wilson's doctor was right when he
told him that religion made people rebellious or guilty. The
clinic was no fair forum to test either AA or spiritual experiences. My friends in the clinic reckoned it was a necessary
evil – and attended to acquire points in the progress book.

   AA laid an emphasis on repudiating the alcoholic life
which I did not share. There were many things in my history
which I valued. If alcoholism is a spiritual search, and I certainly was coming to understand my drinking years in this
way, then the last thing I wanted to be told was to forget my
life up until the moment when I walked through the doors of
my first AA meeting. My search for some kind of harmony
had taken me across the world, to gurus and into political
movements. Disappointment had, in part, led me to the
bottle, but the seeker was well-intentioned. I was fond of her,
my third mad lady, and I had no intention of eradicating her
from my life.

   I sat in the bar of Joe Allen's restaurant, nursing a large

tomato juice, and waiting for the sight of the first friend who was to see the non-drinking me. 'That's a large drink you've got there,' the man next to me said chattily, 'you're drinking it fast for all that vodka.' I swung away on the bar stool, amused at his immediate misconception.

I bluffed for the first hour, and told the truth before we'd finished the meal. It was easier than I'd anticipated. Lucretia didn't have many illusions about my drinking – on two occasions I'd passed out in her living room. But alcoholics have a strange ability to convince themselves that people don't notice their drunken *faux pas*.

One day-patient of the doctor's had once insisted that his neighbours didn't know that he drank though they had expressed disgust at having to clear up the vomit which he had frequently deposited under the fire extinguisher on the landing outside his flat. With the drunk's precision he'd always chosen the same spot to spew up his last meal. But, he added, he never made a noise, never banged into walls. Even that far gone he had preserved a set of manners. When I'd passed out on Lucretia's sofa, I didn't think I'd shown any manners.

I came upstairs after supper on my last night at the clinic.

Alice met me on the landing and took my arm. 'Can I talk to you for a moment?' She steered me into her room.

'What's up?'

'Oh, nothing much . . .' she said. 'I just wanted to know how you felt, about going and all that.'

'OK,' I replied, puzzled, because Alice was usually so direct. I wondered if there was some drama happening outside. 'You know I went to this party last night?'

She nodded.

'It was very strange. I used to live in that house. I've been very drunk there, once took an overdose of heroin there . . . lots of things happened there. Last night, though, I felt a bit like a visitor from another planet. Have you read *The Lost Decade*?'

'Yes.'

'You remember when Trimble says that he just wants to see how people talk and walk and what their clothes are made of, just after he tells his publisher that he's been drunk for ten years? It felt like that.'

'Did you enjoy the party?'

'Yes. It proved certain things.'

'What?'

'That people don't notice you not drinking, that it's just as easy to laugh. And, knowing you're not going to get drunk gives confidence. But it did feel odd. All these people who had known me for years, and none of them knew that I was out for an evening from the bin!'

'Did you want them to know?'

'No.' I shook my head ruefully. 'No, I didn't. I'm still far too nervous for that; far too nervous to admit that I was beaten.'

She clucked. 'Don't be silly – beaten is precisely what you're not. Anyway if you say that nobody noticed you not drinking, then nobody noticed you not getting drunk either, right?' Alice looked at her watch and stood up.

'Come on,' she said. 'Surprise.'

I followed her out of the door, along the by now familiar corridor past the nursing station, where the upper half of the door swung idly on its hinges. She opened the door of the lounge and propelled me in.

The room was full. My leaving party. A huge cake on the coffee table. GOOD LUCK ROSIE etched in yellow cream.

'We wanted to say, Don't get pissed, Rosie,' said Anne who was looking from the cake to me with nervous hesitation. My normally glib and facile tongue ground to an unfamiliar halt. Horrors! I was starting to cry.

'Well, aren't you going to say something?' asked Brian.

'Thanks.' Was this humility, I wondered? 'Thanks.'

The next day, Brian helped me take my belongings home. A great many bags had accumulated in the weeks I'd been in the clinic. William was still away in Kuwait, so I prepared to spend the evening alone.

EIGHTEEN

The early morning shuttle service from Inverness to Glasgow took fifty minutes. From Glasgow on to Birmingham, fifty-five. Rosie had flown thousands of miles, but never in England.

When she and William had arrived home, Rosie's mother was ill. Now, a month later, in early October, Rosie was on her way to her bedside. Charles had rung the day before with the news that she had been operated on and the verdict was cancer, probably malignant. 'They'll know definitely tomorrow,' he said. 'Can you get to Birmingham?'

The early morning commuters drank coffee and shuffled through their briefcases. She sat by the window watching the jigsaw fields slide by. Other people's mothers got cancer, not hers.

'The cancer has spread to the liver. I'm afraid there's nothing we can do. She'll live for three or four months. I'm sorry.' The surgeon was fresh-faced, wholesome, surprisingly youthful.

There were eight beds in the ward, four to each side. The hospital disinfectant mingled with the smell of flowers and talc. Betty was propped up on pillows, wearing her old blue bedjacket. She smiled and held out her right hand. 'Rosel, how lovely to see you . . . how was Scotland? I didn't know you were coming back so soon.'

'William had to go to London, on business,' she lied, 'he dropped me off.'

'I feel so much better,' her mother said. 'I had cancer but it's all gone. I told them about Hugh' – she referred to a family friend – 'about how he had cancer of the bowel, seven years ago, and how he's fit and energetic now.'

They all smiled. We're in a conspiracy, Rosie thought. No one wants to believe. No one wants to say: Cancer, Cancer . . .

Her father drove home. They hardly talked. He was concentrating, she could see, on something in the middle distance. The road? The past? The future? She shuddered. They swerved violently round a bend, and Charles shook himself, straightening the car. 'Sorry,' he said, glumly.

The journey from Birmingham took a little over an hour. Longer that night, because Charles drove slowly. Dreading, she thought, arriving home to a house which, like her mother's body, was now irretrievably changed. They went inside, Rosie seeing, for what felt like the first time, the solid evidence of her mother; her books, her knitting, her letters. She walked upstairs to her parents' room and from the window she watched her father crossing the lawn. The evening was still, warm and calm.

She sat on the edge of her mother's bed. Hanging over the chair was a blue shawl which Betty had been given for Christmas the year before. It was smart and she wondered why her mother hadn't taken it to hospital with her. Rosie felt angry that her mother was still economising, even now. She started to cry, not noisily, not hysterically, rather huge sobs which seemed to emanate from some distant place of anguish. Almost as though someone else was doing the crying.

'I don't know what I'll do without her.' Charles nursed his drink, his eyes filling with tears. They were sitting in the small sitting-room. It was growing dark. They hadn't turned on the lights. They were talking, Rosie thought, as though she were already dead, both worrying how they would manage without her. How awful to say something so selfish, how awful to think it, she thought to herself, but how do you worry for someone else about their death? All you can see is the space they will leave, the space you will have to fill.

Charles told only the immediate family. No friends, no neighbours. The following day he was expecting business colleagues for lunch, and in a leaden trance Rosie shopped in the market town for lamb and cheese. She picked spinach from the garden and fetched potatoes from the shed. She sipped sherry in the kitchen, hoping that it might simultaneously make her feel more connected and further away. Her father went back to the hospital in the afternoon. She stayed at home, expecting William to arrive. He said he would leave Scotland that morning, and come straight to Ludlow. After her father left the house felt like a tomb. She drank and cried, no longer quietly, the sound disturbing the still country air.

When William arrived she was passed out in bed, half in it, half out, her clothes disordered, her breathing shallow.

'You can't go to the hospital like that,' Charles said at breakfast the following morning. Her eyes were puffed, and her hands shook. 'I'm sorry . . .' she said lamely, 'I'm so unhappy.' Then kicked herself because her suffering, she thought, did not equal her father's.

'I need your help and support,' he said. She nodded, inwardly cringing because she felt incapable of giving it, incapable of growing up to a point where she could be an equal to her father, a mother to her mother.

Betty came home after ten days. Rosie cleaned the house from top to bottom, glad that the daily was on her annual holiday in Jersey, glad to have something concrete to contribute.

The vow of silence was now a fact. Neither Betty nor Charles were going to talk. Rosie was torn. She had read about people fighting cancer through sheer strength of will and thought that her mother should decide for herself if she wanted to try.

Charles was similarly concerned. He argued back and forth over whether it was better that she should know, or better that she should live out the rest of her days in optimistic belief about her recovery. Medically she was going to get better before she slid downhill.

But they all knew that silence was mutual protection. The messy business of confronting grief could be avoided, and each could indulge hopeful conjecture. Private mourning, not public turmoil.

Betty's appetite returned and her strength too. Within a few weeks she was up and about. Breakfast in bed was her only concession to illness. Collette came from Denmark and Charles blustered over how to explain his daughter's unexpected visit. She brought news; the impending birth of her fourth child, due at the end of April the following year. Betty was delighted. Collette and Rosie shrank because the thought was ever-present; she won't be here to see her new grandchild.

'I think I only really appreciated Mummy when I had my own children,' Collette said. They were walking down the lane that runs past the house. The day was crisp, autumnal: the oak trees heavy with acorns.

'I used to think you minded – the fact that she always

went to Denmark so automatically, as though it was her right to be there when you had a new baby. I would have thought she would have got in the way.' Collette shook her head. Rosie felt a deep sadness that she had no children, would never know her mother as a grandmother.

Now if she ever had children, this relationship would be in *absentia*. So many things seemed too late; wanting her mother to take pride in her life and work. She felt so inadequate about both. Her mother, she knew intuitively, could see through her relationship with William, to the insecurity and doubt. She knew how much Rosie drank. At times her worries would surface.

'But I don't think you're an alcoholic,' Betty said one morning after Rosie had once again had a bit too much the night before. 'It said in your astrological chart that you would undergo changes when you were thirty, feel more settled, more in touch. You remember?'

Rosie nodded. 'It seemed such a long way off! I was twenty-five then.'

But her drinking was often out of control, and even when it wasn't she was conscious of waiting anxiously for the cocktail hour, for the pre-lunch sherry. The usual comfort she derived from the knowledge that she'd beaten her heroin addiction so easily was wearing thin. Did Collette notice, she wondered, as the two sisters walked through the stubble field?

'What are you going to do?' Collette asked as they clambered over the hunting gate leading down to the river.

'Stay here till Christmas, I think,' she said. 'I'm not likely to find a job in the next six weeks. And, I want to be here. I've been away for almost five years . . . and if there's only three months.'

'What about William?'

'Well, he'll have to look after his business. I suppose he'll be up and down.'

'Are you going to marry him?'

'I don't know,' said Rosie, and changed the subject.

Rosie was thankful that Betty could cope physically. She had never been able to understand her reaction to her mother's body. When she was twenty-two, shortly after she met John, Betty had taken her to Russia. Their helter-skelter schedule took in Leningrad, Moscow and a day trip on the Trans-Siberian Express, all in seven days. On the second day her mother had slipped on the ice while walking back to their hotel from the Hermitage. The doctor pronounced her arm broken. She set it and supplied codeine.

Betty didn't want to go home, but the trip was ruined. The arm was badly set, and the pain caused sleepless nights and hassles with clothes. Rosie was appalled by her injured mother and hated herself for the feeling – which verged on revulsion – which flooded over her when Betty asked her to help her wash. She made a poor job of it; too quick, too uncaring, but Betty was grateful nonetheless. Was it because she had been born from this, she wondered? She had loved her mother's body so much as a child, why now did it fill her with such unease?

By Christmas the topic of the future came up again in conversation. For weeks, it had been avoided. No one had talked about anything that was due to happen the following week, let alone the following year. Collette and her family came for the holiday. Her swelling pregnancy was comforting to Betty, who got out her knitting patterns for bootees and little jackets. Tentatively, they all began to nurture a small hope. Betty took shorter walks, slept a little more and did not regain her full weight; but these facts were easily overlooked in favour of the brightness in her eyes and the return of her infectious laughter.

She dosed herself regularly with homeopathic mistletoe pills, whose poisons are supposed to work against those of cancer.

'She's really getting better, isn't she?' Charles was delighted. He later said that for a period round Christmas he honestly believed that the doctors had made a mistake.

Rosie seethed with anger and sadness. Anger against the cancer, anger against the world for making the impossible happen.

She drank steadily during those winter days. She rarely got very drunk, just enough to take the edge off the pain and confusion. During Christmas, when she cooked, baked and turned out turkeys and tarts for the household of nine, she guiltily kept a bottle of wine upstairs under the bed. She tried to rationalise her guilt, to blame it on the cancer, then felt guilty about that too; conscious that her mother, with her uninvited illness, should not have to bear the responsibility of her indulgence.

Though no one realised it at the time, Charles was contending with two family illnesses. His youngest daughter sank into alcoholism while his wife died of cancer. The self-indulgent behaviour of the drinker seemed the more appalling in the face of the uninvited, fatal growth.

In February Rosie became features editor on a glossy woman's monthly. She took it after first explaining that her mother was dying, and that she would want time off when the inevitable happened.

Every weekend she and William would leave London at five on a Friday, arrive in Ludlow by nine o'clock, and leave again late on Sunday night. Every weekend Betty looked a little worse. Acid accumulated in her stomach, causing it to swell. William and Rosie learnt to play bridge and they spent their evenings in Ludlow alternating between the card table and the television. Rosie cooked enormous meals, experimenting with tastes and spices. The results were too rich for Betty's tastes, but Rosie didn't give up. She was trying to live up to an ideal she thought her mother would approve of. There was so little time and opportunity to make peace with her.

In London they lived in William's mother's flat, which they redecorated with care and trouble. Why so much care, she wondered? She couldn't see herself staying with William; having his children, growing old with him. Sexually, their relationship was what she imagined of a couple married thirty years. Dotage sex: infrequent, unorgasmic. Their weekly coupling brought out in her a Victorian sense of duty: William's right, not her pleasure.

She began to notice, and recoiled from that too, the part that her drinking played in their relationship. During the week, away all day at the office, dealing with a job which she felt confident to handle, happy in the nursery security of an all-female office, her booze consumption would be more or less under control. At the weekends, sipping wine in the kitchen while she cooked, usually drunk by bedtime, she'd wake the following morning haunted by gloom and insecurity. Then, afraid even to think of life without William, she'd welcome him into her arms, into her body. Her mother was dying and leaving her, her father she didn't fully understand, but William seemed to love her, and depend on her.

William's business faltered; he talked about returning to the Middle East; he complained about the times she got drunk; but he never seriously talked about leaving.

As Betty grew worse, Rosie panicked about wanting to say so many things. She wanted to say that, for instance, she felt guilty about what happened in Moscow, that the guilt was more confusing because she couldn't understand it. A girlfriend of hers had once talked to Betty about her own mother and had said that when she was in her teens her mother had had a similar accident. The friend had felt uneasy when helping her mother wash. Betty had nodded, said that she understood this reaction, but there were tears in her eyes. So where did that leave Rosie? Better or worse? She didn't know.

In April Charles took Betty to the Caribbean. She loved sea, heat and sand. By the time they left her stomach had swollen to pregnant proportions. Standing in her underwear, her legs thin, the skin hanging in loose folds no muscle-power would rescue, she reminded Rosie of a starving child. Collette was due to give birth at the end of the month: two swollen bellies, one for life, one for death.

In London she saw little of her old friends. William didn't like them and saw them as competition. 'It's so boring, media gossip,' he had said, the tone of his voice like someone ticking off an inefficient waiter. Rosie shrugged. She gave up trying. The few evenings they'd spent together in the company of what he saw as 'her world' were always painful. William would withdraw into a black cloud. Rosie knew it was embarrassment and insecurity. Other people thought it was pomposity.

She thought about leaving and was appalled by her apathy. Where to go? Where to live? She knew she ought to make a decision. William divorced his wife – a gesture he claimed to have made to free him to marry her. She didn't want to get married. She was too embarrassed to conceive of marrying William, too little in love, not really in love at all. 'Do you love me?' he'd say. 'Oh, you know I do, honestly William.' Her voice carried no conviction.

'We ought to get married . . .' And when she didn't answer, 'Are you just staying here because this is rent-free?'

'No, of course not, how could you . . .'

'Well, what do you want to do? We're not getting any younger.'

'Oh God, let's just go to the bloody registry office and get it over with.'

The rows would come with terrible fierceness.

'I hate him,' she'd mutter to herself, then cook the best dinner she was able to produce.

Then she'd get very drunk. The following morning she would ask William what she'd done the night before.

'Oh, you shouted and ranted. I hope there's not too much truth in *in vino veritas*. Do you really hate me?'

'No,' she would answer, and at that moment, nerves stretching to breaking point, her future without William opening up like the gates to hell, she'd mean it. And hate herself a little more.

Betty returned from the Caribbean, her tan hiding her pallor, her stomach even bigger. She started to spend longer in bed. Collette gave birth to her third son, a red-haired, blue-eyed baby who was named Ivar.

At the end of May Rosie's editor resigned. Rosie applied for her job, certain that she wouldn't get it, but knowing she'd be sunk if she didn't try. She had to show ambition. The staff promised their support.

At the end of June her father called the office to say that Betty had collapsed. Rosie must come home. She packed a bag. William drove her to Ludlow. Betty had improved a little during the day, but she was weak, her breath fitful. Collette and her nursing baby arrived the next day.

'Daddy, we have to tell her . . . have to talk about it now.' Collette sat at the kitchen table, Ivar's hungry mouth firmly attached to her breast. He swelled with life, determined, vocal and tenacious.

'No . . . she's rallying, she could hold on.' Collette sighed and shifted her child. 'Well, I don't know if I'll see her again, and I want to talk to her.'

Collette was the only member of the family who hadn't signed the contract of silence. In Birmingham, when Betty hadn't pursued enquiries about her illness, thereby saying that she didn't want to know, she'd taken Charles and Rosie along in the conspiracy. Charles knew that his wife's ability to hold on stemmed in part from the hopeful silence, and he feared that the truth would so deplete her resources that she would not have the energy to go on living. But Collette, the outsider, could only see the one point of view. Betty was dying; she, Collette, would probably never see her again, and she didn't want to return home empty-handed and fretful.

Later on that night she came and sat on the edge of Rosie's bed. 'I said thank you – you know, for being a good mother. She told me to make sure we encouraged Daddy to remarry. She knew. She's known for a long time. You must talk to her too . . . we can't let her die without that.'

It was now necessary to have a nurse sitting with Betty through the night. The schedule wasn't fully operational so the next night Rosie volunteered to sit up.

'I wanted to say thank you,' she said lamely. 'You've been a wonderful mother.'

Betty smiled, gently. 'You've been a good daughter too.'

Rosie felt choked, wholly inadequate. She had had too much to drink and hoped that Betty wouldn't notice. She wanted to ask if her mother was scared, but was herself too scared to ask.

She stared at her mother's body, at the hump under the blankets where her stomach had tightened like a drum. She couldn't conceive of her actually dying: only of what came after. Already she was treating the world as though her mother was absent, doing anything to avoid thinking of the moment when she stopped breathing.

She fell asleep, her book on her lap. When she woke up, her head groggy and thick, her mother was awake. Her eyes, rested, alert, intelligent, were fixed on her daughter.

'Don't worry, I slept very well,' she said, pre-empting her daughter's apology. Rosie slunk off to get changed, aware that Betty could have died in the night while she was oblivious.

The following day the office called and said they had appointed an outsider to the editor's job. The new editor rang her up. Rosie abused her on the phone. The lunchtime sherry saw to that. Later she was 'forgiven', the incident 'forgotten'. 'Everyone gets drunk when their mothers are dying.'

She went back to London, Collette returned to Denmark.

The weekly commuting began again. Rosie was tired. Her chin was riddled with acne. She slept badly, unless she had had at least four Scotches. The office was an ordeal. The new editor wanted to do the features herself, and it was apparent after a few days that, unless Rosie wanted to play the role of assistant, there was no room for the two of them in the nursery. She wondered, miserably, what to do.

At the end of July Betty collapsed again. Rosie was at home, it was a Friday night. Her breathing was tortured, she was barely conscious. All the feeble strength she had left was going into breathing.

In the morning she was calmer. She ate a little breakfast, smiled, asked Rosie how her week had been. Charles went to the bathroom to shave when the day nurse arrived. Rosie took the sweat-soaked sheets downstairs to the washing machine. On her way back up, the nurse came on to the landing.

'It's over,' she said, her eyes streaked with tears. If only it had been.

Two weeks later she was back at work. The new editor called her into her office. 'Do you want to leave today?'

Although Rosie had spoken to her over the phone four days earlier, saying that she realised there was insufficient work for the two of them, she hadn't anticipated so sudden a move. She wanted to cry, but not in public, and stayed silent. Later she was glad. If she had gone that day, then she'd have resigned. As it turned out, the company had to make her officially redundant, allowing five months on full pay to work out her contract. Humiliation heaped on depression.

The office was sympathetic. They had donated a large sum to Cancer Research on Betty's behalf and her friend Catherine had come all the way to Ludlow for the funeral. Her presence had been comforting, coming as she did from a world that was wholly Rosie's, outside the family and neighbourhood.

At the funeral she wore a cream dress, cream hat and cream sandals. 'White is the colour of light,' she explained rather hopelessly, then wondered if she was making assumptions about the dead. Would her mother really prefer this colour to the traditional black? Betty lay in a coffin at the top of the long aisle of Ludlow Church. Rosie remembered Steve's body in the back of a taxi in India, John's mother hooked up to tubes in a Boulder hospital. How little care she had shown for John; but at the time she'd no idea of what he must have been going through.

At the end of August Charles turned sixty-five. He was retired, widowed, Suddenly he had time and money to do as he pleased, and no one to do it with.

The commuting continued. London to Ludlow. Spending weekends with Charles alone. But now there was no necessity to struggle back through Sunday nights. It didn't matter if she got to the office at lunchtime. The months anticipating Betty's death had in some ways prepared her, but the loss still took her off guard. One day in the newsagents on the way to work, she paid for her copy of *The Times*, then picked up a postcard of a family of mice sitting under a daisy umbrella.

She planned to send it to Betty. Only when she was counting out the change did the thought thud home: Betty's dead.

In the autumn the *Guardian* commissioned a piece on *Spare Rib*'s hundredth edition. Rosie rang her old office and arranged a meeting. She felt they resented her apparent independence from the movement; she, in turn, felt isolated and unwanted by the collective. Though the women seemed happy enough themselves, the magazine was suffering. There was a leaden feel to the pages. She couldn't comment on how it was to work in a collective – her own experience had been too brief for that – but the result lacked sparkle, drive, and personality. There was no triumph in sensing that her original fears about collective organisations were vindicated. Instead, she felt depressed. The movement was missing out on key elements. When she'd finished the piece, which was wholly laudatory, she started work on another, tentatively titled 'Dreams and Expectations'.

'When I was twenty-five,' the working draft began, 'an old friend asked me what I thought I would be doing when I was forty. I was off my guard, and I replied that I imagined I would be living in the country, with a couple of kids and a couple of dogs, growing vegetables and being a wife. He'd looked at me aghast and I wished that I hadn't spoken. "You mean," he queried, "that you imagine that you'll end up like your mother." I'd laughed and said no, it was just idle thinking. But I did think it and as I approach my thirtieth birthday, I realise that I still do.'

At twenty-one, feminist goals had seemed so simple. Change laws and encourage self-confidence, and women would move forward to fill new roles. And fill them happily. What they missed, it seemed to her now, was considering the deep-down wants of women. The deep-down fears that resulted from conditioning. In ten years she'd felt herself no closer to the goals, only riddled with ambiguity. Wanting freedom and success, but terrified by the thought of being alone. Her relationships were no better, neither superficially nor on a deeper level.

To be alone at sixty-five, still working for a living, still struggling with the messy business of life, was a horrendous thought. She knew that she still used her femininity as an excuse for hopelessness, as though being a woman gave her an excuse for not being as good as a man. Allowed her that leeway which covered up the lack of money, the lack of real direction in her life. Hadn't she always been told that a man would pick up the pieces, would ultimately take care of her, and that she could feed on his abundance? But thirty was the age when all this was supposed to have happened, and she was no nearer these goals than she had been at twenty.

While William was away for a few days, trying to organise a deal in Bristol, she went out to dinner with an old friend whom she hadn't seen for a long time. Janet was recently divorced, recently returned from America, and recently a published novelist.

'There's no triumph in singleness,' Janet said, gazing gloomily into her wine. 'After all those feminists telling us to get free and how wonderful it would be, it feels like a burden. There isn't any point in doing something wholly for yourself – at least not for me. And it's crazy, here I have all these things, flat, money, work, published books, going on smart holidays and I have no peace. I can't work because I have no sense of conviction. It isn't enough to do it just for me.'

But was there any more triumph in living with William, Rosie wondered? There wasn't, because she was there for all the wrong reasons; all the reasons which she had scorned in others, put down in other's marriages as signs of over-dependent women. Money, security, fear of the dark, of the big unknown spaces which she was unequipped to deal with.

'But you can't compromise,' Janet continued, 'relation-ships always go sour if you don't respect the man. If you have to pretend to the world that he's good when you know he isn't. Do you ever have to do that?'

'No, yes, sometimes,' Rosie blustered. She was always pre-tending on William's behalf, saying his business was going well when it wasn't. Lacking in respect because she didn't know how to respect him any more, could only hang on to the obvious signs like the devotion he'd showed when Betty died. She sighed; she had tried, she had really tried to be with someone who fitted in, right schools, right accent, right attitudes. The only problem was that she felt she was dying, slowly, like a fox in a snare.

She wrestled between dependence and the wish to be free, and drank to bridge the gap. Her drinking scared her, but not so much as her life did. Drink at least was dependable. It took her past recrimination. Past the sense of madness. Mad because sometimes she drank and drank till she passed out when all she had meant to do was blunt reality, blur its edges with the velvet spirit. Mad because she didn't, at times, know who she was. William blanked out her past, never talked about it – she couldn't understand why he claimed to love her, and she couldn't see how she could change to fit his ideal.

She knew she had the advantage of seeming brave, of pretence, and she knew she was good at it. But the fear of failure kept rearing. She almost took pride in her drinking, in her ability to get shit-faced; she compared it with William's restraint, proof that she'd never fit the mould.

Slowly it dawned how much of her life was derived from her past. She knew her responses, but she wasn't feeling any more. Something had stopped; she was pulling from way back, from tricks learnt at her mother's knee, from old standards of etiquette. Just holding on to a semblance of sanity was a full-time job.

The inner war was divisive. There was the woman who functioned well, who'd played bridge and chatted gaily at dinner parties, who remembered birthdays, who cooked and sewed and made lampshades and wrote articles, who was writing a book, and making money, and rode and fished and exhibited capabilities; then there was the terrified dreamer who always wanted more, who would race, in imagination, from past triumphs to future heights, sneaking, with the Scotch bottle, over the reality of the present. When they clashed, as they inevitably did, this smart country girl and the dreamer, something else would come into play. A third person, a third mad lady, who would pick up a bottle and try to drag the strands together, try to fuse the warring factions. For a few moments, the alcohol would work; the dreams no longer looked ridiculous, even the present assumed possibilities.

The third lady was always there in the morning; they'd wake up together in bed, all temporarily fused in sleep, only to be sent on their way with the clatter of the milkman and the rustle of letters falling into the box. Rosie'd try and eliminate her, send about her business this person who was so capable of wreaking havoc. She wanted the world to be safe; so she turned to bridge and the novels of Alistair MacLean rather than the works of Malcolm Lowry. She understood what people meant when they talked about bags and drives, the price of land and the marriage of the Prince of Wales. She needed minor commotions and could work herself into a rage about the lackadaisical attitudes of the plumber and the builder, when usually she didn't care much about such things. She became competent at ironing, brilliant at cooking, and useful on cold winter mornings, striding through heavy undergrowth, cooing and grunting like a demented pig, banging the bottoms of trees with her walking stick, pushing back the faded green brambles, their leaves withered on purplish branches with menacing thorns, driving roosting pheasants out of their winter hideouts towards the row of waiting guns. Thud, as her stick hit another tree. Thud, went her conscience. Walk to the left, girl, we've got to keep a straight line here, don't want to let any of them get away. Hearty voices with bloodthirsty steps. Rationalisations when the pheasant emerges from the oven, resplendent with crackled skin and white sauce and conversation starts again on the ethics of blood sports, while silver knives and forks clatter on fine bone china.

She was conscious of the disintegration of her humour, her strength, and her honesty. She had an overdraft at the bank, and she had an overdraft on life. Not just an overdraft either, too many accounts, none in credit. At times, she wasn't even sure who was writing the cheques.

She started work on a dictionary of eponyms, and wrote regular magazine articles. Just before her thirtieth birthday William left for the Middle East on a business trip. She saw him off at the airport and drove home. She loathed driving those days: it made her panic and usually she left it to William. Shaky when she arrived, she drank a glass of brandy. It was only seven in the morning and she thought it would send her back to sleep. Fifteen minutes later, she drank another, enjoying the warm feeling, and relishing the thought of a few weeks away from William. She was planning a trip to New York to research the book.

By nine o'clock in the morning she was drunk. The bender lasted for six days. She swarmed in and out of it, but after a day only one drink was needed to bring back all the drunkness, there was so much alcohol coursing through her system. On the night after her birthday – the day itself passed in a haze – she seduced a friend of William's. When he left her bed, abruptly, at four in the morning, the Scotch bottle salvaged what was left of her pride. She was in despair; she wanted to stop, she couldn't, she didn't know why she had started, why she had had the first drink, the second, let alone the third.

Her father arrived from Ludlow, summoned by the slurring sounds on the telephone. He threw away the booze and suggested that she spend the next few nights sleeping at her aunt's nearby. She was too miserable to argue. A doctor came to see her and she minimised the amount she had drunk. He prescribed a sleeping pill and told her to lay off the booze for two months. She shivered and sweated and watched the world turn cartwheels. In the middle of the days she drank a little beer, which curtailed the shakes a bit. While she sat at home, wondering what to do, the phone would ring and ring. She didn't dare answer. Buildings threatened to fall on top of her. She was in acute withdrawal and she didn't know it; just thought she was finally having a nervous breakdown. Madness at last.

The feeling changed. Suddenly her hands stopped shaking and the world resolved into the ordinary three dimensions. It was nearly two weeks after the first brandy. Her father had told her to tell her friends that she was off the booze on medical orders. She had no intention of stopping, of looking a coward, of admitting she couldn't handle the booze, so she kept silent. In New York she researched her book in the public library. In the evenings she got viciously drunk. People were always happy to go and get drunk with her; what they didn't know was that she carried right on drinking, while they took pauses to sober up.

She returned and managed to cut the booze intake back to manageability. William was due back in four days. The day before his return the phone rang.

'Come to Cyprus. We need you. This magazine's going to be great.'

William will object, she thought as she put down the phone, but I've got to go. I'm going crazy here . . . the booze is out of control . . . I need a change.

She ran away from it all, via Heathrow airport to the blue Mediterranean.

NINETEEN

Ten days after I had arrived in the clinic William and I went for a walk down the King's Road in Chelsea. It was a Saturday, the street was full of purple punks with spindly girlfriends. At the street flower stall he stopped to buy me a bunch of orange lilies. I waited, watching the people chatter past and thought: Can they tell? Does it show?

The day after I got out I was walking down a similar busy shopping street in Kensington, still wondering the same things. I was delighted with the sunshine and the gently turning autumn leaves, but I was a marked woman whose emotional overcoat had all the shortcomings of a cheap bargain. I wanted to run away.

William returned from the Middle East. My feelings were no more settled than they had been in the clinic. I was insecure, bruised, living with a secret which he, at least, completely shared. I wasn't being honest, but I countered with the thought that hasty actions in the past had often turned out disastrously.

We settled into fragile domestic harmony, treating each other politely and with reserve. But the dynamic, the drink, had gone: without its skirmishes, what was left between us felt leaden and lifeless.

I returned to the book that I had begun earlier in the year. It wasn't going to earn money, at least not then, but working on it prevented me from having to contact magazines for work and provided a label – writer – both for the public and for my own private needs. Alcoholics are by nature childishly impatient, almost incapable of standing still and letting time pass. To my surprise I found myself enjoying the hours I spent in the library, unearthing eponyms from obscure dictionaries. The discipline was exacting and I tackled it entirely on my own.

I told my friends about the clinic gradually, swearing each to secrecy. But that changed, faster than I would ever have believed.

The more people knew the less I had to lie. Less lying, less repeating of old patterns, and the more people who knew, the more pride stacked against not drinking. I would have lost a lot of face by getting drunk. But as I told the story, I also played my own game with the devil. 'Do you still like me now you know the truth?'

They still seemed to. So I was deeply depressed when an older friend, someone I respected, said, 'God, you surprise me. I thought you were the girl who'd got the seventies beat.' Perhaps it would be better to hush the whole thing up – I noticed that my father was not telling anyone at home in the country. Was I dumb to try and talk about it as though it wasn't shameful?

But even as I thought this, I knew that I would never remain silent, that I didn't feel in any way beaten. I had arrived at a crossroads clearly marked life or death, and made the only choice I could.

But from then on, I saw myself telling the tale in a more frivolous way. I played up the farce, soft-pedalled the seriousness, but I stayed in touch with the clinic. In time I outgrew the need for nursery protection, but I always knew it was there.

'I hate the way people watch me,' I said to Anne one day. 'Hate the fact that I can see them thinking, Oh, being sober is just one more of her mad passions. Like the rest it will fade out in time.'

'You have to expect it . . . after all, what do you think if I don't answer the phone?' she answered quickly. 'You think I'm drunk, don't you?'

True. I did always think that. So if I thought that about Anne, what would someone else, to whom alcoholic drinking was utterly unfathomable, think? In reaction, I became exaggeratedly punctual, afraid that if I was even a few minutes late, someone would think I was back on the booze.

Soon the novelty wore off. I was a recovered drunk; a fact. If I hadn't recovered I'd have been a dead drunk. The escape was no longer close enough to require more congratulation – even from myself. I wanted people to approve of me for being a good girl now, though I didn't want them to make a fuss, particularly by bringing up times in the past when I'd been very bad indeed. I knew this was a kind of regression but it didn't make any difference.

I wanted awareness, but not pity. So when some family friends, hearty drinkers normally, sipped Perrier all through dinner, I felt like a cripple. The lame lady who holds people up in the street because of her slow gait. I squirmed with shame in face of the friendly gesture.

I took my abstem pills daily. My choice. My life. Each pill equalled one more day without booze. I could never decide at the end of each day how much they had helped. All I know is that during the first key months of sobriety, when anyone with a motley drinking history is going to have a lot to deal with, and those who are going to drink again tend to do so, I didn't drink and I didn't want to. I went to my local AA meeting every week. I didn't enjoy them. I didn't enjoy being reduced to a common denominator, nor did I like the assumption that I must be having problems. Though I wasn't tempted to drink, I was very conscious of not-drinking. After three months I saw that these were two sides of the same coin. When I did, I stopped going to AA meetings.

William left for a three-week business trip in the Middle East. One night Brian and I went out to dinner and ended up in bed. It did wonders for my confidence. I arranged to move out and told William the night he returned. I felt guilty but relieved.

Brian went to Switzerland for Christmas. I went to my father's house in the country. For the first time in my life I was voluntarily alone. I finished the eponyms book on Christmas Eve and began making notes for a new one, on how to stop drinking. I'd had the idea before even leaving the clinic; I seriously considered training as a psychotherapist at the same time.

I was zealous about life off the booze and wanted to share the good feeling. Alcoholic textbooks all point to this evangelical 'phase' as a marked part of recovery. I thought it would last for the rest of my life.

I crossed the same fields I'd walked over so many times, hungover, miserable, estranged from the world by a nervous alcohol curtain. Now, kicking through fresh morning snow, I was singing. I hadn't any money, I had nowhere to live, I had an unreliable aristocratic boyfriend (who, judging from his voice on the phone, was already hitting the bottle), the manuscript of a book which would probably sink without trace (and somehow didn't), no job, no visible means of support, and a reputation for being someone who never stays the course. I'd never been happier in my life.

I slept erratic hours, watched video films with breakfast, scribbled notes about drink and, ultimately, found pleasure in my own company. Before, solitude had always meant failure – not having a friend or lover – and unhappiness because I couldn't enjoy things on my own. Now, I found ordinary life a pleasure; waking feeling well, walking, working. I'd seen an incredible amount in the previous decade, most of it far too fast. Now something else was happening. Nerves which had been dumb were coming to life. My three ladies were coalescing into one person and that person was a friend.

I returned to London to a rented flat. Brian returned from Switzerland, fourteen pounds heavier on cherry brandy, apple strudel and fine goat cheeses. He brought with him a large supply of barbiturates acquired over the counter from a lax Swiss pharmacist. He still made love wonderfully, though the barbs and the excess weight took their toll. Within two weeks he'd started to drink again. Drunkenly, he asked me to marry him.

'You'll be a Baroness and have a castle,' he assured me romantically.

I had to admit the idea was attractive. Not that it mattered. By that time Brian was under my skin, temporarily at least, and I said yes. He sighed with relief. What I didn't know was that about the same time he was also proposing to Angie, the rich American from the clinic.

The drinking escalated fast. 'I'm just testing to see that you can stay off it, even if I have a relapse,' Brian announced solemnly. He refused to see a doctor.

I didn't know then, and don't know now, why he drank. But as he continued and my attempts to stop him failed, I started to understand what William had gone through. We never went out – I was too scared of what he would do. I thought I was to blame. 'What have I done wrong – don't you love me any more?' I asked, as though love could conquer his drinking, and as if it were my fault that he fell out of bed at night.

I lied to friends about what we did, not wanting to admit that I was often left watching TV while Brian snored. One day I turned back the mattress on his side of the bed and found twenty-three halves of vodka, empty naturally. I arranged them in a row, waiting for him to arrive. 'What do you expect, I'm an alcoholic,' he said with a grin, adjusting the enormous Stetson he had taken to wearing, which caused me such humiliation in restaurants.

Brian was a geographical man, who took refuge in travel. By the spring he'd decided on another trip. Back to America. Back, so he claimed, to work. He spent hours packing and repacking his copious luggage. I watched miserably. He had no intention of returning. I was too scared to ask. He was too cowardly to tell the truth.

I drove him to the airport. He stank of vodka. 'I'll send a ticket for you,' he said and kissed me goodbye. I hugged him, feeling the familiar outline of the Smirnoff half in his pocket. I knew I wasn't going to see him again.

I phoned the American girl, Angie, and we met for dinner. We swapped notes and let the facts sink in. Brian had been conducting affairs with the two of us in parallel: Angie had the day shift, while I worked, then he returned to me, while she slept him off. Remarkably, he kept up the pace, except for when he passed out, or nodded off over the dinner table.

Despite our mutual indignation, Angie and I couldn't help but laugh.

The following day I woke into a depression the like of which I had not known since my last hangover. The day dragged on my hands and I fretted aimlessly, unable to work. In the evening, clearing out a cupboard, I found a bottle of vodka. Brian must have hidden it while drunk and then forgotten where it was. I poured out a glass and flushed the rest down the sink. I had no thought except Why the hell not? I don't care. Like Raju, like Anne, like Shelagh.

I immediately wanted more and thanked God I'd chucked it out. I had sufficient kick left not to want Brian's memory to have that much satisfaction. But I went to bed miserable; feeling that, in absentia, Brian had scored an enormous victory.

In the morning, my thirty-first birthday (Brian had not even had the decency to hang about for that), I woke up angry: with his duplicity, his lying, with myself for weakening. The emotion was the fuel for recovery.

Brian had been using me as a sucker, a pushover who provided his licence to drink. I'd been using Brian as a crutch for my self-esteem (every time I looked at him I thought, well, at least I'm sober). The day that Brian had collapsed with pancreatitis and I'd hauled him off to the hospital I was confronted with a charming Israeli doctor who took me to one side to explain Brian's drink problem.

'You see,' he said confidentially, holding my arm firmly above the elbow while steering me down the antiseptic corridors, 'he's an alcoholic. He can't drink like you and me. You want to pop over to the pub . . .'

I didn't say anything.

But looking back on the relationship, to which, for a few

weeks at least, I was wholly committed, its destruction was guaranteed before Brian so much as kissed me. He was a losing bet and I was subconsciously allowing myself to be set up. When the inevitable, his departure and his drinking, happened, then I would have every reason to drink and wind up back in the clinic. The opening conversation would have been boringly standard:

'Rosie – you're back, what happened?'

'Well, Brian left, Brian drank, I was so upset I just couldn't take it. '

Sympathetic nods and knowing looks. Readmittance to a room on the always-lit corridor. Try again. The Anne cycle, the Shelagh cycle.

I'd been apologising while Brian drank his vodka. Two wrecks in a storm, we'd clung to each other, aware of mutual weaknesses. There was a kind of safety to begin with, but now I didn't want to be reminded. And I didn't want to apologise again.

While I drank I'd apologise; sober, I was still doing it. Apologising like women have always done. I used to apologise to girlfriends if they saw me ironing William's shirts, apologise because lunch was five minutes late, apologise for talking too much at dinner, apologise for being me. In the wake of Brian's defection, I just thought Sod it.

My evangelical streak died out during the time I spent with Brian, and I grew confident of the value of my story, with or without a useful message to people still on the bottle. I knew I'd never know why I, as against my sister or my father, became an alcoholic; though I knew people would read the book with that question in mind. All I would do was record the facts – hoping they would be salutary in themselves. But how many Rosies were there, I wondered, as

I watched myself change. When would this growth stop, when could I put a pin through it like a dead butterfly and say, 'That's me, and that's how I'll stay.' One day I went round to the clinic to visit Anne, who had checked in for a brief stay following an almighty binge on South African sherry. I felt icy dread as I walked along the corridors and knew it was time to stop going. I didn't need my booster shot of lousy memories to keep me sober.

There were new symptoms of my life, indicators of this change, this growing up. I sewed on buttons and opened and answered letters. Before I'd been too frightened to open official envelopes. My cupboards were ordered. There were ironies too. When I applied for insurance for my mortgage, I was told that it would probably be refused because I would have to own up to having had psychiatric treatment. Wait a year, I was advised. Eighteen months earlier, the mortgage company none the wiser, I'd have had no problem, except, of course, with the payments.

Another irony: whatever alcohol may become to the drinker the initial impulse towards it is one of liberation, euphoria and ecstasy. 'Suddenly I'm above the ordinary,' Don Birnam says as he commences his bender in *The Lost Weekend*, 'I'm walking the tightrope over Niagara Falls. I am one of the great ones. I'm John Barrymore before the movies got him by the throat.'

In my case it began that way too. But I well remember waking up sometimes in my father's house and crawling through the hatch into the dining room (he would have locked the door, aware that I was on the bottle that weekend) to find a drink. No lover in the world has ever evoked such a response and I shudder now at the memory. And being a slave to the bottle meant being a slave to so many other things. Drink cost money; willingly I'd spent it. Drink divided the day into compartments; waiting always for the socially acceptable time to arrive; sweating to reach for the hidden bottle; a handbag full of powerful mouth sprays and strong mints; days hopelessly forfeited to hangovers.

Drunk, I'd sometimes been forced to work late at night, because the previous day's booze intake had wrought such havoc. Sober, I worked all night because I wanted to. Without the booze, I was a free agent. This book – which friends regarded sceptically as a project I'd probably never finish – consumed hours in the way that booze once had. My fears for my third mad lady – and in what particular way she would manifest herself – lulled as I found contentment in work.

The layers peeled off slowly. I was, for a while, still afraid of the truth. I wanted to make my past look good. I wrote the chapter about my schooldays at Cheltenham, confident that I had exposed enough to explain why my life was so adrift.

But as I wrote odd glimpses of unwanted memories circled round the back of my mind. My stories were all too flip; they didn't add up. I hadn't explained what happened to the eager little twelve-year-old, so proud of her school uniform, whose head spun with numbers and who thought that exams were fun.

Could Snoopy, my old friend from Cheltenham, throw some light on the conundrum? We'd been in touch fairly regularly over the last fifteen years, and though our lives had run on dissimilar courses the bonds which school had forged were still strong.

'I'm writing a book,' I told her over the phone. I elaborated, about the clinic, about the drink, about the crack-up.

'I wish you'd told me, there might have been something I

could have done.' I felt relieved, because I still panic when I talk about my alcoholism to someone whose life seems so organised compared to mine.

We sat on the terrace of her house in Kent, watching her two children play in the garden, and talked about the where-abouts of the other Cheltenham Ladies, about funny memories of scrapes and daring.

'What went wrong?' I finally asked. 'What was there about that school that made me so . . . stupid? Why did I do so badly?'

'You had a hell of a time,' she answered, 'we thought you were really dumb. And we didn't like you either. That busi-ness with the sweets,' she continued, looking at me quizzically. Snoopy's face hadn't changed, she could have been the thirteen-year-old I first met.

'When you first came, you used to offer everyone sweets. We'd always take them, then we began to just grab them out of your tin. We'd all been there for two years when you showed up, we needed someone to pick on. And you were such a good person to pick on. You'd do anything we wanted. That day in science, when Kate and I were bored, and we dared you to try and crawl out through the stools. Remember how you bumped into one, spilling chemicals everywhere?'

I nodded, though in truth I didn't really remember. The matter of the sweets had been in my mind, but I'd dismissed it as trivial. Now I saw horrid pictures of myself with an ever-emptying sweet-tin, making trips to the department store where my mother had an account so that I could refill the tin, in dread of the day when no one would speak to me at all because it was empty.

'What else did I do?'

'You were desperate to have Kate and me as your friends. But we never wanted to go when you asked us out to tea! And then we did go once' – yes, I remembered this all right – 'and both of us felt embarrassed in front of the others because we'd been out to tea with you. You know, we never believed that stuff about having been a head girl and doing well in exams.'

'Didn't I show you the picture?' I asked.

'What picture?' she said. What picture . . . remembering the scruffy newspaper clipping torn out of the *Tenbury Advertiser* which shows me, aged twelve, a funny-looking kid, with a great big grin and a pair of skimpy shorts over knobbly legs, holding no less than four silver cups in my hands.

'Your nickname, too,' Snoopy went on. 'I know Oozie is Rosie without the R, but it was more, it was because you were oozy. I mean, all that giving away, of your things, it was . . .'

'Obsequious,' I suggested, praying she wouldn't agree.

'Yes, exactly. Did you really think you'd get friends like that?' A question of pure curiosity, not malice.

'I suppose I must have done. It's left a strange legacy.' The goose bumps were rising on my arms. 'I've always felt inadequate.'

'Did you tell lies at school?' Snoopy asked.

'Not to begin with, but I did later. I remember thinking that I had to construct something fantastic about my home life in order to impress people.'

'You didn't ever steal?' The question shot into the air.

'No, what do you mean?'

She looked embarrassed. 'You know . . . when all those things started to disappear. I suppose it was in your first year and we all thought it was you.'

'God, no,' I replied, feeling close to tears. 'Did you really think that?'

She nodded. 'You must have known that we did.'

The memory lurched into focus. A small girl, with a flat chest, socks always falling down, walking into the dorm one day and overhearing someone say, 'I'm sure it's Oozie.' Turning round and walking out again, too afraid to face it, hoping that it would magically go away. Wondering if she could appease someone by cleaning their shoes.

'God, little girls are so mean to each other,' I said.

'Yes,' answered Snoopy, 'terrifyingly so. When we first came, we were all too scared to be mean. I still shudder to remember what we did to your dress.'

Betty and Charles were not rich in comparison with the parents of most of the Cheltenham Ladies; my clothes were all made at home, theirs came from Fenwicks. I never, ever, mentioned the fact that my father had once sold sheets in Selfridges. I was embarrassed, ashamed, and so I'd either avoid the subject or make up stories which sounded grander.

Mummy had made me a dark blue wool dress, with white lace collar and cuffs. It was pretty, but it was home-made and I was conscious of the fact. One day I walked into the dorm and found my cupboard door open. Stifled giggles came from round the corner. I looked inside: the blue dress had gone.

'Where's my dress?'

More giggles.

'Look outside.'

I went to the window and looked out on to the fire escape. There, twenty feet down, my dress hung limply, caught on a rusty girder by its sleeve.

My tormentors chanted, 'Oozie's lost her dress . . . lost her dress . . .' to the tune of 'London Bridge'. I opened the window and crept down the ladder, tears springing to my eyes.

'Your mother always knew that you were unhappy, didn't she?' Snoopy said.

'Yes, I think she did. How did you know?'

'Partly because she told me something about it later, and also because of all those postcards. Honestly Rosie, she was amazing the way she did that.'

My mother had sent a card, or a letter, every day for my first two terms. I eventually became embarrassed by this gesture too, though I loved getting them, and with a toss of my head would have to say, 'Oh, it's only old Mum, writing again,' while other girls would look up from their love-letters, smirking.

'Your memory's incredible,' I said to her, grinning, wanting it to stop, yet knowing I had to keep on finding out more about that first year. I was appalled at the whitewash job I had done, even more appalled to rediscover the truth.

'And you couldn't write either,' said Snoopy. 'They were sods to make you learn italic in the third year. They should never have tried. That probably had a lot to do with us all thinking you were so stupid.'

Italic: the dreaded script. My handwriting had to be undone, relearned. I spent Saturday mornings writing out 'the cat jumped over the fox' in the new script and I'd already learnt how to write at five.

'Is this upsetting you?'

'No,' I said, only half truthfully. 'It explains a lot. Ever since I've thought that what I actually am is not good enough. I've always had to do things which were so extreme that I didn't have to lie about them afterwards.

Like the fisherman's prayer, the one that goes, "God grant me the strength to catch a fish, so large that even I, when telling of it afterwards, may never need to lie."'

I laughed. Snoopy looked relieved.

'Is that why you always did outrageous things? Could that one year really have made such a difference? I always saw you as someone who needed to be popular. You always needed lots of boyfriends, far more than I did.'

'I suppose, yes, that a lot of it does go back to that. I think that stuff you really bury is important – you wouldn't bother if not. It's like the fact that you can only dislike qualities in others which are in you – or like them for that matter. I've always hated people who grovel – and for a time I was the biggest groveller of all. Come to that, I haven't eaten sweets since I left Cheltenham.'

It was Snoopy's turn to laugh. That little girl at Cheltenham seemed so sad. I wanted to cuddle her, to tell her that she was not so bad, really, and that she didn't need to apologise for her existence. Apologising ever since; inadequate ever since, keeping a full sweet-tin handy, in case.

The past sloughed off like snakeskin. As I wrote about it, it became just that; the past, not a myth from which I was trying to derive my present. I followed the story chronologically, ringing long-forgotten numbers and renewing friendships on the way. I came to my life in Colorado. Like Cheltenham, it stank of unfinished business.

'You ran away. You ran away,' I wrote the words, then immediately made arrangements to go back, aware that I was, in a medical sense, doing something wholly dotty. Colorado represented my version of the lion's den, the ultimate test of my sobriety.

I timed my visit to coincide with a festival celebrating Jack Kerouac's *On the Road*, written twenty-five years earlier. My first sober flight. The plane circled in over Denver. Seven years is a long time to not lay eyes on two very important people – a guru and an old lover. I was jumping with nervous excitement.

John had married in the meantime. I was unwelcome in his new world. We'd spoken on the phone before my arrival and I'd told him about the book. 'I gave up drink for six months,' he said, 'but I got so bored I just started again.' He seemed surprised when I said that I never got bored.

I looked forward to picking up the conversation but that wasn't to be. His new wife held tight reins, which weren't flexible enough to include spending even an hour with an old girlfriend. At a party one night in the Boulderado – nostalgia shrieking off the walls – John was drunk and maudlin. He apologised for not being able to see me. I remembered a time when William had put the phone down on John with a curt 'She doesn't live here any more.' At the time, I'd been angry, but too weak and paranoid to complain. Now I shrugged. 'Dinner in another seven years.'

I stayed with old friends who were close to Rinpoche. They offered to arrange an interview. 'How will you feel about his drinking?' Thinking, they later told me, Will the guru's influence make you start again? I was fairly confident of the answer, but had no idea what my feelings would be. A guru who drinks to excess is not an easy example. So while I waited for the interview I went to see José Arguelles, who runs the Buddhist Alcoholic Group.

Early morning outside Jose's mountain home we sat on the porch and wondered what we had in common. We had both stopped drinking overnight to rush back to life, not away from it. No shame, no apologies, no guilt.

'Do you call it enlightenment?' I asked, with some embarrassment.

'Maybe,' he answered. 'No one knows what enlightenment is, but something changed in me, altered the downward spiral, something that was so strong that I can't explain it. Shit man, did I drink! I can't explain to other people how I managed to just give up drink – without any effort – and how I've never been happier, more fulfilled and more directed. Buddhists say enlightenment is living in the now – well, I'm doing that.'

'The rage to live. It's a good way of putting it,' I said. 'You know what Jung said to the founder of AA – that alcohol is the craving for spiritual wholeness and that he had only known people stop drinking after undergoing some kind of spiritual experience.'

Jose nodded. How else to explain such enormous changes? Spiritual experiences don't have to come flashing in on lightning clouds.

'It's wonderful to be back,' I said. And it was. Boulder had changed. The paranoid ranks which once ranged themselves around Rinpoche had settled into order. And in that order there was space. Finally, I felt I fitted in, and told Jose as much.

'Seven years in the wilderness . . . not half bad,' he laughed.

'How do you deal with Rinpoche's drinking?' I had heard that it had escalated and I wondered how a recovered alcoholic student dealt with a living god who was skunked most of the time.

'It's hard to talk about. Hard to live with. If I say he's alcoholic then I'm making a heretical statement. If I ignore it, I don't feel I'm being truthful. The example is tricky for the students who do drink . . .'

I saw the example two days later. Rinpoche had acquired a new town house which his students called The Court. Outside it resembled any other large weatherbeaten mountain house, opulent suburbia with room for a kindergarten of children in the back yard. Inside, Tibet had invaded and dragons romped on the carpets.

I wondered if he would remember me. I had reread Rinpoche's books in the clinic and there had been times when I'd crawled back to the high I'd experienced in prison, when the moment was enough in itself; freedom in the palm of my hand. My past, which before I had always regarded as more real than my generally distasteful present, was now only the past. I waited to confront a piece of the past which, if my sweating palms were any indication, was also a major part of the present.

'Oh, it's you,' he said with a pleased grin and held out his hand. He was a little fatter, a little more paralysed and a lot more drunk. The skin on his arms was sunburnt and the peel line ran from wrist to elbow like a watermark in a bathtub. I told him about the clinic.

'Very dramatic,' he hiccuped and put an arm round me. 'Will you stay the night?'

'Why?'

'Why not?'

'Because I'd find it too confusing.'

He smiled, I relaxed and suddenly we were just two people sitting in a room. I felt as though he had simultaneously lifted a weight and given me a gift. The gift, in a funny way, of equality. Now all the sex business was out of the way, we could just get on.

I thanked him for what I limply described as his assistance while I was in the nuthouse. His eyebrows rose above his slanted eyes and questioned me silently. 'You made sense, for the first time ever. What you always used to say – still do, I suppose – about being able to deal with our neurosis and our manure. To be able to use all that's potentially negative because it's also pure energy.'

He nodded. 'It still sounds very dramatic. Did you have any fun in there?'

I giggled. I was sitting on the floor at his feet and his arm was loosely round my shoulder. 'I did meet one nice person.'

'That's better,' Rinpoche answered, taking another huge slug of his drink. I wondered how Brian was getting on.

'Why do you drink so much? Don't you know it upsets a lot of people?'

'People don't understand me.'

'But they care.' I might have been talking to a wall.

A few minutes later I got up to go, kissed him goodbye and wondered when I would see him again. I didn't wonder if, only when.

The hostess on the plane back to New York offered doughnuts. The coffee beaker was stamped with the rubric AA. American Airlines. I had grown up a little. My mother died in the year that preceded my own near-death. The scales of my life had been lightly balanced; so easy to have gone either way. So little the weight that turned the balance back to life; just a nudge which grew to be a certainty.

I was lucky to be so greedy for happiness, to be young enough to be flexible. I thought of Taylor in his nursing home. Years earlier I'd been circling east across South Dakota choking down my breakfast vodka. One year before, another flight which seemed to herald, when I landed at London airport from Cyprus too drunk to stand, the end of my world. In a way it was. It was time to let go.

I have a few wrinkles, and I do not dislike them. Now there is something inordinately satisfactory about the passage of time, about the sense of survival. I have things on which I can depend which mitigate the fear of the future. And though I occasionally feel nostalgic for the popping of corks, the world is a far more pleasurable place in my sober state.

I do not live silently, nor on the terms which society dictates to ex-inmates of mental institutions, or reformed alcoholics. I have my own freedom now, to live and to live out loud.

EPILOGUE

The first version of *A Nice Girl Like Me* ran to almost six hundred pages, and I delivered it to the offices of Chatto & Windus and the arms of my editor and friend Carmen Callil in an old suitcase. Then I went and sat in a coffee house, and cried. I was pregnant and I'd given up smoking. I felt as though I had lost the temporary umbrella that writing a book provides, but more than that, I felt I had almost certainly condemned myself to a future living on the margins of life. No one, I reasoned, would ever want to employ a woman who was not only an alcoholic, but who had stuck needles in her arms, wound up in a Thai jail and voluntarily shown herself capable of so many acts that verged all too regularly on lunacy.

When the book was published, I was surprised by how well it was received and by the number of lives my story touched. While I was by no means the first woman to confess publicly to being an alcoholic, there was still a stigma attached to female drinkers: the hand that rocks the cradle can't also hold the gin bottle. Revealing my own secrets made it possible for other women to reveal their secrets to me. I was inundated with letters from readers – most of them female drinkers or mothers or wives of alcoholics – both wanting advice and wanting to share their stories. Far from proving a liability, having told the truth turned into an invisible armour. There was nothing anyone could say about me that I hadn't said already, and as I established my career in London I found the book worked as a shield. I'd talked and written about being an alcoholic, and as the years rolled by that fact became a public part of me, written into profiles along with standard descriptive lines such as 'blonde and blue-eyed'.

But not all the reactions were positive. The one person whose approval I so craved was the one who was most distraught: my father. His first letter, after reading the proof, lambasted me for revealing so many 'family secrets'. Several more were to follow, each more hurtful, full of rage. I couldn't figure out quite what had upset him the most: the details of my drinking, the stories about my sex life, or the portrayal of his tough transition from army major to working civilian. We were still not speaking when the book was published. He returned his invitation to the launch party, torn into little pieces.

More than his letters, or his stony silence, that torn-up invitation cut like a knife. I wanted him to be there, I wanted him to be proud of me; above all, I didn't want to fail him – yet this seemed to be exactly what I had done. But by then it was far too late to grab back the book and cut it to pieces – removing every trace of him, every family secret. And even though a part of me wanted to do just that, I also knew that those very same family secrets were what had made me into the person I was. I could no more ignore them than I could ignore the effects of all that vodka, all those drugs and journeys and quests. Secrets, as I was to learn much later, keep you sick. They're part of the denial process that every addict goes through if they're going to get to the other side and into recovery. When I look back on my descriptions of my childhood, I now think that I underplayed the effects of those early years. Decades of future therapy unmasked layers of shame, layers laid down as my parents struggled to come to terms with their sudden loss of status. It was this shame that they passed on to me, an invisible baton that I absorbed into my being. But with that realisation there also came a sense of immense pride in my father. It wasn't until I was in my forties – the same age as he had been when he left the army – that I could start to comprehend just how awful it must have been for him, teetering on the verge of middle age, jobless, unemployable, a man who had grown up to believe that it was part of his masculine destiny to look after his wife and children, suddenly rendered incapable of doing either. Collectively, we breathed in shame. It lodged itself inside me like a piece of netting tangled inside a doomed fish.

By the time the book came out, all my friends knew what had happened to me. And as days rolled into months and I never felt the urge to drink, I began to think that being sober – and most crucially, staying sober – was a relatively easy business. I went to AA meetings for a few months, but as my confidence rose, my attendance dipped from regular, to infrequent, to never. All I needed to do, I argued, was not pick up that first drink. Even though my fellow patients were not faring so well, I was supremely confident in my own ability to cope. I stayed in touch with Max Glatt, my original therapist, until the day I told him I was about to marry another alcoholic, David Leitch, the brilliant writer and journalist – and who, coincidentally, had seen Max too. Max's reaction took me aback. 'It's not a good idea, Rosie. Two alcoholics, unless they have years of recovery behind them, are a recipe for disaster.'

I didn't want to listen. I didn't listen, although I did remember. I was pregnant and sublimely happy. David was sober and I thought that our mutual vulnerability would prove to be a strength if and when times grew tough. My ongoing tendency to strike bargains with the Almighty had left me convinced that my survival through my twenties had been achieved at a very low cost and that the hidden price would prove to be an inability to have a child. When Daisy was born on 9 August 1983, weighing in at 6lb 3oz and utterly perfect in every way, I felt as though I'd finally come home.

My worries about going to parties, about finding the highs in life, vanished within months. The smell of booze made me shudder and I revelled in the knowledge that I could do anything and go anywhere and not have to pay the awful price of drunken humiliation and crippling hangovers. A sober life did not have to equate to a boring life and life with David was anything but boring, until the day when his extended period of sobriety suddenly ended and he disappeared on a three-day bender with an old university friend of his who lectured at York University. He returned, chastened, white, shaking, and went to bed for two days. I forgave and tried to forget, but I was unable to shake off the sense that maybe this was my fault, that I was in some way a failure. Otherwise, why would he have needed to drink? I could see the irony, since I had written about the effects of active alcoholism on the spouse and the family, and intellectually at least, I knew that its symptoms, while real enough, were also at heart a falsehood. Every drinker has his or her own path to follow, just as every alcoholic who chooses the path to recovery has to accept that it is his or her responsibility to keep to it. What I didn't grasp in those early days – and indeed, was not to grasp fully for another twenty years – was that sobriety has to be the single major goal of any recovering addict's life. It can't sit alongside your family, your job, your passions. It has to stand above, alone and sacred, as without it you have no chance of having any of the others.

Sadly, though, David was by then drinking again fairly regularly. Sometimes he would simply be loud and gregarious, sometimes his complex and tortured demons would explode. His own history was messy, a romantic and tortured saga that had once seemed so attractive to me. Given away as a tiny baby through an advertisement on the front page of the *Daily Express* in October 1937, he'd spent his life searching for roots, for his own sense of belonging. Like me, he'd had a vast thirst for life and – like John Steinbeck – harboured the notion that peace, of a precarious sort, could only be found in war zones, whether real, fabricated or imagined. Both John and David, I came to realise, were hopeless at dealing with the everyday, with the mundanity of gas bills and mortgages, of shopping and just coping with what my lifelong friend and mentor Martha Gelhorn described as 'the kitchen of life'.

Six years into our marriage I relapsed myself. One Sunday, cooking lunch for several of David's newly discovered relatives, I found my hand reaching towards an open wine bottle, pouring a glass, and glugging it down. The effect was immediate: like an injection of cocaine the alcohol flew through my body, a distant and neglected friend, a tantalising devil with a crooked finger beckoning me back. Why did I do it? I was scared of my marriage collapsing, I was exhausted and I thought that you could have just one glass, that six years of sobriety had earned me the right to have that mood-altering hit, the guaranteed balm against anxiety, and that that would be it. I ended up drinking the entire bottle.

My own sobriety was now acutely vulnerable, but I continued to believe that I was capable of dealing with my addiction by myself. Looking back, I understand that even though I'd stayed clean and sober for about two thousand days, I had neglected the inner work and the deep-seated changes that every addict needs to make so that when that finger beckons, your toolbox is primed.

I made no attempts to change my behaviour or my circumstances, instead plunging into work with a vengeance that verged on mania. For well over two years I lived in an emotionally paralysing limbo, unhappily married, still having the occasional drink. Work always kept me from going over the edge, but I knew I was living my life on a tightrope with no safety nets. Martha, as ever, came to my rescue. A short note arrived in the post one morning saying 'It is far better to be a woman alone with a child, than to be a woman trapped in a doomed marriage.'

David and I parted and I thought I had once again banished my demons as my career became increasingly successful. At that point too, my father came back into my life, slowly and tentatively. He adored his granddaughter and took enormous pride in her achievements. I loved to see his love of her and hers of him. He helped me pay the mortgage as the property crash of the early nineties left me with sole responsibility for bills I couldn't pay and a flat I couldn't sell. Later, when I left the relatively safe waters of editing *Esquire* magazine for the choppy uncertainties of editing the *Independent on Sunday*, his constant phone calls kept my nerves intact. I remember calling him one day and saying that I was overwhelmed, uncertain of my abilities to do the job. 'Stick it for one year,' he said, 'then leave if it still frightens you so much.' It was the best advice to give a single scared woman, and over the coming years, before he declined into the horrifying grip of Alzheimer's, we became close friends. It was a blessed peace even though we never mentioned the book. No one understands how much their parents love them until they have children of their own, and it slowly dawned on me that perhaps his anger about *A Nice Girl Like Me* was simply because it revealed to the world that maybe he hadn't protected me enough and that possibly he could have spared me some of the pain. I don't know. I never will.

When I became the editor of *Esquire* – the first woman ever to do so – an American journalist came over to London to interview me. She took her research very seriously and trekked up to Shropshire to talk to my father. He told her that while he wouldn't talk about the book, he did keep a copy in the house. On my many visits I used to hunt around surreptitiously for it, and when it came time for my sister Collette and me to clear out the house, after he had finally gone into a care home, I stayed up all through one long wintry night, poking into drawers, under beds and through boxes, in the vain hope that I'd find it. I never did.

I had never expected to end up as a newspaper editor, but when I left the *Express* in 2001 – the third national newspaper of my six-year stint in the newspaper world – after the title had been bought by the multimillionaire pornographer Richard Desmond, I wasn't remotely prepared for the shock. I felt as though my sense of self, and self-esteem, had plunged off the side of a cliff. Work, I realised, had taken the place of booze in the addictive landscape of my being.

Even though I had remarried, to a childhood friend who was both loving and endlessly supportive, was financially secure, and had been able to leave the *Express* with my head held high, I found myself wading through an abyss of depression, drowned by a complete loss of identity and self. I loathed myself for it: it seemed self-indulgent, almost ridiculous, yet I was waking up in the mornings in tears, unsure of how I would get through the day, and like an amoeba with undefined edges, I felt myself falling rapidly to pieces. Even with all I had achieved, I felt empty and hollow. It wasn't long before I started drinking again, a relapse that was to last for almost a year, culminating in a car crash that almost resulted in the loss of my right leg and left me on crutches for twenty months. I went back to rehab – a very different experience the second time round. Now there were no excuses. I couldn't hide behind the veil of ignorance, of pretending I didn't know I was an alcoholic.

What I realised was that I couldn't do it by myself. Pride and gritted teeth were useless tools when the chips were down. I was forced to face the fact that I needed help and that I needed to surrender completely to my powerlessness over alcohol. Accolades and trophies count for nothing when you wake in the morning unable to remember what you did the night before.

I realised, and continue to realise, that there is no substitute for the therapeutic benefit of one addict helping another. The disease is at once physical, mental and spiritual – a slithery concept for most people to grasp and one that only another alcoholic truly understands. Even most doctors don't really understand it, although luckily more and more of them are prepared to refer patients to AA, rather than recommend antidepressants as a cure. Because of course there is no cure, in the traditional sense. I will always only be a 'recovering alcoholic', never a 'recovered' one.

In the grip of addiction, my world had dwindled to a tiny

speck. I had been incapable of looking outside of my own sense of panic and isolation. Only when I began to embrace others did I start to see, once again, the wonder of the world around me.

Did I need this relapse to make me finally understand? Perhaps. You can't unmake the past, you can only – as Beckett says – fail again, but fail better. When I reread *A Nice Girl Like Me* now, I think that if I made any mistakes in writing it, my error was to make it sound too easy. Or perhaps that's really what I felt at the time. I had only recently begun to make my way down the path to recovery and I was confident, revelling in my newly sober state. I was enjoying the new symptoms of my life: the order, the sense of survival. I had yet to realise that instead of distracting myself with work and family, a deep-seated change was necessary and that staying sober has to be the primary responsibility of my life.

On a lousy day, when things go wrong, I'm stressed and I haven't accomplished anything, as long as I go to bed without having had a drink, knowing that my head hits the pillow in a sober state, then I have, in fact, accomplished the most important thing of all.

RMB
May 2009